1 MONTH OF
FREE
READING

at
www.ForgottenBooks.com

By purchasing this book you are eligible for one month membership to ForgottenBooks.com, giving you unlimited access to our entire collection of over 1,000,000 titles via our web site and mobile apps.

To claim your free month visit:
www.forgottenbooks.com/free882917

ISBN 978-0-265-74149-8
PIBN 10882917

THE

BERWICK HYMNAL

Arnold EDITED BY THE

REV. A. W. OXFORD, M.A.

Vicar of St. Luke's, Berwick Street, Soho

REVISED EDITION

London

T. FISHER UNWIN

26 PATERNOSTER SQUARE

MDCCCLXXXVIII

To

THE PARISHIONERS

OF

ST. LUKE'S, BERWICK STREET.

PREFACE.

——◆◆——

I HAVE to thank the following authors and owners
of copyright for permission to use the hymns written
or owned by them : Professor Felix Adler, Rev.
Dendy Agate, Mrs. Alexander, Rev. S. Baring-
Gould, Professor Blackie, Rev. A. G. W. Blunt,
Rev H. Bonar, Miss Jane Borthwick, Rev. S. A.
Brooke, Rev. Phillips Brooks, Rev. T. W. Chignell,
Rev. S. Childs-Clarke, Miss Cobbe, Rev. J Eller-
ton, the Bishop of Exeter, Rev. T. W. Freckelton,
Canon Furse, for hymns of the late Dr. Monsell ;
Mr. T. H. Gill, Rev. E. Hatch, Miss Havergal, for
hymns of the late Miss F. R. Havergal ; Mr. J. T.
Hayes, for hymns of the late Dr. Neale ; Mr. O.
W. Holmes, Rev. J. Page Hopps, Mr. T. Hughes,
Rev. E. Husband, Mr. A. C. Jewitt, Rev. R. F.
Littledale, Mrs. Lynch, for hymns of the late Rev.
T. T. Lynch ; Mr. H. C. Maxwell Lyte, for hymns
of the late Rev. H. F. Lyte ; Mr. W. Maccall, Rev.
W. T. Matson, Miss Edith Miles, Rev. H. Austin
Mills, for hymns of the late Rev. E. Caswall ;
Cardinal Newman, Mr. F. T. Palgrave, Very Rev.
E. H. Plumptre, Mr. C. Smith, Rev. W. C. Smith,
Rev. S. J. Stone, Rev. Godfrey Thring, Rev. L.
Tuttiett, Miss A. L. Waring, Mr. G. Watson, and
Miss Wiglesworth.

The right of publishing some of Miss Procter's hymns has been purchased from Messrs. George Bell and Sons, and of publishing Hymn 53 from Mr. W. Chatterton Dix.

Special thanks must be given to Rev. J. V. Blake, of Chicago, Rev. J. W. Chadwick, of Brooklyn, Rev. J. F. Clarke, of Boston, Mass., Rev. W. C. Gannett, of Chicago, Rev. F. L. Hosmer, of Chicago, Rev. S. Longfellow, of Cambridge, Mass., Rev. M. J. Savage, of Boston, Mass., who have given me free permission to use their hymns. Mr. Longfellow has also given me permission to use the hymns of the late Rev. S. Johnson, and any others from "Hymns of the Spirit."

I have also to thank the Rev. W. Garrett Horder for much valuable assistance in preparing both editions of the Hymnal.

I hope that any involuntary infringement of copyright may be forgiven.

This hymn-book has been prepared solely for the use of my own congregation. It includes therefore no hymns for children, for whose use another book has already been compiled.

HYMNS.

Sunday. 8.6.8.4.

HAIL, sacred day of earthly rest,
From toil and trouble free ;
Hail, day of light, that bringest light
And joy to me.

A holy stillness, breathing calm
On all the world around,
Uplifts my soul, O God, to Thee,
Where rest is found.

No sound of jarring strife is heard,
As weekly labours cease ;
No voice, but those that sweetly sing
Sweet songs of peace.

I hear the organ loudly peal,
And soaring voices raise
To Thee, their great Creator, hymns
Of deathless praise.

All earthly things appear to fade,
As, rising high and higher,
The yearning voices strive to join
The heavenly choir.

For those who sing with saints below
  Glad songs of heavenly love,
Shall sing, when songs on earth have ceased,
  With saints above.

Accept, O God, my hymn of praise
  That Thou this day hast given,
Sweet foretaste of that endless day
  Of rest in heaven.

G. Thring.

2   *The day of rest.*   10.6.

THOU givest thy rest, O Lord; the din is stilled
  Of man's unquiet care;
A sacred calm, with thy deep presence filled,
  Breathes through the silent air.

O leave us not, through long and darkened hours,
  In night of woe and sin,
But pour thy day with all its radiant powers
  Upon the world within.

Purge from our hearts the stains so deep and foul,
  Of wrath and pride and care;
Send thine own holy calm upon the soul,
  And bid it settle there.

Banish this craving self, that still has sought
  Lord of the soul to be ;
Teach us to turn to fellow-men our thought;
  Teach us to turn to Thee.

Teach us to love thy creatures great and small
  To live as in thine eye,
Thou who hast freely given thy love to all,
  Thou who to all art nigh.

Anon.

THIS is the day of light :
　Let there be light to-day ;
O Day-spring, rise upon our night,
　And chase its gloom away.

This is the day of rest :
　Our failing strength renew ;
On weary brain and troubled breast
　Shed Thou thy freshening dew.

This is the day of peace:
　Thy peace our spirits fill ;
Bid Thou the blasts of discord cease,
　The waves of strife be still.

This is the day of prayer :
　Let earth to heaven draw near ;
Lift up our hearts to seek Thee there,
　Come down to meet us here.

This is the first of days :
　Send forth thy quickening breath,
And wake dead souls to love and praise,
　O Vanquisher of death.

J. Ellerton.

LORD, in this sacred hour
Within thy courts we bend,
And bless thy love, and own thy power,
Our Father and our Friend.

But Thou art not alone
In courts by mortals trod,
Nor only is the day thine own
When man draws near to God.

Thy temple is the arch
Of yon unmeasured sky ;
Thy sabbath, the stupendous march
Of grand eternity.

'Lord, may that holier day
Dawn on thy servants' sight,
And purer worship may we pay
In heaven's unclouded light.

S. G. Bulfinch.

5   *Morning.*   10.10.10.10.6.

FOR the dear love that kept us through the night,
And gave our senses to sleep's gentle sway ;
For the new miracle of dawning light
Flushing the east with prophecies of day,
       We thank Thee, O our God.

For the fresh life that through our being flows
With its full tide to strengthen and to bless ;
For calm sweet thoughts, upspringing from repose,
To bear to Thee their song of thankfulness,
       We praise Thee, O our God.

Day uttereth speech to-day, and night to night
Tells of thy power and glory. So would we,
Thy children, duly, with the morning light,
Or at still eve, upon the bended knee
       Adore Thee, O our God.

Thou know'st our needs, thy fulness will supply ;
Our blindness ;—let thy hand still lead us on,
Till, visited by the dayspring from on high,
Our prayer, one only, 'Let thy will be done,'
       We breathe to Thee, O God.

W. H. Burleigh.

6   *Morning.*   L.M.

LORD God of morning and of night,
We thank Thee for thy gift of light:
As in the dawn the shadows fly,
We seem to find Thee now more nigh.

Fresh hopes have wakened in the heart,
Fresh force to do our daily part;
Thy thousand sleeps our strength restore,
A thousand-fold to serve Thee more.

Yet whilst thy will we would pursue,
Oft what we would we cannot do;
The sun may stand in zenith skies,
But on the soul thick midnight lies.

O Lord of lights, 'tis Thou alone
Canst make our darkened hearts thine own:
Though this new day with joy we see,
Great Dawn of God, we cry for Thee.

Praise God, our Maker and our Friend;
Praise Him through time, till time shall end;
Till psalm and song his name adore
Through heaven's great day of Evermore.

F. T. Palgrave.

7   *Morning.*   L.M.

O TIMELY happy, timely wise,
Hearts that with rising morn arise,
Eyes that the beam celestial view
Which evermore makes all things new.

New every morning is the love
Our wakening and uprising prove;
Through sleep and darkness safely brought,
Restored to life, and power, and thought.

New mercies, each returning day,
Hover around us while we pray;
New perils past, new sins forgiven,
New thoughts of God, new hopes of heaven.

If on our daily course our mind
Be set to hallow all we find,
New treasures still, of countless price,
God will provide for sacrifice.

Old friends, old scenes will lovelier be,
As more of heaven in each we see;
Some softening gleam of love and prayer
Shall dawn on every cross and care.

The trivial round, the common task,
Will furnish all we need to ask;
Room to deny ourselves, a road
To bring us daily nearer God.

Only, O Lord, in thy dear love
Fit us for perfect rest above;
And help us, this and every day,
To live more nearly as we pray.

J. Keble.

8 *Morning.* C.M.

I WAKE this morn, and all my life
  Is freshly mine to give;
The future, with sweet promise rife,
  Has crowns of joy to give.

New words to speak, new thoughts to hear,
  New love to give and take;
Perchance new burdens I may bear
  To-day, for love's sweet sake.

New hopes to open in the sun ;
　New efforts worth the will ;
Or tasks, with yesterday begun,
　More bravely to fulfil.

Fresh seeds for all the time to be
　Are in my hand to sow,
Whereby, for others and for me,
　Undreamed-of fruit may grow.

And if, when eventide shall fall
　In shade across my way,
It seems that nought my thoughts recall
　But life of every day,—

Yet if each step in shine or shower
　Shall be with Thee for guide,
Then blest be every happy hour
　That keeps me at thy side.
　　　　　　　　From ' Chambers' Journal.'

9　　　　　　*Evening.*　　　　S.M.

Our day of praise is done ;
　The evening shadows fall ;
But pass not from us with the sun,
　True Light that lightenest all.

Around the throne on high,
　Where night can never be,
The white-robed harpers of the sky
　Bring ceaseless hymns to Thee.

Too faint our anthems here ;
　Too soon of praise we tire :
But O the strains how full and clear
　Of that eternal choir !

Yet, Lord, to thy dear Will
  If Thou attune the heart,
We in thine angels' music still
  May bear our lower part.

'Tis thine each soul to calm,
  Each wayward thought reclaim,
And make our life a daily psalm
  Of glory to thy name.

A little while, and then
  Shall come the glorious end;
And songs of angels and of men
  In perfect praise shall blend.

                           J. Ellerton.

10   *Evening.*   7s.

Lord of power, Lord of might;
  God and father of us all;
Lord of day and Lord of night,
  Listen to our solemn call;
Listen, whilst to Thee we raise
Songs of prayer, and songs of praise.

Light and love and life are thine,
  Great Creator of all good;
Fill our souls with light divine;
  Give us, with our daily food,
Blessings from thy heavenly store,
Blessings rich for evermore.

Graft within our heart of hearts
  Love undying for thy name;
Bid us, ere the day departs,
  Spread afar our Maker's fame:
Young and old together bless,
Clothe our souls with righteousness.

Full of years and full of peace,
　　May our life on earth be blest;
When our trials here shall cease,
　　And at last we sink to rest,
Fountain of eternal Love,
Call us to our home above.

G. Thring.

11　　　　　　　*Evening.*　　　　　8.7.8.7.7.7.

FATHER, now the day is over,
　　As the sun sinks in the west,
Ere the night creep slowly round us,
　　Ere soft slumber be our guest,
　　　　Let us bless Thee that to-day,
　　　　Thou, O God, hast been our stay.

Lord, we need no earthly temple,
　　For, where we thy love have found,
All thy humblest creatures teach us
　　Where we are is holy ground:
　　　　Lord, we need no holier place
　　　　Than where we thy love can trace.

For the birds and flowers we thank Thee,
　　For each song and perfume sweet,
For the faith that dare address Thee,
　　For the love that may Thee greet;
　　　　Most, that we for every gift
　　　　May our souls to Thee uplift.

For the love of friends we bless Thee,
　　Who to-day our joys have shared,
Whose true hearts spread out before us,
　　Have thy love to us declared;
　　　　For each thought of truth and love
　　　　They have echoed from above.

For the mystic band which binds us
  Each to each, and all to Thee,
And with all the past entwines us,
  In the world's long harmony;
    For each striving human soul
    Which is part of thy great whole.

For each gift Thou hast withholden
  From our foolish, grasping hands;
For each pang which quick has chidden
  Every breach of thy commands;
    For the weariness and pain
    Which Thou hast not sent in vain.

Pour thy Spirit, Lord, upon us,
  Guard us in unconscious sleep;
Be that Spirit ever with us,
  While death slumbers o'er us creep;
    And, our life's long journey past,
    We are safe with Thee at last.

E. B.

12   *Evening.*   8.6.

O SHADOW in a sultry land,
  We gather to thy breast,
Whose love, enfolding us like night,
  Brings quietude and rest;
Glimpse of a fairer life to be,
  In foretaste here possessed.

From all our wanderings we come,
  From drifting to andfro,
From tossing on life's restless deep
  Amid its ebb and flow;
The grander sweep of tides serene
  Our spirits yearn to know.

That which the garish day has lost
   The twilight vigil brings,
While softlier the vesper bell
   Its silver cadence rings,—
The sense of an immortal trust,
   The touch of angel wings.

Drop down behind the solemn hills,
   O day with golden skies;
Serene, above its fading glow,
   Night, starry-crowned, arise;
So beautiful may heaven be
   When life's last sunbeam dies.

Caroline M. Packard.

13   *Evening.*   C.M.

O LOVE divine, of all that is
   The sweetest still and best,
Fain would I come and rest to-night
   Upon thy tender breast:
I pray Thee turn me not away;
   For, sinful though I be,
Thou knowest every thing I need,
   And all my need of Thee.

And yet the spirit in my heart
   Says, Wherefore should I pray
That Thou shouldst seek me with thy love,
   Since Thou dost seek alway?
And dost not even wait until
   I urge my steps to Thee;
But in the darkness of my life
   Art coming still to me.

But Thou wilt hear the thought I mean,
   And not the words I say ;
Wilt hear the thanks among the words,
   That only seem to pray.
Still, still thy love will beckon me,
   And still thy strength will come
In many ways to bear me up
   And bring me to my home.

I would not have Thee otherwise
   Than what Thou still must be;
Yea, Thou art God, and what Thou art
   Is ever best for me.
And so, for all my sighs, my heart
   Doth sing itself to rest,
O Love divine, most far and near,
   Upon thy tender breast.

J. W. Chadwick.

14   *Evening.*   7s.

Now that day its wings has furled
   And the earth has gone to rest ;
Take me, Shepherd of the world,
   Home to sleep upon thy breast.

All the night from dream to dream,
   Keep my spirit pure and bright ;
Fill the darkness with the stream
   Of thine everlasting light.

If I waken, calm and fair
   Be the thoughts that in me rise ;
And thy presence in the air
   Make my heart a Paradise.

But if trouble in my heart,
  Or fierce pain me restless keep,
Then to me thy peace impart;
  Give to thy belovèd sleep.

So when morning with his wing
  Wakens me to work and play,
I may rise with joy and sing—
  'God has turned my night to day.'
S. A. Brooke.

15   *Evening.*   8.7.

Now on land and sea descending,
  Brings the night its peace profound;
Let our vesper-hymn be blending
  With the holy calm around.
Soon as dies the sunset glory,
  Stars of heaven shine out above,
Telling still the ancient story—
  Their Creator's changeless love.

Now our wants and burdens leaving
  To his care, who cares for all,
Cease we fearing, cease we grieving,
  At his touch our burdens fall.
As the darkness deepens o'er us,
  Lo, eternal stars arise;
Hope and Faith and Love rise glorious
  Shining in the spirit's skies.
S. Longfellow.

16   *Evening.*   7.7.7.7.3.

Holy Father, who this day
Hast vouchsafed to guide our way,
Be Thou near to soothe and bless,
Cheering night's dark loneliness
          With thy light.

In our hearts bid tumult cease;
Fill our minds with heavenly peace;
Breathe thy calm o'er earthly strife;
Troubled ones in this stern life
    Lead aright.

Send thy comfort from on high,
Blessing those in pain who lie;
Whisper to them words of love—
How for aye in realms above
    They shall rest.

Those, now far from home in sin,
Bring, O Father, safely in;
Lead their trembling steps to Thee;
With thy dear ones may they be
    Ever blest.

Hush complaints; bend every will
Ne'er to doubt, but trust Thee still;
On the path now overcast
With dark clouds and shadows vast
    Send thy peace.

We are blind, and see not why
Grief is sent and troubles try;
From too heavy weight of care,
Gloom, and darkness of despair,
    Grant release.

Steer us onward to that shore
Where all pain and grief are o'er;
Guard in tempest our frail bark,
Guide it through the gathering dark
    To the light.

Edith Miles.

17 *Evening.* 105.

Go down, great sun, into thy golden west,
  The day is done, the hours of labour past;
The night's dark shadows deepen all around;
The day is over; rest has come at last.

And so our life to eventide draws nigh,
  Our days of change their course have almost
    run;
And soon the storms of winter will be past,
And then comes summer, and th' unsetting sun.

And in that holier world of joy and peace,
  Our sun shall rise upon a land so blest,
That none in this poor world have words to tell
  How great the joy of that pure heavenly rest.

But there the Light that never dies shines on
  Undimmed, unclouded through th' eternal
    years;
And souls shall find, in that sweet home of
    Love,
The hand that wipes away the mourners' tears.
                              E. Husband.

18 *Evening.* 10.4.

FATHER Supreme, Thou high and holy one,
      To Thee we bow,
Now, when the burden of the day is gone,
      Devoutly, now.

When the glad morn upon the hills was spread,
      Thy smile was there;
Now, as the darkness gathers overhead,
      We feel thy care.

Night spreads her shade upon another day
    For ever past;
So o'er our faults, thy love, we humbly pray,
    A veil may cast.

Silence and calm, o'er hearts by earth distrest,
    Now sweetly steal;
So every fear that struggles in the heart
    Shall faith conceal.

Thou, through the dark, wilt watch above our
    sleep
    With eye of love;
And Thou wilt wake us, when the sunbeams
    leap
    The hills above.

From age to age unchanging, still the same
    All-good Thou art;
Hallowed for ever be thy holy name
    In every heart.

                                     Anon.

19   *Evening.*   8.7.

EVENSONG is hushed in silence
    And the hour of rest is nigh;
Strengthen us for work to-morrow,
    God Almighty, God Most High.
Sinful men and sinful women,
    Help us in the narrow way,
Till Thou bring us to thy city
    Whence thy sons can never stray.
    We are weary of life-long toil,
    Of sorrow, and pain, and sin;
But there is a city with streets of gold,
    And all is peace within.

When we enter that bright city,
    What the vision we behold?
Gates of pearl and walls of jasper,
    Streets of pure transparent gold.
Are the many mansions empty?
    Lone the terraces so fair?
Jesus and our brethren pace them;
    How they long to see us there.
      We are weary, &c.

There the dear ones who have left us
    We shall some day meet again;
There will be no bitter partings,
    No more sorrow, death, or pain.
Evensong has closed in silence,
    And the hour of rest is nigh;
Lighten Thou our darkness, Father,
    God Almighty, God Most High.
      We are weary, &c.
                 J. Purchas.

20   *Evening.*   C.M.

As darker, darker, fall around
    The shadows of the night,
We gather here, with hymn and prayer,
    To seek the Eternal Light.

Father in heaven, to Thee are known
    Our many hopes and fears,
Our heavy weight of mortal toil,
    Our bitterness of tears.

We pray Thee for our absent ones,
    Who have been with us here;
And in our secret heart we name
    The distant and the dear.

For weary eyes, and aching hearts,
   And feet that from Thee rove,
The sick, the poor, the tried, the fallen,
   We pray Thee, God of love.

We pray Thee for the little bark
   Just launched upon life's sea ;
Are not the depths of parents'·love,
   O Father, known to Thee?

We bring to Thee our hopes and fears,
   And at thy footstool lay ;
And, Father, Thou who lovest all
   Wilt hear us as we pray.

Anon.

21   *Evening.*   L.M.

AGAIN, as evening's shadow falls,
We gather in these hallowed walls ;
And vesper hymn and vesper prayer
Rise mingling on the holy air.

May struggling hearts that seek release
Here find the rest of God's own peace;
And, strengthened here by hymn and prayer,
Lay down the burden and the care.

O God, our Light, to Thee we bow ;
Within all shadows standest Thou ;
Give deeper calm than night can bring ;
Give sweeter songs than lips can sing.

Life's tumult we must meet again,
We cannot at the shrine remain ;
But, in the spirit's secret cell,
May hymn and prayer for ever dwell.

S. Longfellow.

22　　　　　*Evening.*　　　　　10s.

ABIDE with me ; fast falls the eventide,
The darkness deepens ; Lord, with me abide ;
When other helpers fail, and comforts flee,
Help of the helpless, O abide with me.

Swift to its close ebbs out life's little day ;
Earth's joys grow dim, its glories pass away ;
Change and decay in all around I see ;
O Thou who changest not, abide with me.

I need thy presence every passing hour ;
What but thy grace can foil temptation's power ?
Who like thyself my guide and stay can be ?
Through cloud and sunshine, Lord, abide with
　　me.

I fear no foe with Thee at hand to bless ;
Ills have no weight, and tears no bitterness ;
Where is death's sting ? Where, grave, thy
　　victory ?
I triumph still, if Thou abide with me.

Hold Thou the cross before my closing eyes,
Shine through the gloom, and point me to the
　　skies ;
Heaven's morning breaks, and earth's vain
　　shadows flee ;
In life, in death, O Lord, abide with me.
　　　　　　　　　　　　　　　H. F. Lyte.

23　　　　　*Evening.*　　　　　6.4.6.6.

THE hills and vales grow dark,
　　The shades descend ;
Let prayer of human hearts
With nature's vespers blend.

As earth is hushed and wrapt
  In starry night;
My soul would give herself
To rest and slumber light.

For all thy gifts we bless;
  For eve and morn,
For earth in new leaves dressed,
For gold of autumn born.

For lightnings, rain, and snow,
  For winds and storms,
For all this world's delight,
All nature's wondrous forms.

For virtue, friendship, love,
  Souls wise and good,
Divine society,
And tranquil solitude.

Above all other things
  We love Thee.   Come,
O spirit of light, life,
Make Thou our heart thy home.

Now wearied nature sinks
  To silent sleep,
And all is hushed and still,
Rest grant us sweet and deep.

As falls the evening dew
  On tender flower,
Thine influence, O breathe
In this still evening hour.

T. W. Chignell.

24   *Evening.*   C.M.

THE twilight falls, the night is near;
    We put our work away,
And kneel to Him who bends to hear
    The story of the day.

The common story; yet we kneel
    To tell it at thy call,
And cares grow lighter when we feel
    Our Father knows them all.

Yes, all! the morning and the night,
    The joy, the grief, the loss,
The mountain track, the valley bright,
    The daily thorn and cross.

Thou knowest all: we lean our head,
    Our wearied eyelids close;
Content and glad awhile to tread
    The way our Father knows.

And He has loved us! all our heart
    With answering love is stirred;
And poverty and toil and smart,
    Find healing in that word.

So here we lay us down to rest,
    As nightly shadows fall;
And lean, confiding on his breast,
    Who knows and pities all;

And holds the morrows, far and near,
    Within his love alway:
Let come what will, He bends to hear
    The story day by day.

                                    Anon.

25 *Evening.* C.M.

THE shadows of the evening hours
  Fall from the darkening sky ;
Upon the fragrance of the flowers
  The dews of evening lie :
Before thy throne, O Lord of heaven,
  We kneel at close of day :
Look on thy children from on high,
  And hear us while we pray.

The sorrows of thy servants, Lord,
  O do not Thou despise ;
But let the incense of our prayers
  Before thy mercy rise ;
The brightness of the coming night
  Upon the darkness rolls ;
With hopes of future glory chase
  The shadows from our souls.

Slowly the rays of daylight fade ;
  So fade within our heart
The hopes of earthly love and joy
  That one by one depart ;
Slowly the bright stars, one by one,
  Within the heavens shine ;
Give us, O Lord, fresh hopes in heaven,
  And trust in things divine.

Let peace, O Lord,—thy peace, O God,—
  Upon our souls descend ;
From midnight fears and perils Thou
  Our trembling hearts defend :
Give us a respite from our toil ;
  Calm and subdue our woes ;
Through the long day we suffer, Lord,
  O give us now repose.

Adelaide A. Procter.

26　　　　　*Evening.*　　　　　8.8.8.4.

THE radiant morn hath passed away,
　And spent too soon her golden store;
·The shadows of departing day
　　　　Creep on once more.

Our life is but an autumn day,
　Its glorious noon how quickly past;
Lead us through Christ, the living way,
　　　　Home, Lord, at last.

O, by thy soul-inspiring grace
　Uplift our hearts to realms on high;
Help us to look to that bright place
　　　　Beyond the sky;

Where light, and life, and joy, and peace
　In undivided empire reign,
And thronging angels never cease
　　　　Their deathless strain;

Where saints are clothed in spotless white,
　And evening shadows never fall;
Where Thou, eternal Light of Light,
　　　　Art Lord of all.
　　　　　　　　G. Thring.

27　　　　　*Evening.*　　　　　7s.

SLOWLY by thy hand unfurled,
Down around the weary world
Falls the darkness; O how still
Is the working of thy will!

Mighty Maker, here am I;
Work in me as silently;
Veil the day's distracting sights,
Show me heaven's eternal lights.

From the darkened sky come forth
Countless stars, a wondrous birth :
So may gleams of glory dart
From this dim abyss, my heart.

Living worlds to view be brought
In the boundless realms of thought ;
High and infinite desires,
Flaming like those upper fires.

Holy Truth, Eternal Right,
Let them break upon my sight ;
Let them shine, serene and still,
And with light my being fill.

Thou who dwellest there, I know,
Dwellest here within me too ;
May the perfect peace of God
Here, as there, be shed abroad,

Let my life attunèd be
To the heavenly harmony
Which, beyond the power of sound,
Fills the universe around.

W. H. Furness.

28   *Evening.*   L. M.

O LIGHT of life, O Saviour dear,
Before we sleep bow down thine ear :
Through dark and day, o'er land and sea,
We have no other hope but Thee.

Oft from thy royal road we part,
Lost in the mazes of the heart :
Our lamps put out, our course forgot,
We seek for God and find Him not.

What sudden sunbeams cheer our sight !
What dawning risen upon the night !
Thou giv'st Thyself to us, and we
Find Guide and Path and all in Thee.

Through day and darkness, Saviour dear,
Abide with us more nearly near ;
Till on thy face we lift our eyes,
The Sun of God's own Paradise.

Praise God, our Maker and our Friend ;
Praise Him through time, till time shall end ;
Till psalm and song his name adore
Through heaven's great day of Evermore.

F. T. Palgrave.

29   *Evening.*   10s.

SAVIOUR, again to thy dear name we raise,
With one accord our parting hymn of praise ;
We stand to bless Thee ere our worship cease,
Then, lowly kneeling, wait thy word of peace.

Grant us thy peace upon our homeward way ;
With Thee began, with Thee shall end, the day ;
Guard Thou the lips from sin, the hearts from
    shame,
That in this house have called upon thy name.

Grant us thy peace, Lord, through the coming
    night,
Turn Thou for us its darkness into light ;
From harm and danger keep thy children free,
For dark and light are both alike to Thee.

Grant us thy peace throughout our earthly life,
Our balm in sorrow and our stay in strife :
Then, when thy voice shall bid our conflict cease,
Call us, O Lord, to thine eternal peace.

J. Ellerton.

30   *Close of Worship.*   C.M.

THE Lord be with us as we bend
   His blessing to receive ;
His gift of peace upon us send,
   Before his courts we leave.

The Lord be with us as we walk
   Along our homeward road ;
In silent thought, or friendly talk,
   Our hearts be still with God.

The Lord be with us till the night
   Enfold our day of rest ;
Be He of every heart the Light,
   Of every home the Guest.

The Lord be with us through the hours
   Of slumber calm and deep ;
Protect our homes, renew our powers,
   And guard his people's sleep.
                     J. Ellerton.

31   *Part in Peace.*   8.7.

PART in peace ! is day before us ?
   Praise his name for life and light :
Are the shadows lengthening o'er us ?
   Bless his care who guards the night.

Part in peace ! with deep thanksgiving,
   Rendering, as we homeward tread,
Gracious service to the living,
   Tranquil memory to the dead.

Part in peace ! from sweet reposing,
   And with heavenly thoughts refreshed,
In the morn our eyes unclosing,
   May we bless the Ever-blessed.

Part in peace ! such are the praises
   God our Maker loveth best ;
Such the worship that upraises
   Human hearts to heavenly rest.
Sarah F. Adams.
Ver. 3, *S. A. Brooke.*

32   *The Benediction of Peace.*   8.7.

FATHER, give thy benediction,
   Give thy peace before we part ;
Still our minds with truth's conviction,
   Calm with trust each anxious heart.

Let thy voice, with sweet commanding,
   Bid our griefs and struggles end ;
Peace which passeth understanding
   On our waiting spirits send.
S. Longfellow.

33   *Advent.*   C.M.

HARK the glad sound ! the Saviour comes,
   The Saviour promised long :
Let every heart prepare a throne,
   And every voice a song.

On Him the Spirit largely poured
   Exerts its sacred fire ;
Wisdom and might, and zeal and love,
   His holy breast inspire.

He comes the prisoners to release
   In evil bondage held ;
The gates of brass before Him burst,
   The iron fetters yield.

He comes the broken heart to bind,
   The bleeding soul to cure ;
And with the treasures of his grace
   To enrich the humble poor.

Our glad hosannas, Prince of peace,
   Thy welcome shall proclaim ;
And heaven's eternal arches ring
   With thy belovèd name.

P. Doddridge.

34   *Advent.*   7s.

WATCHMAN, tell us of the night,
   What its signs of promise are ;
Traveller, o'er yon mountain's height
   See that glory-beaming star.
Watchman, doth its beauteous ray
   Aught of hope or joy foretell ?
Traveller, yes ! it brings the day,
   Promised day of Israel.

Watchman, tell us of the night ;
   Higher yet that star ascends ;
Traveller, blessedness and light,
   Peace and truth its course portends.
Watchman, will its beams alone
   Gild the spot that gave them birth ?
Traveller, ages are its own,
   And it bursts o'er all the earth.

Watchman, tell us of the night,
  For the morning seems to dawn ;
Traveller, darkness takes its flight,
  Doubt and terror are withdrawn.
Watchman, let thy wanderings cease ;
  Hie thee to thy quiet home ;
Traveller, lo ! the Prince of Peace,
  Lo ! the Lord of Love is come.

Sir J. Bowring. •

35 *John and Jesus.* S.M.

A VOICE by Jordan's shore,
  A summons stern and clear :—
'Repent, be just, and sin no more ;
  God's judgment draweth near.'

A voice by Galilee,
  A holier voice I hear :—
'Love God ; thy neighbour love ; for see,
  God's mercy draweth near.'

O voice of Duty, still
  Speak forth, I hear with awe ;
In thee I own the sovereign will,
  Obey the sovereign law.

Thou higher voice of Love,
  Yet speak thy word in me ;
Through duty let me upward move
  To thy pure liberty.

S. Longfellow.

36 *Christmas.* 7.9.6.8.

O LITTLE town of Bethlehem,
  How still we see thee lie ;
Above thy deep and dreamless sleep,
  The silent stars go by ;

Yet in thy dark streets shineth
  The everlasting light ;
The hopes and fears of all the years
  Are met in thee to-night.

For Christ is born of Mary ;
  And gathered all above,
While mortals sleep, the angels keep
  Their watch of wondering love.
O morning stars, together
  Proclaim the holy birth,
And praises sing to God the King,
  And peace to men on earth.

How silently, how silently
  The wondrous gift is given ;
So God imparts to human hearts
  The blessings of his heaven.
No ear may hear his coming ;
  But in this world of sin,
Where meek souls will receive Him still,
  The dear Christ enters in.

O holy Child of Bethlehem,
  Descend to us, we pray ;
Cast out our sin and enter in ;
  Be born in us to-day.
We hear the Christmas angels
  The great glad tidings tell ;
O come to us, abide with us,
  Our Lord Emmanuel.

Phillips Brooks.

37   *Christmas.*   8.7.

Now the joyful Christmas morning,
  Breaking o'er the world below,
Tells again the wondrous story
  Of the Christ-child long ago.

Hark ! we hear again the chorus
　　Echoing through the starry sky,
And we join the heavenly anthem,
　　' Glory be to God on high.'

Out of every clime and people
　　Under every holy name,
Is the everlasting gospel
　　Good and glad for aye the same :
So we, in our happy Christmas,
　　Breathe the universal creed,
Clasping hands with distant ages
　　In a brotherhood indeed.

Sing aloud, then, hearts and voices ;
　　Shout, O new world, free and strong ;
Hail of light the deathless triumph,
　　Join the old world's birthday song,—
' Glory be to God the Highest ;
　　Peace on earth, goodwill to men.'
'Twas the morning stars that pealed it ;
　　Let the world respond again.
Mrs. M. N. Meigs. (v. 1.)

38　　　　　　　*Christmas.*　　　　　　　C.M.

LONG, long ago, in manger low
　　Was cradled from above
A little Child, in whom God smiled,
　　A Christmas gift of love.

When hearts were bitter and unjust,
　　And cruel hands were strong,
The noise He hushed with hope and trust,
　　And peace began her song.

Whene'er the Father's Christmas gifts
　　Seem only frost and snow,
And anxious stress and loneliness
　　And poverty and woe ;

Straightway provide a welcome wide,
    Nor wonder why they came;
They stand outside our hearts and bide
    Knocking in Jesus' name.

For trouble cold, and dreary care,
    Are angels in disguise;
And greeted fair, with trust and prayer,
    As peace and love they rise.

They are the manger, rude and low,
    In which a Christ-child lies;
O welcome guest, thy cradle nest
    Is always God's surprise.
            Jane Andrews and W. C. Gannett.

39   *Peace on earth.*   C.M.

It.came upon the midnight clear,
    That glorious song of old,
From angels bending near the earth,
    To touch their harps of gold:—
'Peace to the earth, goodwill to men
    From heaven's all-gracious King.'
The world in solemn stillness lay
    To hear the angels sing.

Still through the cloven skies they come,
    With peaceful wings unfurled;
And still their heavenly music floats
    O'er all the weary world.
Above its sad and lowly plains
    They bend, on hovering wing,
And ever o'er its Babel-sounds
    The blessed angels sing.

But with the woes of sin and strife
   The world has suffered long :
Beneath the angel-strain have rolled
   Two thousand years of wrong ;
And man, at war with man, hears not
   The love-song which they bring :
O hush the noise, ye men of strife,
   And hear the angels sing.

And ye, beneath life's crushing load,
   Whose forms are bending low,
Who toil along the climbing way
   With painful steps and slow ;
Look now ! for glad and golden hours
   Come swiftly on the wing :
O rest beside the weary road,
   And hear the angels sing.

For lo, the days are hastening on,
   By prophet bards foretold,
When, with the ever-circling years,
   Comes round the age of gold ;
When peace shall over all the earth
   Its ancient splendours fling,
And the whole world give back the song
   Which now the angels sing.

E. H. Sears.

40   *Christmas.*   8.7.

In the old time, runs the story,
   There was once a wondrous night,
When from out the unseen glory
   Burst a ray of glad delight :
It was when the stars were gleaming,
   Shepherds watched their flocks, and then
In their waking, or their dreaming,
   Angels sang, ' Goodwill to men.'

Since that day the children's voices
 Have caught up the glad refrain ;
And to-day the heart rejoices
 That the hour comes round again
And the children are our angels ;
 With one loud acclaim they cry,
Answering back the glad evangel's
 ' Glory be to God on high.'

Each new child's a new Messiah,
 Whether cot or palace born,
Leading on the race still higher
 Toward the glad redemption morn ;
Each new child's a word new spoken,
 God to earth come down again
With His promise never broken,
 ' Peace on earth, goodwill to men.'

M. J. Savage.

41 *Christmas.* C.M.

CALM, on the listening ear of night,
 Come heaven's melodious strains,
Where wild Judæa stretches forth
 Her silver-mantled plains.
Celestial choirs, from courts above,
 Shed sacred glories there ;
And angels, with their sparkling lyres,
 Make music on the air.

The answering hills of Palestine
 Send back the glad reply ;
And greet, from all their holy heights,
 The day-spring from on high ;
O'er the blue depths of Galilee,
 There comes a holier calm :
And Sharon waves, in solemn praise,
 Her silent groves of palm.

'Glory to God.' The lofty strain
   The realm of ether fills,
How sweeps the song of solemn joy
   O'er Judah's sacred hills.
'Glory to God.' The sounding skies
   Loud with their anthems ring,
'Peace on the earth; goodwill to men
   From heaven's Eternal King.'

This day shall Christian tongues be mute,
   And Christian hearts be cold?
O catch the anthem that from heaven
   O'er Judah's mountains rolled,
When burst upon that listening night
   The high and solemn lay:
'Glory to God, on earth be peace,'
   Salvation comes to-day.
              E. H. Sears.

42   *Christmas.*   C.M.

TO-DAY be joy in every heart,
   For lo, the angel throng
Once more above the listening earth
   Repeats the advent song:

'Peace on the earth, goodwill to men!'
   Before us goes the star
That leads us on to holier births
   And life diviner far.

Ye men of strife, forget to-day
   Your harshness and your hate;
Too long ye stay the promised years
   For which the nations wait.

And ye upon the tented field,
   Sheathe, sheathe to-day the sword ;
By love, and not by might, shall come
   The kingdom of the Lord.

O star of human faith and hope,
   Thy light shall lead us on,
Until it fades in morning's glow,
   And heaven on earth is won.

F. L. Hosmer.

43   *Christmas.*   7s.

THROUGH the starry midnight dim
O'er the hills of Bethlehem,
Loud awoke the angels' hymn,
      Hallelujah.

And the shepherds who their sheep
Kept among the meadows steep,
Feared, but soon had joy as deep.
      Hallelujah.

' Fear not,' cried the angel bright,
' There is born to you this night
A Saviour, Jesus, King of Light.'
      Hallelujah.

' He is Christ the Lord ; arise,
Seek Him where He lowly lies,
In a manger, hid from eyes.'
      Hallelujah.

Joyful were the shepherds then,
When the Gospel tidings ran,
' Peace on earth, goodwill to Man.'
      Hallelujah.

And all heaven at the word,
Sang aloud—'O, be adored
In the highest, God the Lord.'
        Hallelujah.
              S. A. Brooke.

44   *Christmas.*   L.M .

'WHAT means this glory round our feet,'
The magi mused, 'more bright than morn?'
And voices chanted clear and sweet,
'To-day the Prince of Peace is born.'

'What means that star,' the shepherds said,
'That brightens through the rocky glen?'
And angels, answering overhead,
Sang, 'Peace on earth, goodwill to men.'

'Tis eighteen hundred years and more
Since those sweet oracles were dumb;
We wait for Him like them of yore;
Alas, He seems so slow to come.

But it was said in words of gold,
No time or sorrow e'er shall dim,
That little children might be bold,
In perfect trust to come to Him.

All round about our feet shall shine
A light like that the wise men saw,
If we our willing hearts incline
To that sweet Life which is the Law.

So shall we learn to understand
The simple faith of shepherds then,
And kindly clasping hand in hand,
Sing, 'Peace on earth, goodwill to men.'

For they who to their childhood cling,
And keep their natures fresh as morn,
Once more shall hear the angels sing,
To-day the Prince of Peace is born.'

J. R. Lowell.

45   *Christmas.*   7.6.7.7.7.7.

STILL the night, holy the night!
Sleeps the world! yet the light
Shines where Mary watches there
Her child Jesus sweet and fair.
   Sleeping in heavenly rest;
   Sleeping in heavenly rest.

Still the night, holy the night!
Shepherds first told aright
How the Angel-Hallelujah
Rang so loud from near and far;
   Jesus, a Saviour, is born;
   Jesus, a Saviour, is born.

Still the night, holy the night!
Little Child, O how bright
Love is smiling from thy face!
Now there strikes the hour of grace;
   Jesus, our Master, is here;
   Jesus, our Master, is here.

German, tr. S. A. Brooke.

46   *Christmas.*   C.M.

As shadows, cast by cloud and sun,
   Flit o'er the summer grass,
So, in thy sight, Almighty One,
   Earth's generations pass.

And while the years, an endless host,
    Come pressing swiftly on,
The brightest names that earth can boast
    Just glisten, and are gone.

Yet doth the star of Bethlehem shed
    A lustre pure and sweet;
And still it leads, as once it led,
    To the Messiah's feet.

O Father, may that holy star
    Grow every year more bright,
And send its glorious beams afar
    To fill the world with light.

W. C. Bryant.

47   *Epiphany.*   C.M.

A THOUSAND years have come and gone,
    And near a thousand more,
Since happier light from heaven shone
    Than ever shone before;
And in the hearts of old and young
    A joy most joyful stirred,
That sent such news from tongue to tongue
    As ears had never heard.

And we are glad, and we will sing,
    As in the days of yore;
Come all, and hearts made ready—bring
    To welcome back once more
The day when first on wintry earth
    A summer change began,
And dawning in a lowly birth
    Uprose the Light of man.

For trouble such as men must bear
    From childhood to fourscore,
Christ shared with us, that we might share
    His joy for evermore ;
And twice a thousand years of strife,
    Of conflict, and of sin,
May tell how large the harvest-sheaf
    His patient love shall win.

T. T. Lynch.

48   *Jesus.*   C. M.

IMMORTAL by their deed and word
    Like light around them shed,
Still speak the prophets of the Lord,
    Still live the sainted dead.

The voice of old by Jordan's flood
    Yet floats upon the air ;
We hear it in beatitude,
    In parable and prayer.

And still the beauty of that life
    Shines star-like on our way,
And breathes its calm amid the strife
    And burden of to-day.

Earnest of life for evermore,
    That life of duty here,—
The trust that in the darkest hour
    Looked forth and knew no fear.

Spirit of Jesus, still speed on,
    Speed on thy conquering way,
Till every heart the Father own,
    And all his will obey.

F. L. Hosmer.

49   *Jesus.*   8.7.

JESUS, by thy simple beauty,
  By thy depth of love unknown,
We are drawn to earnest duty,
  We come near the Father's throne.

When we read the thrilling pages
  Of that life so pure and true,
Stars of hope across the ages,
  Rise in glory on our view.

Faith and hope and love shine o'er us,
  Make our daily lives divine ;
Friend and Brother gone before us,
  Be our thoughts and deeds like thine.

Thanks for ever, heavenly Father,
  That when human eyes grow dim,
And when shadows darkly gather,
  Shines a holy light through Him.

50   *Jesus.*   7.7.5.

WHEN the Lord of Love was here,
Happy hearts to Him were dear,
  Though his heart was sad ;
Worn and lonely for our sake,
Yet He turned aside to make
  All the weary glad.

Meek and lowly were his ways,
From his loving grew his praise,
  From his giving, prayer :
All the outcasts thronged to hear,
All the sorrowful drew near
  To enjoy his care.

When He walked the fields, He drew
From the flowers, and birds, and dew
   Parables of God;
For within his heart of love
All the soul of man did move,
   God had his abode.

Lord, be ours thy power to keep
In the very heart of grief,
   And in trial, love;
In our meekness to be wise,
And through sorrow to arise
   To our God above.

Fill us with thy deep desire,
All the sinful to inspire,
   With the Father's life:
Free us from the cares that press
On the heart of worldliness,
   From the fret and strife.

And when in the fields and woods
We are filled with nature's moods,
   May the grace be given
With thy faithful heart to say,
'All I see and feel to-day,
   Is my Father's heaven.'

S. A. Brooke.

51   *Of such is the kingdom of God.*   8.8.8.6.

IT fell upon a summer day,
When Jesus walked in Galilee,
The mothers of the village brought
   Their children to his knee.

He took them in his arms, and laid
His hands on each remembered head;
'Suffer these little ones to come
    To Me,' He gently said.

'Forbid them not; unless ye bear
The childish heart your hearts within,
Unto my kingdom ye may come,
    But may not enter in.'

Master, I fain would enter there;
O let me follow Thee, and share
Thy meek and lowly heart, and be
    Freed from all worldly care.

Of innocence, and love, and trust,
Of quiet work, and simple word,
Of joy, and thoughtlessness of self
    Build up my life, good Lord.

All happy thoughts, and gentle ways,
And loving-kindness daily given,
And freedom through obedience gained,
    Make in my heart thine heaven.

And all the wisdom that is born
Of joy and love that question not,
The child's bright vision of the earth,
    Be mine, O Lord, unsought.

O happy thus to live and move;
And sweet this world, where I shall find
God's beauty everywhere, his love,
    His good in all mankind.

Then, Father, grant this childlike heart,
That I may come to Christ, and feel
His hands on me in blessing laid,
    So pure, so strong to heal.

So when, far fled from earth, I come
Before Thee, happy and forgiven,
The heavenly host may cry with joy,
   ' A child is born in heaven.'

S. A. Brooke.

52   *Follow Me.*   L.M.

BESIDE the shore of Galilee,
A voice was heard athwart the sea—
A voice at once of tender tone,
Yet grave, with meaning all its own:
And humble fishers as they heard,
Forgot their nets, obeyed its word,
Left all, disciples true to be,
For Christ had uttered—' Follow Me.'

When, seated at the custom's board,
The faithful Levi saw the Lord,
Then in his heart the bell was rung
For worship from that fruitful tongue:
He left his trade, he left his gold;
His heart grew large, his breast was bold;
He went disciple true to be,
For Christ had uttered—' Follow Me.'

Christ calls us not to come by creed,
But by the truthful faith of deed;
And we who would obey his call,
Must make his teachings lord of all,
Must learn his love, and cease from strife,
And mould our minds to his through life,
If we disciples true would be,
For Christ has uttered—' Follow Me.'

And still e'en now we hear that voice :
Hark, silvery strains, rejoice, rejoice ;
Above the clouds, beyond the air,
Up highest heaven's sapphire stair,
Beyond life's gate of mortal bar,
From sky to sky, from star to star,
It quivereth, echoeth, floweth free,
For Christ still calleth—' Follow Me.'

G. Barmby.

53　　　　　　　*Come unto Me.*　　　　　　7.6.

' Come unto Me, ye weary,
　And I will give you rest.'
O blessèd voice of Jesus,　　　.
　Which comes to hearts opprest :
It tells of benediction,
　Of pardon, grace, and peace,
Of joy that hath no ending,
　Of love which cannot cease.

' Come unto Me, ye wanderers,
　And I will give you light.'
O loving voice of Jesus,
　Which comes to cheer the night ;
Our hearts were filled with sadness,
　And we had lost our way ;
But He has brought us gladness
　And songs at break of day.

' Come unto Me, ye fainting,
　And I will give you life.'
O cheering voice of Jesus,
　Which comes to aid our strife ;
The foe is stern and eager,
　The fight is fierce and long ;
But He has made us mighty,
　And stronger than the strong.

'And whosoever cometh,
   I will not cast him out.'
O welcome voice of Jesus,
   Which drives away our doubt;
Which calls us, very sinners,
   Unworthy though we be
Of love so free and boundless,
   To come to God with Thee.
                      W. C. Dix.

54   *Come unto Me.*   C.M.

I HEARD the voice of Jesus say,
   'Come unto Me and rest;
Lay down, thou weary one, lay down
   Thy head upon my breast.'
I came to Jesus as I was,
   Weary, and worn, and sad;
I found in Him a resting-place,
   And He has made me glad.

I heard the voice of Jesus say,
   'Behold, I freely give
The living water, thirsty one,
   Stoop down, and drink, and live.'
I came to Jesus, and I drank
   Of that life-giving stream;
My thirst was quenched, my soul revived,
   And now I live in Him.

I heard the voice of Jesus say,
   I am this dark world's Light;
Look unto Me, thy morn shall rise,
   And all thy day be bright:'
I looked to Jesus, and I found
   In Him my Star, my Sun;
And in that light of life I'll walk
   Till travelling days are done.
                      H. Bonar.

55 *Follow Me.* 8.5.8.3.

ART thou weary, art thou languid,
  Art thou sore distrest?
'Come to Me,' saith One, 'and coming
            Be at rest.'

Hath He marks to lead me to Him,
  If He be my guide?
'In his feet and hands are wound-prints,
            And his side.'

Hath He diadem as monarch
  That his brow adorns?
'Yea, a crown in very surety,
            But of thorns.'

If I find Him, if I follow,
  What his guerdon here?
'Many a sorrow, many a labour,
            Many a tear.'

If I still hold closely to Him,
  What hath He at last?
'Sorrow vanquished, labour ended,
            Jordan past.'

If I ask Him to receive me,
  Will He say me nay?
'Not till earth and not till heaven
            Pass away.'

Finding, following, keeping, struggling,
  Is He sure to bless?
'Angels, Martyrs, Prophets, Virgins,
            Answer, Yes.'
            Stephen the Sabaite, tr. J. M. Neale.

56   *The story of Jesus.*   7.6.

TELL me the old, old story,
   To lift my heart above,
Of Jesus and his glory,
   Of Jesus and his love ;
Tell me the story simply,
   As to a little child,
For I am weak and wayward
   And oft am sin-defiled.

Tell me the story softly,
   With earnest tones and grave,
That I, like Him, may struggle
   For all that's high and brave ;
Tell me the story, tell it,
   To shame me from the fear
That God's own truth and beauty
   Can ever cost too dear.

Tell me the story slowly,
   The world has heard so long,
As fresh to-day as ever
   To save a heart from wrong ;
Tell it in noble measures, -
   Tell it to every soul,
Tell us the old, old story,
   And it shall make us whole.

57   *I am the Way, the Truth, and the Life.*   10s.

O THOU great Friend to all the sons of men,
   Who once appeared in humblest guise below,
Sin to rebuke, to break the captive's chain,
   And call thy brethren forth from want and woe,

We look to Thee ; thy truth is still the light
   Which guides the nations, groping on their way,
Stumbling and falling in disastrous night,
   Yet hoping ever for the perfect day.

Yes, Thou art still the Life ; Thou art the Way
The holiest know,—Light, Life, and Way of
heaven ;
And they who dearest hope, and deepest pray,
Toil by the Light, Life, Way, which Thou hast
given.

T. Parker.

58　　　　　　*The Lost Sheep.*　　　　　IRR.

I WAS wandering and weary,
When the Shepherd came unto me ;
For the ways of sin grew dreary,
And the world had ceased to woo me :
And I thought I heard Him say,
As He came along his way,
'O wandering souls, come near Me ;
My sheep shall never fear Me ;
I am the Shepherd true.'

At first I would not hearken,
And put off until the morrow ;
But life began to darken,
And I was sick with sorrow.
And I thought I heard Him say,
As He came along his way,
'O wandering souls,' etc.

At last I stopped to listen,
His voice could not deceive me ;
I saw his kind eyes glisten,
So anxious to relieve me :
And I thought I heard Him say,
As He came along his way,
'O wandering souls,' etc.

He took me on his shoulder,
 And tenderly He kissed me;
He bade my love be bolder,
 And said how He had missed me;
And I'm sure I heard Him say,
As He went along his way,
  'O wandering souls,' etc.

I thought his love would weaken,
 As more and more He knew me;
But it burneth like a beacon,
 And its light and heat go through me.
And I ever hear Him say,
As He goes along his way,
  'O wandering souls,' etc.

         F. W. Faber.

59 *Behold, I stand at the door and knock.* 7.7.8.7.8.7.

KNOCKING, knocking! who is there?
Waiting, waiting, O how fair!
'Tis a Pilgrim, strange and kingly,
 Never such was seen before;
Ah! my soul, for such a wonder,
 Wilt thou not undo the door?

Knocking, knocking! Still He's there,
Waiting, waiting, wondrous fair;
But the door is hard to open,
 For the weeds and ivy-vine,
With their dark and clinging tendrils,
 Ever round the hinges twine.

Knocking, knocking! What, still there?
Waiting, waiting, grand and fair;
Yes, the piercèd hand still knocketh,
 And beneath the crownèd hair
Beam the patient eyes so tender,
 Of Thy Master, waiting there.

        Harriet B. Stowe.

60   *On the Mount.*   L.M.

Not always on the mount may we
Rapt in the heavenly vision be ;
The shores of thought and feeling know
The Spirit's tidal ebb and flow.

Lord, it is good abiding here--
We cry, the heavenly presence near ;
The vision vanishes, our eyes
Are lifted into vacant skies.

Yet hath one such exalted hour
Upon the soul redeeming power,
And in its strength through after days
We travel our appointed ways ;

Till all the lowly vale grows bright
Transfigured in remembered light,
And in untiring souls we bear
The freshness of the upper air.

The mount for vision,—but below
The paths of daily duty go,
And nobler life therein shall own
The pattern on the mountain shown.

F. L. Hosmer.

61   *Work and Worship.*   10S.

Stay, Master, stay upon this heavenly hill :
A little longer, let us linger still ;
With all the mighty ones of old beside,
Near to the Awful Presence still abide ;
Before the throne of light we trembling stand,
And catch a glimpse into the spirit-land.

Stay, Master, stay; we breathe a purer air;
This life is not the life that waits us there:
Thoughts, feelings, flashes, glimpses come and go;
We cannot speak them—nay, we do not know;
Wrapt in this cloud of light we seem to be
The thing we fain would grow—eternally.

'No!' saith the Lord, 'the hour is past,—we go;
Our home, our life, our duties lie below.
While here we kneel upon the mount of prayer,
The plough lies waiting in the furrow there:
Here we sought God that we might know his will;
There we must do it,—serve Him,—seek Him still.'

If man aspires to reach the throne of God,
O'er the dull plains of earth must lie the road.
He who best does his lowly duty here,
Shall mount the highest in a nobler sphere:
At God's own feet our spirits seek their rest,
And he is nearest Him who serves Him best

S. Greg.

62   *Charity.*   8.5.

Thou, who on that wondrous journey
  Sett'st thy face to die,
By thy holy, meek example
  Teach us Charity.

Thou, who that dread cup of anguish
  Did'st not put from Thee;
O most Loving of the loving,
  Give us Charity.

Thou who reignest, by thy meekness,
  Over earth and sky,
O, that we may share thy triumph,
  Grant us Charity.

Send us Faith, that trusts thy promise;
    Hope, with upward eye;
But more blest than both, and greater,
    Send us Charity.

Dean Alford.

63   *Which temple ye are.*   10S.

'DESCEND to thy Jerusalem, O Lord!'
Her faithful children cry with one accord;
Come, ride in triumph on! behold, we lay
Our guilty lusts and proud wills in thy way.

Thy road is ready, Lord; thy paths, made straight,
In longing expectation seem to wait
The consecration of thy beauteous feet:
And hark, Hosannas loud thy footsteps greet.

Welcome, O welcome to our hearts, Lord, here
Thou hast a temple too, and full as dear
As that in Sion, and as full of sin:
How long shall thieves and robbers dwell therein?

Enter and chase them forth, and cleanse the floor;
Destroy their strength, that they may never more
Profane with traffic vile that holy place,
Which Thou hast chosen, there to set thy face.

And then, if our stiff tongues shall silent be
In praises of thy finished victory,
The temple-stones shall cry, and loud repeat,
Hosanna, and thy glorious footsteps greet.

Bishop J. Taylor.

64   *Passiontide.*   L.M.

SIGN of a glorious life afar,
    The holy cross with joy we take,
Sign of a peace strife could not mar,
    Sign of a faith death could not shake.

It tells how truth, once crucified,
　　Now throned in majesty doth reign ;
How love is blessed and glorified,
　　That once on earth was mocked and slain.

Up, children of the cross ! and dare
　　Follow where Jesus goes before ;
Be strong to take, be strong to bear,
　　For love and right, the cross He bore.
　　　　　　L. A. Gotter, tr. Catherine Winkworth.

65　　　　　*The cross of Christ.*　　　8.7.

In the cross of Christ I glory,
　　Towering o'er the wrecks of time ;
All the light of sacred story
　　Gathers round its head sublime.

When the woes of life o'ertake me,
　　Hopes deceive, and fears annoy,
Never shall the cross forsake me ;
　　Lo, it glows with peace and joy.

When the sun of bliss is beaming
　　Light and love upon my way,
From the cross the radiance streaming
　　Adds more lustre to the day.

Bane and blessing, pain and pleasure,
　　By the cross are sanctified ;
Peace is there, that knows no measure,
　　Joys that through all time abide.

In the cross of Christ I glory,
　　Towering o'er the wrecks of time ;
All the light of sacred story
　　Gathers round its head sublime.
　　　　　　　　　　Sir J. Bowring.

THOU say'st, 'Take up thy cross,
  O man, and follow Me';
The night is black, the feet are slack,
  Yet we would follow Thee.

But, O dear Lord, we cry,
  That we thy face could see,
Thy blessed face one moment's space,—
  Then might we follow Thee.

Dim tracts of time divide
  Those golden days from me;
Thy voice comes strange o'er years of change;
  How can we follow Thee?

Comes faint and far thy voice
  From vales of Galilee;
Thy vision fades in ancient shades?
  How should we follow Thee?

O heavy cross—of faith
  In what we cannot see;
As once of yore Thyself restore
  And help to follow Thee.

If not as once Thou cam'st
  In true humanity,
Come yet as guest within the breast
  That burns to follow Thee.

Within our heart of hearts
  In nearest nearness be;
Set up thy throne within thine own :—
  Go, Lord : we follow Thee.

                      F. T. Palgrave.

67   *Looking unto Jesus.*   6.6.10.

THOU, who in life below
Didst drain the cup of woe,
And glorify the cross of agony,
    Thy blessèd labours done,
    Thy crown of victory won,
Hast passed from earth, passed to thy home
    on high.

It was no path of flowers,
Through this dark world of ours,
Belovèd of the Father, Thou didst tread ;
    And shall we in dismay
    Shrink from the narrow way,
When clouds and darkness are around it
    spread ?

Dear image of our life,
Look on us through the strife ;
Thy own meek head by rudest storms was
    bowed ;
    Raise Thou our eyes above,
    To see a Father's love
Beam, like a bow of promise, through the
    cloud.

E'en through the awful gloom
Which hovers o'er the tomb,
That light of love our guiding star shall be;
    Our spirits shall not dread
    The shadowy way to tread,
Friend, Guardian, Saviour, which doth lead
    to Thee.

Sarah E. Miles.

68   *Let this cup pass from Me.*   L.M.

A VOICE upon the midnight air,
   Where Kedron's moonlit waters stray,
Weeps forth, in agony of prayer,
   O Father, take this cup away.

Ah, Thou, who sorrow'st unto death,
   We conquer in thy mortal fray ;
And earth for all her children saith,
   ' O God, take not this cup away.'

O Man of sorrows, nobly die ;
   Thou'lt heal or hallow all our woe ;
Thy peace shall still the mourner's sigh,
   Thy strength shall raise the faint and low.

O King of earth, the cross ascend ;
   O'er climes and ages, 'tis thy throne ;
Where'er thy fading eye may bend
   The desert blooms and is thine own.

Great Chief of faithful souls, arise ;
   None else can lead the martyr-band,
Who teach the brave how peril flies,
   When faith unarmed lifts up the hand.

Thy parting blessing, Lord, we pray :
   Make but one fold below, above ;
And when we go the last lone way,
   O give the welcome of thy love.
                    J. Martineau.

69   *Gethsemane and Calvary.*   7s.

WHEN my love to God grows weak,
When for deeper faith I seek,
Then in thought I go to thee,
Garden of Gethsemane.

There I walk amid the shades,
While the lingering twilight fades;
See that suffering, friendless One
Weeping, praying there alone.

When my love for man grows weak,
When for stronger faith I seek,
Hill of Calvary, I go
To thy scenes of fear and woe;

There behold his agony
Suffered on the bitter tree;
See his anguish, see his faith,
Love triumphant still in death.

Then to life I turn again,
Learning all the worth of pain,
Learning all the might that lies
In a full self-sacrifice.

J. R. Wreford and S. Longfellow.

70   *Stabat Mater.*   8.8.7.

Jews were wrought to cruel madness,
Christians fled in fear and sadness,
    Mary stood the cross beside.
At its foot her foot she planted,
By the dreadful scene undaunted,
    Till the gentle Sufferer died.

Poets oft have sung her story,
Painters decked her brow with glory,
    Priests her name have deified;
But no worship, song, or glory
Touches like that simple story,—
    Mary stood the cross beside.

And when under fierce oppression
Goodness suffers like transgression,
   Christ again is crucified.
But if love be there, true-hearted,
By no grief or terror parted,
   Mary stands the cross beside.

                      W. J. Fox.

71   *It is finished.*   7s.

' It is finished '—all the pain,
All the sorrow, all the stain ;
Death has freed the Lord of life
From the burden of his strife.

' It is finished '—all the days,
Led through many weary ways ;
Now at last his eyelids close
On the hatred of his foes.

' It is finished '—all the toil
Sin and trial could not spoil ;
Never could his spirit fleet,
Till the work was all complete.

' It is finished '—all the Word,
Poor, and sinners, gladly heard ;
All the Father's love made known,
Human goodness fully shown.

' It is finished '—all the love,
Deep as his that dwells above ;
Saving others, all He gave,
. But Himself He would not save.

'It is finished '—Hark, the cry,
Uttered in Love's agony,
Is the seal, below, above,
Of the Victory of Love.
     Hallelujah.
S. A. Brooke.

72   *Strength from the cross.*   8.8.7.

'IT is finished !' Man of sorrows,
From thy cross our frailty borrows
  Strength to bear and conquer thus.

While extended there we view Thee,
Mighty Sufferer, draw us to Thee,
  Sufferer victorious.

Not in vain for us uplifted,
Man of sorrows, wonder-gifted,
  May that sacred emblem be ;

Lifted high amid the ages,
Guide of heroes, saints, and sages,
  May it guide us still to Thee ;

Still to Thee, whose love unbounded
Sorrow's depths for us has sounded,
  Perfected by conflicts sore.

Honoured be thy cross for ever,
Star, that points our high endeavour
  Whither Thou hast gone before.
F. H. Hedge.

73   *It is finished.*   8.8.8.6.

O WHO is this that on a tree
Of shame and pain and mockery,
Hangs by the hill of Calvary ?
  'Tis Jesus, Lord of Love.

Mercy could not from Him depart;
His arms, outstretched in piteous art,
Dropt blood, like love, upon the heart
    Of all the sinful world.

O deep the passion, great the woe,
He long endured to slay the foe;
That we the depths of love might know,
    The love that died for men.

Yet in the woe, a joy as deep
Mingled, and laid the pain asleep;
And we are glad, although we weep
    With John, beneath his cross.

For through the gloom that veiled the hill,
A heavenly vision came to fill
His heart with joy ineffable;
    The vision of the end.

The whole of mankind gathered in,
His sheep, his own belovèd kin,
Saved from themselves, and saved from sin
    By God the Father's love.

Then sank his head upon his breast,
Then was his heart, at last, at rest,
Holy and undefiled and blest!
    'All is fulfilled,' He said.

O Jesu, who thus died that we
Might know Life's deepest mystery,
Lead us, through love like thine to see
    Our Father, face to face.

S. A. Brooke.

74   *Our Calvary.*   10.4.

GOD draws a cloud over each gleaming morn :
    Would we ask why ?
It is because all noblest things are born
    In agony.

Only upon *some* cross of pain or woe
    God's son may lie ;
Each soul redeemed from self and sin must know
    Its Calvary.

Yet we must crave neither for joy nor grief,
    God chooses best :
He only knows our sick soul's best relief,
    And gives us rest.

More than our feeble hearts can ever pine
    For holiness,
The Father, in his tenderness divine,
    Yearneth to bless.

He never sends a joy not meant in love,
    Still less a pain :
Our gratitude the sunlight falls to prove ;
    Our faith the rain.

In his hands we are safe.   We falter on
    Through storm and mire :
Above, beside, around us, there is One
    Will never tire.

What though we fall, and bruised and wounded
    lie,
    Our lips in dust?
God's arm shall lift us up to victory :
    In Him we trust.

For neither life, nor death, nor things below,
    Nor things above,
Shall ever sever us, that we should go
    From his great love.

Frances P. Cobbe.

75   *Easter.*   8.4.4.6.8.6.

YE happy bells of Easter Day!
Ring, ring your joy
Through earth and sky;
Ye ring a glorious word;
The notes that swell in gladness tell
The rising of the Lord.

Ye glory-bells of Easter Day!
The hills that rise
Against the skies
Re-echo with the word—
The victor breath that conquers death—
The rising of the Lord.

Ye passion-bells of Easter Day!
The bitter cup
He lifted up,
Salvation to afford;
Ye saintly bells, your passion tells
The rising of the Lord.

Ye victor bells of Easter Day!
The thorny crown
He layeth down;
Ring, ring, with strong accord,
The mighty strain of love and pain—
The rising of the Lord.

76   *Easter.*   8.8.8.4.

PAST are the cross, the scourge, the thorn,
The scoffing tongue, the gibe, the scorn,
And brightly breaks the Eastern morn.
                   Hallelujah !

Gone are the gloomy clouds of night ;
The shades of death are put to flight ;
And from the tomb beams heavenly light.
                   Hallelujah !

And so, in sorrow dark and drear,
Though black the night, the morn is near ;
Soon shall the heavenly day appear.
                   Hallelujah !

And when death's darkness dims our eyes,
From out the gloom our souls shall rise
In deathless glory to the skies.
                   Hallelujah !

Then let us raise the glorious strain,
Love's triumph over sin and pain,
Faith's victory over terror's reign.
                   Hallelujah !
                 A. C. Jewitt.

77   *Easter.*   8.7.

STANDING on the shore at morning,
    I beheld the shining sea,
Saw the wreathing vapours mounting
    Into heaven silently.

Standing on the hill at evening,
    Clouds stooped gently over me,
Softly from the west ascending,
    And the rain fell silently.

So I cried, my Spirit's incense
   Sure returneth unto me;
Upward breathing, falls in blessing
   From our Father, silently.

So my life up-striving, soaring,
   Where nor eye nor thought can see,
Comes again descending on me,
   Filled with immortality.

And the bliss of hope awakens;
   Earth and sky I clearer see;
And I carol, in my gladness,
   Joyful hymn and melody.

J. V. Blake.

78   *Easter.*   7.7.7.3.

THERE is gladness in the air,
All around and everywhere,
For the spring, so fresh and fair,
    Comes again;
And with verdure clad anew,
'Neath a dome of cloudless blue,
Decks with garb of varied hue
    Hill and plain.

With an endless beauty rife,
Newly quickened into life,
'Mid the world's discordant strife,
    Hear it say,
' Every winter ushers spring,
Each night's gloom the morn shall bring,
And its heaviness shall fling
    Far away.'

Easter triumph, Easter joy,
Tell of bliss without alloy ;
Life, no death can e'er destroy,
    Has begun.
Hear again the welcome word,
Through successive ages heard,
' Christ is risen, Christ the Lord ! '
    Lo, 'tis done.

                    S. Childs-Clarke.

79   *Easter.*   C.M. Chorus L.M.

The buds are bursting on the trees,
    The earth awakes again,
The birds are singing out their glees,
    For Christ again doth reign.
Awake and alleluias sing,
For death is slain, and Christ is king ;
Awake and let the chorus swell
With voice and harp and Easter bell.

Come let us all sweet blossoms bring
    The risen Lord to greet,
And make our hearts an offering,
    And lay them at his feet.
        Awake, etc.

No longer death and hopeless gloom
    Shall grieve our souls distressed ;
For Christ has trodden through the tomb
    A pathway for the blest.
        Awake, etc.

                  Mabel G. Osgood.

80   *Easter.*   7.6.

Let the merry church-bells ring ;
    Hence with tears and sighing ;
Frost and cold have fled from spring ;
    Life hath conquered dying.

Flowers are smiling, fields are gay,
  Sunny is the weather ;
With our risen Lord to-day
  All things rise together.

Let the birds sing out again
  From their leafy chapel,
Praising Him, with whom in vain
  Sin hath sought to grapple.
Sounds of joy come loud and clear,
  As the breezes flutter ;
'He arose and is not here,'
  Is the strain they utter.

Let the past of grief be past ;
  This our comfort giveth,
He was slain on Friday last,
  But to-day He liveth.
Mourning heart must needs be gay
  Out of sorrow's prison,
Since the very grave can say,
  ' Christ, He hath arisen.'

J. M. Neale.

81   *Easter.*   8.7.8.7.7.7.

EASTER flowers, Easter carols,
  Deck the altar, fill the air ;
Glorious dawns the happy morning
  O'er a world so bright and fair.
      Alleluia let us sing,
      Alleluia to our King.

Now the clouds of night are broken,
  Doubt and darkness flee away,
And on this bright Easter morning
  Sing we now the triumph lay.
      Alleluia let us sing,
      Alleluia to our King.

Past is all the gloom and sadness,
 Easter joys around us shine,
Turned is sorrow into gladness,
 Death is changed to life divine.
  Alleluia let us sing,
  Alleluia to our King.

82   *Immortality.*   11.9.11.9.11.6.

FATHER Omnipotent, joyful and thankful,
 Bring we the praises to Thee belong;
Hopefulness, joyfulness in thy great mercy
 Fill our waked spirits with sounding song.
Hallowed this festival, when life immortal
  Shines through open portal :

Open to faithfulness, open to sorrow,
 Open to vision of saint and seer.
Death, where thy victory? where thy great anguish?
 Hope cometh mighty, outcasting fear.
O hope victorious, on us descending,
  Earth and heaven blending !

Glory and majesty break forth upon us,
 Like unto splendours of morning skies.
Light beatifical, life everlasting,
 With thy great glory on us arise ;
Lighten our heaviness, shine on our sorrow,
  Life's eternal morrow.

          J. V. Blake.

83   *The Ascension.*   7s.

HE is gone—beyond the skies,
A cloud receives Him from our eyes ;
Gone beyond the highest height
Of mortal gaze or angel's flight ;

Through the veils of time and space,
Passed into the holiest place;
All the toil, the sorrow done,
All the battle fought and won.

He is gone—and we return,
And our hearts within us burn;
Olivet no more shall greet,
With welcome shout, his coming feet;
Never shall we track Him more
On Gennesareth's glistening shore,
Never in that look, or voice,
Shall Zion's walls again rejoice.

He is gone—and we remain
In this world of sin and pain;
In the void which He has left,
On this earth, of Him bereft,
We have still his work to do,
We can still his path pursue,
Seek Him both in friend and foe,
In ourselves his image show.

He is gone—towards the goal
World and Church must onward roll:
Far behind we leave the past,
Forward are our glances cast:
Still his words before us range
Through the ages, as they change;
Wheresoe'er the truth shall lead,
He will give whate'er we need.

He is gone—but we once more
Shall behold Him as before,
In the heaven of heavens, the same
As on earth He went and came;

In the many mansions there,
Place for us He will prepare,
In that world unseen, unknown,
He and we may yet be one.

He is gone—but not in vain;
Wait, until He comes again;
He is risen, He is not here,
Far above this earthly sphere;
Evermore in heart and mind,
There our peace in Him we find;
To our own Eternal Friend,
Thitherward let us ascend.

Dean Stanley.

84　　　*Venite, sancte Spiritus.*　　　7s.

COME, Thou Holy Spirit, come;
And from thy celestial home
　Shed a ray of light divine:
Come, Thou Father of the poor,
Come, Thou source of all our store,
　Come, within our bosoms shine:

Thou of Comforters the best,
Thou the soul's most welcome guest,
　Sweet refreshment here below:
In our labour rest most sweet,
Grateful coolness in the heat,
　Solace in the midst of woe.

O most blessèd Light divine,
Shine within these hearts of thine,
　And our inmost being fill:
Where Thou art not, man hath nought,
Nothing good in deed or thought,
　Nothing free from taint of ill.

Heal our wounds; our strength renew;
On our dryness pour thy dew;
　　Wash the stains of guilt away:
Bend the stubborn heart and will;
Melt the frozen, warm the chill;
　　Guide the steps that go astray.

On the faithful, who adore
And confess Thee evermore,
　　In thy gracious gifts descend:
Give them virtue's sure reward,
Give them thy salvation, Lord,
　　Give them joys that never end.

Robert II. of France, tr. based on that of E. Caswall.

85　　　　　*The Comforter.*　　　　　7.7.7.6.

In the hour of my distress,
When temptations me oppress,
And when I my sins confess,
　　Sweet Spirit, comfort me.

When I lie within my bed,
Sick in heart and sick in head,
And with doubts discomfited,
　　Sweet Spirit, comfort me.

When the house doth sigh and weep,
And the world is drowned in sleep,
Yet mine eyes the watch do keep,
　　Sweet Spirit, comfort me.

When God knows I'm tossed about,
Either with despair or doubt,
Yet, before the glass be out,
　　Sweet Spirit, comfort me.

When the tempter me pursu'th
With the sins of all my youth,
And half slays me with untruth,
   Sweet Spirit, comfort me.

When the judgment is revealed,
And that opened which was sealed,
When to Thee I have appealed,
   Sweet Spirit, comfort me.

R. Herrick.

86   *Prayer for Grace.*   7s.

GRACIOUS Spirit, dwell with me ;
I myself would gracious be,
And, with words that help and heal,
Would thy life in mine reveal ;
And with actions bold and meek
Christ's own gracious spirit speak.

Truthful Spirit, dwell with me ;
I myself would truthful be ;
And with wisdom kind and clear
Let thy life in mine appear ;
And with actions brotherly
Follow Christ's sincerity.

Tender Spirit, dwell with me ;
I myself would tender be ;
Shut my heart up like a flower
At temptation's darksome hour ;
Open it when shines the sun,
And his love by fragrance own.

Silent Spirit, dwell with me ;
I myself would quiet be,
Quiet as the growing blade
Which through earth its way has made ;
Silently, like morning light,
Putting mists and chills to flight.

Mighty Spirit, dwell with me;
I myself would mighty be,
Mighty so as to prevail
Where unaided man must fail;
Ever by a mighty hope
Pressing on and bearing up.

Holy Spirit, dwell with me;
I myself would holy be;
Separate from sin, I would
Choose and cherish all things good;
And whatever I can be,
Give to Him who gave me Thee.

T. T. Lynch.

87   *The Spirit of God.*   S.M.

BREATHE on me, Breath of God,
Fill me with life anew,
That I may love what Thou dost love,
And do what Thou wouldst do.

Breathe on me, Breath of God,
Until my heart is pure,
Until with Thee I will one will,
To do or to endure.

Breathe on me, Breath of God,
Till I am wholly thine,
Till all this earthly part of me
Glows with thy fire divine.

Breathe on me, Breath of God,
So shall I never die,
But live with Thee the perfect life
Of thine eternity.

E. Hatch.

88   *The Divine Spirit.*   C.M.

Spirit divine, attend our prayer,
  And make our hearts thy home ;
Descend with all thy gracious power ;
  Come, Holy Spirit, come.

Come, glorious Light, to waiting minds
  That long the truth to know,
Reveal the narrow path of right,
  The way of duty show.

Come, cleansing Fire, enkindle now
  The sacrificial flame,
That all our souls an offering be
  To love's redeeming name.

Come as the dew ; on hearts that pine
  Descend in this still hour,
Till every barren place shall own
  With joy thy quickening power.

Come, Wind of God, sweep clean away
  What dead within us lies,
And search and freshen all our souls
  With living energies.
            A. Reed and S. Longfellow.

89   *Inspiration.*   7s.

Holy Spirit, Truth divine,
Dawn upon this soul of mine ;
Word of God, and inward Light,
Wake my spirit, clear my sight.

Holy Spirit, Love divine,
Glow within this heart of mine ;
Kindle every high desire ;
Perish self in thy pure fire.

Holy Spirit, Power divine,
Fill and nerve this will of mine ;
By Thee may I strongly live,
Bravely bear and nobly strive.

Holy Spirit, Right divine,
King within my conscience reign ;
Be my Law, and I shall be
Firmly bound, forever free.

Holy Spirit, Peace divine,
Still this restless heart of mine ;
Speak to calm this tossing sea,
Stayed in thy tranquility.

Holy Spirit, Joy divine,
Gladden Thou this heart of mine ;
In the desert ways I sing
'Spring, O Well, forever spring.'

S. Longfellow.

90　　　　*The Everlasting Word.*　　　　8s.

OUT from the heart of nature rolled
The burdens of the Bible old ;
The litanies of nations came,
Like the volcano's tongue of flame,
Up from the burning core below,
The canticles of love and woe.

The word unto the prophet spoken
Was writ on tables yet unbroken ;
Still floats upon the morning wind,
Still whispers to the willing mind.
One accent of the Holy Ghost
The heedless world has never lost.

R. W. Emerson.

91   *Love divine.*   L.M.

O LOVE divine, whose constant beam
    Shines on the eyes that will not see,
And waits to bless us while we dream
    Thou leav'st us when we turn from Thee;

All souls that struggle and aspire,
    All hearts of prayer by Thee are lit;
And, dim or clear, thy tongues of fire
    On dusky tribes and centuries sit.

Nor bounds, nor clime, nor creed Thou know'st;
    Wide as our need thy favours fall;
The white wings of the Holy Ghost
    Stoop, unseen, o'er the heads of all.

                       J. G. Whittier.

92   *The Thought of God.*   C.M.

ONE thought I have, my ample creed,
    So deep it is and broad,
And equal to my every need,—
    It is the thought of God.

Each morn unfolds some fresh surprise,
    I feast at life's full board;
And rising in my inner skies
    Shines forth the thought of God.

At night my gladness is my prayer;
    I drop my daily load,
And every care is pillowed there
    Upon the thought of God.

I ask not far before to see,
    But take in trust my road;
Life, death, and immortality
    Are in my thought of God.

To this their secret strength they owed
   The martyr's path who trod;
The fountains of their patience flowed
   From out their thought of God.

Be still the light upon my way,
   My pilgrim staff and rod,
My rest by night, my strength by day,
   O blessèd thought of God.

F. L. Hosmer.

93   God.   11.11.11.5.

FATHER Almighty, bless us with thy blessing,
Answer in love thy children's supplication;
Hear Thou our prayers, the spoken and unspoken:
     Hear us, our Father.

Shepherd of souls, who bringest all who seek Thee
To pastures green, beside the peaceful waters;
Tenderest Guide, in ways of cheerful duty,
     Lead us, Good Shepherd.

Spirit of mercy, from thy watch and keeping
No place can part, nor hour of time remove us;
Give us thy good, and save us from our evil,
     Infinite Spirit.

L. J. W.

94   Our Refuge.   C.M.

OUR God, our help in ages past,
   Our hope for years to come,
Our shelter from the stormy blast,
   And our eternal home:

Under the shadow of thy throne
   Thy saints have dwelt secure ;
Sufficient is thine arm alone,
   And our defence is sure.

Before the hills in order stood,
   Or earth received her frame,
From everlasting Thou art God,
   To endless years the same.

A thousand ages in thy sight
   Are like an evening gone ;
Short as the watch that ends the night
   Before the rising sun.

The busy tribes of flesh and blood,
   With all their lives and cares,
Are carried downwards by thy flood,
   And lost in following years.

Time, like an ever-rolling stream,
   Bears all its sons away ;
They fly forgotten, as a dream
   Dies at the opening day.

Our God, our help in ages past,
   Our hope for years to come,
Be Thou our guard while troubles last,
   And our eternal home.

I. Watts.

95   *The Mystery of God.*   C.M

O Thou, in all thy might so far,
   In all thy love so near,
Beyond the range of sun and star,
   And yet beside us here,—

What heart can comprehend thy name
  Or, searching, find Thee out,
Who art within, a quickening flame,
  A presence round about?

Yet though I know Thee but in part,
  I ask not, Lord, for more :
Enough for me to know Thou art,
  To love Thee and adore.

O sweeter than aught else besides,
  The tender mystery
That like a veil of shadow hides
  The light I may not see !

And dearer than all things I know
  Is childlike faith to me,
That makes the darkest way I go
  An open path to Thee.

F. L. Hosmer.

96　　　　　*The Greatness of God.*　　　　C.M.

My God, how wonderful Thou art,
  Thy majesty how bright,
How beautiful thy mercy-seat,
  In depths of burning light.

How dread are thine eternal years,
  O everlasting Lord,
By prostrate spirits day and night
  Incessantly adored.

How wonderful, how beautiful,
  The sight of Thee must be,
Thine endless wisdom, boundless power,
  And awful purity.

O how I fear Thee, living God,
  With deepest, tenderest fears,
And worship Thee with trembling hope,
  And penitential tears.

Yet I may love Thee too, O Lord,
  Almighty as Thou art,
For Thou has stooped to ask of me
  The joy of my poor heart.

No earthly father loves like Thee,
  No mother, e'er so mild,
Bears and forbears as Thou hast done
  With me thy sinful child.

Only to sit and think of God,
  O what a joy it is;
To think the thought, to breathe the name,
  Earth has no higher bliss.

Father of mankind, love's reward,
  What rapture will it be,   :
To know thy righteousness at last,
  And lose ourselves in Thee.
                              F. W. Faber.

97   *Found.*   C.M.

'O NAME, all other names above,
  What art Thou not to me,
Now I have learned to trust thy love
  And cast my care on Thee. ·

What is our being but a cry,
  A restless longing still,
Which Thou alone canst satisfy,
  Alone thy fulness fill.

Thrice blessèd be the holy souls
  That lead the way to Thee,
That burn upon the martyr-rolls
  And lists of prophecy.

And sweet it is to tread the ground
  O'er which their faith hath trod;
But sweeter far when Thou art found,
  The soul's own sense of God.

The thought of Thee all sorrow calms;
  Our anxious burdens fall;
His crosses turn to triumph-palms
  Who finds in God his all.

F. L. Hosmer.

98   *O that I knew where I might find Him.*   C.M.

Go not, my soul, in search of Him,
  Thou wilt not find Him there,—
Or in the depths of shadow dim.
  Or heights of upper air.

For not in far-off realms of space
  The Spirit hath its throne;
In every heart it findeth place
  And waiteth to be known.

Thought answereth alone to thought,
  And soul with soul hath kin;
The outward God he findeth not
  Who finds not God within.

And if the vision come to thee
  Revealed by inward sign,
Earth will be full of Deity ¯
  And with his glory shine.

Thou shalt not want for company
   Nor pitch thy tent alone ;
The indwelling God will go with thee
   And show thee of his own.

O gift of gifts, O grace of grace,
   That God should condescend
To make thy heart his dwelling-place
   And be thy daily Friend.

Then go not thou in search of Him,
   But to thyself repair ;
Wait thou within the silence dim
   And thou shalt find Him there.
                            F. L. Hosmer.

99   *God all in all.*   L.M.

THE flowing soul, nor low nor high,
   Is perfect here, is perfect there.
Each drop in ocean orbs the sky ;
   And seeing eyes make all things fair.

The evening clouds, the wayside flower,
   Surpass the Andes and the rose ;
And wrapped in every hasty hour
   Is all the lengthened year bestows.

Therefore, erase thy false degrees ;
   From stock and stone strike stars and fire ;
Lo, even in the ' least of these '
   Dwells that Lord-Christ whom ye desire.

100   *Love and Law.*   L.M.

ONE Lord there is, all lords above,—
His name is Truth, his name is Love,
His name is Beauty, it is Light,
His will is Everlasting Right.

But ah, to wrong what is his name?
This Lord is a Consuming Flame
To every wrong beneath the sun;
He is One Lord, the Holy One.

Lord of the Everlasting Name,
Truth, Beauty, Light, Consuming Flame,
Shall I not lift my heart to Thee,
And ask Thee, Lord, to rule in me?

If I be ruled in other wise,
My lot is cast with all that dies,
With things that harm, and things that hate,
And roam by night, and miss the Gate,—

Thy happy Gate, which leads us where
Love is like sunshine in the air,
And Love and Law are both the same,
Named with the Everlasting Name.

W. B. Rands.

101   *Whatsoever road I take joins the highway
that leads to Thee.*   7s.

WHEN the night is still and far,
    Watcher from the shadowed deeps;
When the morning breaks its bar,
    Life that shines and wakes and leaps;
When old Bible-verses glow,
    Starring all the deep of thought,
Till it fills with quiet dawn,
    From the peace our years have brought,—
        Sun within both skies, we see
        How all lights lead back to Thee.

'Cross the field of daily work
    Run the footpaths, leading—where?
Run they east or run they west,
    One way all the workers fare.

Every awful thing of earth,—
   Sin and pain and battle-noise ;
Every dear thing,—baby's birth,
   Faces, flowers, or lover's joys,—
     Is a wicket-gate where we
     Join the great highway to Thee.

Restless, restless, speed we on,—
   Whither in the vast unknown ?
Not to you and not to me
   Are the sealèd orders shown :
But the Hand that built the road,
   And the Light that leads the feet,
And this inward restlessness,
   Are such invitation sweet,
     That where I no longer see,
     Highway still must lead to Thee.

W. C. Gannett.

102   *The Eternal Father.*   C.M.

FATHER, the sweetest, dearest name
   That men or angels know,
Fountain of Life, that had no fount
   From which itself could flow ;

Thou comest not, Thou goest not ;
   Thou wert not, wilt not be ;
Eternity is but a thought
   By which we think of Thee.

Lost in thy greatness, Lord, I live,
   As in some gorgeous maze ;
Thy sea of unbeginning light
   Blinds me, and yet I gaze.

Thy grandeur is all tenderness,
　All motherlike and meek ;
The hearts that will not come to it
　Humbling itself to seek.

Thou feign'st to be remote, and speak'st
　As if from far above,
That fear may make more bold with Thee,
　And be beguiled to love.

On earth thou hidest, not to scare
　Thy children with thy light ;
Then showest us thy face in heaven,
　When we can bear the sight.

F. W. Faber.

103　　　*The greatness of God.*　　　C.M.

O GOD, thy power is wonderful,
　Thy glory passing bright ;
Thy wisdom, with its deep on deep,
　A rapture to the sight.

Yet more than all, and ever more,
　Should we thy creatures bless,
Most worshipful of attributes,
　Thine awful holiness.

There's not a craving in the mind
　Thou dost not meet and still ;
There's not a wish the heart can have
　Which Thou dost not fulfil.

Thy justice is the gladdest thing
　Creation can behold ;
Thy tenderness so meek, it wins
　The guilty to be bold.

All things that have been, **all that are,**
 All things that can be dreamed,
All possible creations, made,
 Kept faithful, or redeemed,—

All these may draw upon thy power,
 Thy mercy may command
And still outflows thy silent sea,
 Immutable and grand.

O little heart of mine, shall pain
 Or sorrow make thee moan,
When all this God is all for thee,
 A Father all thine own?

F. W. Faber.

104   *The Lord of all.*   C.M.

SING forth his high eternal name
 Who holds all powers in thrall,
Through endless ages still the same,—
 The mighty Lord of all.

His goodness, strong and measureless,
 Upholds us lest we fall;
His hand is still outstretched to bless,—
 The loving Lord of all.

His perfect law sets metes and bounds,
 Our strong defence and wall;
His providence our life surrounds,—
 The saving Lord of all.

He every thought and every deed
 Doth to his judgment call;
O may our hearts obedient heed
 The righteous Lord of all.

When, turning from forbidden ways,
    Low at his feet we fall,
His strong and tender arms upraise,—
    The pardoning Lord of all.

Unwearied He is working still,
    Unspent his blessings fall,
Almighty, Loving, Righteous One,—
    The only Lord of all.
                      S. Longfellow.

105   *Who by searching can find out God?*   11.10.

I CANNOT find Thee. Still on restless pinion
    My spirit beats the void where Thou dost dwell;
I wander lost through all thy vast dominion,
    And shrink beneath thy light ineffable.

I cannot find Thee. E'en when most adoring,
    Before thy shrine I bend in lowliest prayer;
Beyond these bounds of thought, my thought up-
      soaring,
    From furthest quest comes back: Thou art not
      there.

Yet high above the limits of my seeing,
    And folded far within the inmost heart,
And deep below the deeps of conscious being,
    Thy splendour shineth: there, O God, Thou
      art.

I cannot lose Thee. Still in Thee abiding,
    The end is clear, how wide soe'er I roam;
The law that holds the worlds my steps is guiding,
    And I must rest at last in Thee, my home.
                    Eliza Scudder.

106   *The thought of God.*   C.M.

THE thought of God, the thought of Thee
    Who liest in my heart,
And yet beyond imagined space
    Outstretched and present art :—

It is a thought which ever makes
    Life's sweetest smiles from tears ;
And is a daybreak to our hopes,
    A sunset to our fears.

It is not of his wondrous works,
    Nor even that He is ;
Words fail it—but it is a thought
    That by itself is bliss.

Within a thought so great, our souls
    Little and modest grow ;
And by its vastness awed, we learn
    The art of walking slow.

The very thinking of the thought,
    Without or praise or prayer,
Gives light to know, and life to do,
    And marvellous strength to bear.
              F. W. Faber.

107   *Thought of God.*   8s.

I SAW the beauty of the world
Before me like a flag unfurled,
The splendour of the morning sky,
And all the stars in company ;
I thought, How beautiful it is :
My soul said, ' There is more than this.'

I saw the pomps of death and birth,
The generations of the earth;
I looked on saints and heroes crowned,
And love as wide as heaven is round;
I thought, How beautiful it is:
My soul said, 'There is more than this.'

Sometimes I have an awful thought
That bids me do the thing I ought;
It comes like wind, it burns like flame,
How shall I give that thought a name?
It draws me like a loving kiss:
My soul says, 'There is more than this.'

Yea, there is One I cannot see
Or hear, but He is Lord to me:
And in the heavens and earth and skies,
The good which lives till evil dies,
The love which I cannot withstand,
God writes his Name with his own hand.

W. B. Rands.

108   *Lord God Almighty.*   5.8.8.5.

LORD God Almighty,
Who hearest all who cry to Thee,
To Thee I cry,—O hear Thou me,
Lord God Almighty.

Lord God Almighty,
Who lovest all who trust in Thee,
Both small and great,—O love Thou me,
Lord God Almighty.

Lord God Almighty,
Who healest all who come to Thee;
In faith I come,—O heal Thou me,
Lord God Almighty.

Lord God Almighty,
Who savest all who saved would be ;
I fear, I faint,—O save Thou me,
Lord God Almighty.

Lord God Almighty,
Which was, and is, and is to be,
All praise and glory be to Thee,
Lord God Almighty.

G. *Thring.*

109 *Praise.* 11S.

IMMORTAL, invisible, God only wise,
In light inaccessible, hid from our eyes,
Most blessèd, most glorious, the Ancient of Days,
Almighty, victorious, thy great name we praise.

Unresting, unhasting, and silent as light,
Nor wanting, nor wasting, Thou rulest in might ;
Thy justice like mountains high soaring above
Thy clouds which are fountains of goodness and
     love.

To all, life Thou givest—to both great and small ;
In all life Thou livest, the true life of all ;
We blossom and flourish as leaves on the tree,
And wither and perish—but nought changeth Thee.

To-day and To-morrow with Thee still are Now ;
Nor trouble, nor sorrow, nor care, Lord, hast Thou;
Nor passion doth fever, nor age doth decay,
The same God for ever that was yesterday.

Great Father of glory, pure Father of light,
Thine angels adore Thee, all veiling their sight ;
But of all thy rich graces this grace, Lord, impart—
Take the veil from our faces, the veil from our
     heart.

All laud we would render; O help us to see,
'Tis only the splendour of light hideth Thee;
And so let thy glory almighty impart,
Through Christ in the story, thy Christ to the
    heart.

W. C. Smith.

110   *Praise.*   7s.

LET the whole Creation cry
Glory to the Lord on high;
Heaven and earth, awake and sing
' God is good, and therefore King.'

Praise Him, all ye hosts above,
Ever bright and fair in love;
Sun and moon, uplift your voice,
Night and stars, in God rejoice.

Chant his honour, ocean fair;
Earth, soft rushing through the air;
Sunshine, darkness, cloud and storm,
Rain and snow, his praise perform.

All the elemental powers,
Forests, plains, and secret bowers,
Vales and mountains, burst in song;
Rivers, roll his praise along.

Let the blossoms of the earth
Join the universal mirth;
Birds, with morn and dew elate,
Sing with joy at heaven's gate.

All the beasts that haunt the woods,
And the fish that cleave the floods,
Insects, and all creeping things,
Loud exalt the King of kings.

Warriors fighting for the Lord,
Prophets·burning ·with his word,
Those to whom the arts belong,
Join the rushing of the song.

Kings of knowledge and of law,
To the glorious circle draw;
All who work and all who wait,
Sing, 'The Lord is good and great.'

Men and women, young and old,
Raise the anthem manifold;
And let children's happy hearts
In this worship bear their parts.

From the north to southern pole
Let the mighty chorus roll—
Holy, Holy, Holy One,
Glory be to God alone.

S. A. Brooke.

111   *Psalm cxxxvi.*   7ˢ.

LET us with a gladsome mind
Praise the Lord, for He is kind;
    For his mercies shall endure,
    Ever faithful, ever sure.

He with all-commanding might,
Filled the new-made world with light.

He the golden-tressèd sun
Caused all day his course to run.

And the moon to shine by night
'Mong her spangled sisters bright.

He hath with a piteous eye
Looked upon our misery.

All things living He doth feed,
His full hand supplies their need.

Le us therefore warble forth
His high majesty and worth.

J. Milton.

112   *The Lord of Life.*   L.M.

LORD of all being, throned afar,
Thy glory flames from sun and star;
Centre and soul of every sphere,
Yet to each loving heart how near.

Sun of our life, thy quickening ray
Sheds on our path the glow of day:
Star of our hope, thy softened light
Cheers the long watches of the night.

Our midnight is thy smile withdrawn;
Our noontide is thy gracious dawn;
Our rainbow arch thy mercy's sign:
All, save the clouds of sin, are thine.

Lord of all life, below, above,
Whose light is Truth, whose warmth is Love;
Before thy ever-blazing throne
We ask no lustre of our own.

Grant us thy truth to make us free,
And kindling hearts that burn for Thee,
Till all thy living altars claim
One holy light, one heavenly flame.

O. W. Holmes.

113 *The Omnipresent God.* L.M.

FATHER and Friend, thy light, thy love,
Beaming through all thy works we see;
Thy glory gilds the heavens above,
And all the earth is full of Thee.

·Thy voice we hear, thy presence feel,
Whilst Thou, too pure for mortal sight,
Involved in clouds, invisible,
Reignest, the Lord of life and light.

We know not in what hallowed part
Of the wide heavens thy throne may be,
But this we know, that where Thou art,
Strength, wisdom, goodness, dwell with Thee.

Thy children shall not faint or fear,
Sustained by this inspiring thought;
Since Thou, their God, art everywhere,
They cannot be where Thou art not.
Sir J. Bowring.

114 *Psalm civ.* 10.10.11.11.

O WORSHIP the King all-glorious above;
O gratefully sing his power and his love;
Our Shield and Defender, the Ancient of Days,
Pavilioned in splendour, and girded with praise.

O tell of his might, O sing of his grace,
Whose robe is the light, whose canopy space;
His chariots of wrath the deep thunder clouds
        form,
And dark is his path on the wings of the storm.

The earth with its store of wonders untold,
Almighty, thy power hath founded of old;
Hath stablished it fast by a changeless decree,
And round it hath cast, like a mantle, the sea.

Thy bountiful care what tongue can recite?
It breathes in the air, it shines in the light;
It streams from the hills, it descends to the plain,
And sweetly distils in the dew and the rain.

Frail children of dust, and feeble as frail,
In Thee do we trust, nor find Thee to fail;
Thy mercies how tender, how firm to the end,
Our Maker, Defender, Redeemer and Friend.

O measureless Might, ineffable Love,
While angels delight to hymn Thee above,
Thy ransomed creation, though feeble their lays,
With true adoration shall sing to thy praise.
Sir R. Grant.

115 *Praise the Lord.* 8.7.

PRAISE, my soul, the King of heaven,
  To his feet thy tribute bring;
Ransomed, healed, restored, forgiven,
  Evermore his praises sing;
    Alleluia! Alleluia!
  Praise the everlasting King.

Praise Him for his grace and favour
  To our fathers in distress;
Praise Him, still the same as ever,
  Slow to chide and swift to bless;
    Alleluia! Alleluia!
  Glorious in his faithfulness.

Father-like, He tends and spares us,
  Well our feeble frame He knows;
In his hands He gently bears us,
  Rescues us from all our foes;
    Alleluia! Alleluia!
  Widely yet his mercy flows.

Angels in the height, adore Him :
  Ye behold Him face to face ;
Saints triumphant, bow before Him,
  Gathered in from every race ;
    Alleluia ! Alleluia !
  Praise with us the God of grace.
H. F. Lyte.

116   *Praise.*   7s.

ALL that's good, and great, and true,
  All that is and is to be,
Be it old, or be it new,
  Comes, O Father, comes from Thee.

Mercies dawn with every day,
  Newer, brighter than before ;
And the sun's declining ray,
  Layeth others up in store.

Not a bird that doth not sing
  Sweetest praises to thy name,
Not an insect on the wing
  But thy wonders doth proclaim.

Every blade and every tree,
  All in happy concert sing,
And in wondrous harmony
  Join in praises to their King.

Far and near, o'er land and sea,
  Mountain-top and wooded dell,
All, in singing, sing of Thee,
  Songs of love ineffable.

Fill us then with love divine ;
  Grant that we, though toiling here
May, in spirit being thine,
  See and hear Thee everywhere.

May we all with songs of praise,
  Whilst on earth, thy name adore,
Till with angel choirs we raise
  Songs óf praise for evermore.

G. Thring.

117   *Praise.*   Irr.

BLESSÈD be thy name for ever,
Thou of life the Guard and Giver !
Thou who slumberest not nor sleepest,
Blest are they Thou kindly keepest.

God of stillness and of motion,
Of the rainbow and the ocean,
Of the mountain, rock, and river,
Blessèd be thy name for ever.

God of evening's peaceful ray,
God of every dawning day,
Rising from the distant sea,
Breathing of eternity !

Thine the flaming sphere of light,
Thine the darkness of the night :
God of life that fade shall never,
Glory to thy name for ever.

J. Hogg.

118   *Praise.*   L.M.

THOU One in all, Thou All in one,
Source of the grace that crowns our days,
For all thy gifts 'neath cloud or sun,
We lift to Thee our grateful praise.

We bless Thee for the life that flows,
A pulse in every grain of sand,
A beauty in the blushing rose,
A thought and deed in brain and hand.

For life that Thou hast made a joy,
For strength to make our lives like thine,
For duties that our hands employ,—
We bring our offerings to thy shrine.

Be thine to give and ours to own
The truth that sets thy children free,
The law that binds us to thy throne,
The love that makes us one with Thee.

S. C. Beach.

119   *All ye creatures.*   8.7.8.8.7.

ANGELS holy, high and lowly,
  Sing the praises of the Lord ;
Earth and sky, all living Nature,
Man, the stamp of thy Creator,
  Praise ye, praise ye God the Lord.

Sun and moon bright, night and noon-light
  Starry temples azure-floored,
Cloud and rain, and wild winds' madness,
Sons of God that shout for gladness,
  Praise ye, praise ye God the Lord.

Ocean hoary, tell his glory ;
  Cliffs, where tumbling seas have roared ;
Pulse of waters, blithely beating,
Wave advancing, wave retreating,
  Praise ye, praise ye God the Lord.

Rock and highland, wood and island,
  Crag where eagle's pride hath soared,
Mighty mountains, purple-breasted,
Peaks cloud-cleaving, snowy-crested,
  Praise ye, praise ye God the Lord.

Rolling river, praise Him ever,
    From the mountain's deep vein poured,
Silver fountain, clearly gushing,
Troubled torrent, madly rushing,
    Praise ye, praise ye God the Lord.

Bond and free man, land and sea man,
    Earth, with peoples widely stored,
Wanderer lone o'er prairies ample,
Full-voiced choir, in costly temple,
    Praise ye, praise ye God the Lord.

Praise Him ever, Bounteous Giver,
    Praise Him, Father, Friend, and Lord;
Each glad soul its free course winging,
Each glad voice its free song singing,
    Praise the great and mighty Lord.

                                J. S. Blackie.

120   *Consecration to God.*   11.11.11.5.

FATHER, O hear us, seeking now to praise Thee,
Thou art our hope, our confidence, our saviour;
Thou art the refuge of the generations,
    Lord God Almighty.

Maker of all things, loving all thy creatures,
God of all goodness, infinite in mercy,
Changeless, eternal, holiest, and wisest,
    Hear Thou thy children.

We are thy children, asking Thee to bless us,
Banded together for a full obedience,
Mutual help and mutual refreshing,
    Lord, in thy service.

Childhood shall learn to know Thee and revere
    Thee;
Manhood shall serve Thee, strong in power and
    knowledge;
Old age shall trust Thee, having felt thy mercy,
      E'en 'mid the shadows.

Bless Thou our purpose, consecrate our labours,
Keep us still faithful to the best and truest,
Guide us, protect us, make us not unworthy
      Learners of Jesus.

Glory and honour, thanks and adoration,
Still will we bring, O God of men and angels,
To Thee, the holy, merciful, and mighty,
      Father, our Father.

D. Walmsley.

121   *In all.*   L.M.

GOD of the earth, the sky, the sea,
    Maker of all above, below,
Creation lives and moves in Thee,
    Thy present life through all doth flow.

Thee in the lonely woods we meet,
    On the bare hills or cultured plains,
In every flower beneath our feet,
    And e'en the still rock's mossy stains.

Thy love is in the sunshine's glow,
    Thy life is in the quickening air;
When lightnings flash and storm-winds blow,
    There is thy power; thy law is there.

We feel thy calm at evening's hour,
    Thy grandeur in the march of night;
And, when the morning breaks in power,
    We hear thy word, ' Let there be light.'

But higher far, and far more clear,
   Thee in man's spirit we behold;
Thine image and Thyself are there,—
   The Indwelling God, proclaimed of old.

                       S. Longfellow.

122   *Rejoice.*   6.6.6.6.8.8.

REJOICE, the Lord is King,
   Your Lord and King adore;
Mortals, give thanks and sing,
   And triumph evermore :
Lift up your heart, lift up your voice;
Rejoice, in prayer and praise rejoice.

His wintry north-winds blow,
   Loud tempests rush amain;
Yet his thick showers of snow
   Defend the infant grain :
Lift up your heart, lift up your voice;
Rejoice, in prayer and praise rejoice.

He wakes the genial spring,
   Perfumes the balmy air;
The vales their tribute bring,
   And summer flowers are fair :
Lift up your heart, lift up your voice;
Rejoice, in prayer and praise rejoice.

His autumn crowns the year;
   His flocks the hills adorn;
He fills the golden ear,
   And loads the field with corn :
O happy mortals, raise your voice;
Rejoice, in prayer and praise rejoice.

Lead on your fleeting train,
　Ye years, and months, and days;
O bring the eternal reign
　Of love, and joy, and praise:
Lift up your heart, lift up your voice;
Rejoice, in prayer and praise rejoice.

J. Taylor.

123　　*What shall I render unto the Lord?*　　6.4.

To do thy holy Will,
　To bear the cross;
To trust thy mercy still
　In pain or loss;
Poor gifts are these to bring,
　Dear Lord, to Thee,
Who hath done everything
　For all, and me.

For all thy glorious earth,
　Thy stars and flowers,
For love and gentle mirth,
　For happy hours,
For good by which we live,
　For sweet sunshine;
What recompense can give
　This heart of mine?

Thou, who enthroned above
　Dost hear our call;
O can our faithful love
　Pay Thee for all?
Poor recompense to bring,
　Dear Lord, to Thee,
Who hast done everything
　For man, and me.

G. Cooper.
Ver. 2, S. A. Brooke.

124 *Thanksgiving.* 7s.

For the beauty of the earth,
  For the glory of the skies,
For the love which from our birth
  Over and around us lies,
    Lord of all, to Thee we raise
    This our grateful hymn of praise.

For the wonder of each hour
  Of the day and of the night,
Hill and vale, and tree and flower,
  Sun and moon, and stars of light,
    Lord of all, to Thee we raise
    This our grateful hymn of praise.

For the joy of human love,
  Brother, sister, parent, child,
Friends on earth, and friends above,
  Pleasures pure and undefiled,
    Lord of all, to Thee we raise
    This our grateful hymn of praise.

For thy Church that evermore
  Lifteth holy hands above,
Offering up on every shore
  Her full sacrifice of love,
    Lord of all, to Thee we raise
    This our grateful psalm of praise.
                                    F. S. Pierpoint.

125 *Thanksgiving.* 7.6.

O father of our spirits,
  Whence life, love, beauty roll
Unasked, full, like a river
  To every human soul,

We thank Thee for our coming
    Into this world of thine,
Voice of eternal silence,
    Stream from the sea divine.

For the green earth we thank Thee,
    With beast, and bird, and tree ;
For sky that o'er us floateth,
    So blue, so bright, so free;
Thanks for the morning sunshine,
    And for the living air ;
For sight of man, earth, heaven,
    Thy universe so fair ;

For mother and for father,
    For home of childhood's years,
Its shelter, warmth, and bounty,
    Its laughter and its tears ;
For knowledge, for high models
    That beckoned to ascend,
Encouragements, restrainings,
    From parent, teacher, friend.

Thanks for an occupation,
    That calls forth all our powers,
That shelters us from wasting
    Our short life's precious hours ;
Makes food and sleep the sweeter,
    And grief the easier borne,
And brings down from the heaven,
    ' Thou worker true, well done.'

Thanks for the world's great gospel,
    That dawned on eastern shore,
God loves the bird, the flower,
    He loveth man much more ;

For no neglects or follies
  Will God a man e'er shun ;
For ever and for ever
  He loves and seeks his son.

And man for man his brother
  Throughout the world shall care,
And plenty, freedom, wisdom,
  Each shall with other share.
Who in man's form appeareth
  Beneath the outspread sky,
Shall call forth awe and service,
  As home of Deity ?

Thanks for the holy circle
  In deathless friendship bound,
Who with us work and worship,
  Or sleep beneath the ground :
O that our lives so gifted,
  Our daily thoughts and ways,
May make to ear of heaven,
  Unbroken hymns of praise.

              T. W. Chignell.

126   *Before Thee.*   7s.

Lo, we stand before Thee now,
And our silent, inward vow
Thou dost hear, in that profound
Where is neither voice nor sound.

Not by any outward sign
Dost Thou show thy will divine ;
Deep within thy voice doth cry,
And our quickened souls reply.

Thou dost hear, and Thou wilt bless
With thy strength and tenderness ;
Lo, we come to do thy will ;
With thy life our spirits fill.

J. W. Chadwick.

127　　　*Worship.*　　　L.M.

O GOD, whose presence glows in all
Within, around us, and above,
Thy word we bless, thy name we call,
Whose word is Truth, whose name is Love.

That truth be with the heart believed
Of all who seek this sacred place,
With power proclaimed, in peace received,—
Our spirits' light, thy Spirit's grace.

That love its holy influence pour,
To keep us meek and make us free,
And throw its binding blessing more
Round each with all, and all with Thee.

Send down its angel to our side,
Send in its calm upon the breast ;
For we would need no other guide,
And we can need no other rest.

N. L. Frothingham.

128　　　*Worship.*　　　8.8.7.

GRACIOUS Power, the world pervading,
Blessing all, and none upbraiding,
　We are met to worship Thee ;

Not in formal adorations,
Nor with servile deprecations,
　But in spirit true and free.

By thy wisdom mind is lighted,
By thy love the heart excited,
   Light and love all flow from Thee ;

And the soul of thought and feeling,
In the voice thy praises pealing,
   Must thy noblest homage be.

Not alone in our devotion,
In all being, life, and motion,
   We the present Godhead see.

Gracious Power, the world pervading,
Blessing all, and none upbraiding,
   We are met to worship Thee.

                      W. J. Fox.

129   *Invocation.*   L.M.

UNTO thy temple, Lord, we come
   With thankful hearts to worship Thee ;
And pray that this may be our home
   Until we touch eternity ;—

The common home of rich and poor,
   Of bond and free, and great and small ;
Large as thy love for evermore,
   And warm and bright and good to all.

And dwell Thou with us in this place,
   Thou and thy Christ, to guide and bless ;
Here make the well-springs of thy grace
   Like fountains in the wilderness.

May thy whole truth be spoken here;
Thy gospel light for ever shine;
Thy perfect love cast out all fear,
And human life become divine.

R. Collyer.

130   *Glories that remain.*   8.7.

FAIRER grows the earth each morning
To the eyes that watch aright;
Every dew-drop sparkles warning
Of a miracle in sight,
Of some unsuspected glory
Waiting in the old and plain;
Poet's dream nor traveller's story
Words such wonders as remain.

Everywhere the gate of Beauty
Fresh across the pathway swings,
As we follow truth or duty
Inward to the heart of things;
And we enter, foolish mortals,
Thinking now the heart to find,—
There to gaze on vaster portals;
Still the Glory lies behind.

Faith I love. I love you deeper
As I press your portals through,
Heeding not the call of keeper,
Heeding sole the vision new.
All our creeds are hinting only
Of a faith of nobler strain:
God is living; are we lonely,
'Mid his glories that remain?

W. C. Gannett.

131 *Worship above and below.* 7s.

PLEASANT are thy courts above
In the land of light and love;
Pleasant are thy courts below
In this land of sin and woe:
O my spirit longs and faints
For the converse of thy Saints,
For the brightness of thy face,
For thy fulness, God of grace.

Happy birds that sing and fly
Round thy altars, O Most High;
Happier souls that find a rest
In a heavenly Father's breast;
Like the wandering Dove that found
No repose on earth around,
They can to their ark repair,
And enjoy it ever there.

Happy souls, their praises flow
In this vale of sin and woe;
Waters in the desert rise,
Manna feeds them from the skies;
On they go from strength to strength,
Till they reach thy Throne at length,
At thy feet adoring fall,
Who hast led them safe through all.

Lord, be mine this prize to win,
Guide me through a world of sin,
Keep me by thy saving grace,
Give me at thy side a place;
Sun and shield alike Thou art,
Guide and guard my erring heart;
Grace and glory flow from Thee:
Shower, O shower them, Lord, on me.

H. F. Lyte.

132 *A Litany of Work and Worship.* 8.8.8.4.

O THOU to whom our voices rise,
King of the earth, and air, and skies,
For all the blessings that we prize,
 We thank Thee, Lord.

For work and rest, for home and friends,
For health and strength thy mercy sends,
That we may serve the noblest ends,
 We thank Thee, Lord.

For idle word and trifling thought,
For selfish pleasure we have sought,
When all for Thee we should have wrought,
 Forgive us, Lord.

From anger, pride, and selfish care,
From want of faith in work or prayer,
From sin that we would rashly dare,
 O save us, Lord.

We trust thy wisdom, love, and power:
When all is bright, when sorrows lower,
Through all our life, in death's last hour,
 Be with us, Lord.

       D. Agate.

133 *Nature's Worship.* C.M.

THE ocean looketh up to heaven,
 As 't were a living thing;
The homage of its waves is given,
 In ceaseless worshipping.

They kneel upon the sloping sand
 As bends the human knee;
A beautiful and tireless band,
 The priesthood of the sea.

The mists are lifted from the rills,
  Like the white wing of prayer;
They kneel above the ancient hills,
  As doing homage there.

The forest-tops are lowly cast
  O'er breezy hill and glen,
As if a prayerful spirit passed
  On nature as on men.

The sky is as a temple's arch;
  The blue and wavy air
Is glorious with the spirit march
  Of messengers at prayer.

J. G. Whittier (*his original version*).

134　　　*The Book of Nature.*　　　C.M.

THERE is a book, who runs may read,
  Which heavenly truth imparts,
And all the lore its scholars need,
  Pure eyes and Christian hearts.

The works of God, above, below,
  Within us and around,
Are pages in that book to show
  How God Himself is found.

The glorious sky, embracing all,
  Is like the Maker's love,
Wherewith encompassed, great and small
  In peace and order move.

The dew of heaven is like thy grace,
  It steals in silence down;
But, where it lights, the favoured place
  By richest fruits is known.

One Name, above all glorious names,
  With its ten thousand tongues
The everlasting sea proclaims,
  Echoing angelic songs.

The raging fire, the roaring wind
  Thy boundless power display ;
But in the gentler breeze we find
  Thy Spirit's viewless way.

Two worlds are ours : 'tis only sin
  Forbids us to descry
The mystic heaven and earth within,
  Plain as the sea and sky.

Thou, who hast given me eyes to see
  And love this sight so fair,
Give me a heart to find out Thee,
  And read Thee everywhere.

                              J. Keble.

135   *The garment thou seest Him by.*   C.M.
THY seamless robe conceals Thee not
  From earnest hearts and true :
The glory of thy perfectness
  Shines all its texture through.
And on its flowing hem we read,
  As Thou dost linger near,
The message of a love more deep
  Than any depth of fear.

And so no more our hearts shall plead
  For miracle and sign ;
Thy order and thy faithfulness
  Are all in all divine.

These are thy revelations vast
From earliest days of yore ;
These are our confidence and peace :
We cannot wish for more.

J. W. Chadwick.

136   *The people of God.*   8.7.8.7.8.8.7.

WE come unto our fathers' God ;
Their rock is our salvation ;
The eternal arms, their dear abode,
We make our habitation :
We bring Thee, Lord, the praise they
brought,
We seek Thee as thy saints have sought
In every generation.

Their joy unto their Lord we bring ;
Their song to us descendeth ;
The Spirit who in them did sing
To us his music lendeth.
His song in them, in us, is one ;
We raise it high, we send it on,
The song that never endeth.

Ye saints to come, take up the strain,
The same sweet strain endeavour ;
Unbroken be the golden chain ;
Keep on the song for ever.
Safe in the same dear dwelling place,
Rich with the same eternal grace,
Bless the same boundless Giver.

T. H. Gill.

137   *God our help.*   8.5.

UNTO Thee abiding ever,
Look I in my need,
Strength of every good endeavour,
Holy thought and deed.

Thou dost guide the stars of heaven,
  Heal the broken heart,
Bring in turn the morn and even,—
  Love and Law Thou art.

Clouds and darkness are about Thee,
  Just and sure thy throne ;
Not a sparrow falls without Thee,
  All to Thee is known.

Origin and end of being,
  All things in and through,
Light Thou art of all my seeing,
  Power to will and do.

Through my life, whate'er betide me,
  Thou my trust shalt be ;
Whom have I on earth beside Thee,
  Whom in heaven but Thee ?
                              F. L. Hosmer.

138　　　　*God's Law and Love.*　　　　L. M.

O GOD, in whom we live and move,
Thy love is law, thy law is love ;
Thy present spirit waits to fill
The soul which comes to do thy will.

Unto thy children's spirits teach
Thy love, beyond the power of speech ;
And make them know, with joyful awe,
The encircling presence of thy law.

That law doth give to truth and right,
Howe'er despised, a conquering might,
And makes each fondly-worshipped lie
And boasting wrong, to cower and die.

Its patient working doth fulfil
Man's hope, and God's all-perfect will,
Nor suffers one true word or thought
Or deed of love to come to nought.

Such faith, O God, our spirits fill,
That we may work in patience still;
Who works for justice works with Thee,
Who works in love, thy child shall be.

S. Longfellow.

139   *The pilgrim's joy.*   L.M.

O GOD, Thou art my God alone:
Early to Thee my soul shall cry;
A pilgrim in a land unknown,
A thirsty land whose springs are dry.

More dear than life itself, thy love
My heart and tongue shall still employ,
And to declare thy truth shall prove
My peace, my glory, and my joy.

In blessing Thee with grateful songs
My happy life shall glide away,
The praise that to thy name belongs
With lifted hands I hourly pay.

Thy name, O God, before I sleep,
Dwells on my lips, and fires my thought,
Thy presence in the midnight deep,
Sure comfort to my soul has brought.

And when I wake at morn, thy love
Is sweeter than the light to me:
O whom have I in heaven above,
Or what on earth compared to Thee?

Therefore awake, my grateful voice ;
O happy heart, awake and sing
Of God, who bids my heart rejoice
Beneath the shadow of his wing.

J. Montgomery and S. A Brooke.

140   *The Spirit of Truth.*   C.M.

THOU long disowned, reviled, oppressed,
　Strange friend of human kind,
Seeking through weary years a rest
　Within our hearts to find ;—

How late thy bright and awful brow
　Breaks through these clouds of sin :
Hail, Truth divine, we know thee now,
　Angel of God, come in.

Come, though with purifying fire,
　And swift-dividing sword,
Thou of all nations the desire ;
　Earth waits thy cleansing word.

Struck by the lightning of thy glance,
　Let old oppressions die :
Before thy cloudless countenance
　Let fear and falsehood fly.

Anoint our eyes with healing grace,
　To see, as not before,
Our Father in our brother's face,
　Our Maker in his poor.

Flood our dark life with golden day ;
　Convince, subdue, enthrall ;
Then to a mightier yield thy sway,
　And Love be all in all.

Eliza Scudder.

141   *The silent Presence.*   C.M.

UNHEARD the dews around me fall,
    And heavenly influence shed;
And silent on this earthly ball,
    Celestial footsteps tread.

Night moves in silence round the pole,
    The stars sing on unheard,
Their music pierces to the soul,
    Yet borrows not a word.

Noiseless the morning flings its gold,
    And still the evening's place;
And silently the earth is rolled
    Amidst the vast of space.

In quietude thy Spirit grows
    In man from hour to hour;
In calm eternal onward flows
    Thy all-redeeming power.

Lord, grant my soul to hear at length
    Thy deep and silent voice:
To work in stillness, wait in strength,
    With calmness to rejoice.
               S. A. Brooke.
               Ver. 1, *Anon.*

142   *Whom but Thee.*   10s.

THOU Life within my life, than self more dear,
Thou veilèd Presence infinitely dear,
From all my nameless weariness I flee
To find my centre and my rest in Thee.

Take part with me against these doubts that rise
And seek to throne Thee far in distant skies:
Take part with me against this self that dares
Assume the burden of these sins and cares.

How can I call Thee who art always here?
How shall I praise Thee who art still most dear?
What may I give Thee save what Thou hast given?
And whom but Thee have I in earth or heaven?

Eliza Scudder.

143   *The Love of God.*   C.M.

Thou Grace divine, encircling all,
　A shoreless, soundless sea,
Wherein at last our souls must fall;
　O Love of God most free!

When over dizzy heights we go,
　One soft hand blinds our eyes,
The other leads us safe and slow;
　O Love of God most wise!

And though we turn us from thy face,
　And wander wide and long,
Thou hold'st us still in thine embrace;
　O Love of God most strong!

The saddened heart, the restless soul,
　The toil-worn frame and mind,
Alike confess thy sweet control,
　O Love of God most kind!

But not alone thy care we claim,
　Our wayward steps to win;
We know Thee by a dearer name,
　O Love of God within.

And, filled and quickened by thy breath,
　Our souls are strong and free
To rise o'er sin and fear and death,
　O Love of God, to Thee!

Eliza Scudder.

144   *The Love of God.*   S.M.

I PRAY to know thy peace,
I long to feel thy love,
Each day I yearn the way to learn
Unto thy home above.
O love of God most full,
O love of God most free,
Come warm my heart, come fill my soul,
Come lead me unto Thee.

Warm as the glowing sun
So shines thy love on me,
It wraps me round with kindly care,
It draws me unto Thee.
O love of God, &c.

No foe can face me down,
No fear can make me flee,
No sorrow fill my life with ill;
Thy love surroundeth me.
O love of God, &c.

The wildest sea is calm,
The tempest brings no fear,
The darkest night is full of light,
Because thy love is near.
O love of God, &c.

I triumph over sin,
I put temptation down,
The love of God doth give me strength
To win the victor's crown.
O love of God most full,
O love of God most free,
Thou warm'st my heart, thou fill'st my soul,
With might thou strengthenest me.

O. Clute.

145   *The Will of God.*   C.M.

I worship Thee, sweet Will of God;
    And all thy ways adore;
And every day I live, I long
    To love Thee more and more.

When obstacles and trials seem
    Like prison-walls to be,
I do the little I can do,
    And leave the rest to Thee.

I have no cares, O blessèd Will,
    For all my cares are thine:
I live in triumph, Lord, for Thou
    Hast made thy triumphs mine.

Man's weakness waiting upon God
    Its end can never miss;
For men on earth no work can do
    More angel-like than this.

Ride on, ride on triumphantly,
    Thou glorious Will, ride on;
Faith's pilgrim sons behind Thee take
    The road that Thou hast gone.

He always wins who sides with God,
    To him no chance is lost:
God's will is sweetest to him when
    It triumphs at his cost.

Ill that God blesses is our good,
    And unblest good is ill;
And all is right that seems most wrong,
    If it be his dear will.

F. W. Faber.

146   *God our Possession.*   6.6.6.6.8.8.

IF only God I have,
If only He is mine,
If, fearless to the grave,
My thoughts to God incline ;
Then can I nought of sorrow know,
And all my griefs to rapture grow.

If only I have God,
All else I glad forsake,
And on the appointed road
My pilgrim-staff I take,
Letting the heedless multitude
Proclaim the broadest path the good.

If only I have God,
How calm and sweet my sleep ;
Though tears my eyes o'erflowed,
I still would love to weep,
For He, thy Father, turns my tears
To balm for the eternal years.

If only I have God,
The universe I own,
Blest am I on earth's sod,
As seraph by thy throne ;
Rapt in beholding, loving Thee,
I fear not earthly misery.

If only I have Thee,
I have my fatherland ;
As heritage, rich, free,
Each gift flows to my hand ;
Brethren long lost I find again
In hearts renewed of living men.

Novalis.
tr. W. Maccall.

147   *A Present Heaven.*   C.M.

FATHER in heaven, thy dwelling-place
    Nought but a heaven can be;
O come, inhabit Thou my soul,
    And make thy heaven in me.

I know, O God, that where Thou art
    Either I cannot be
Or must, though but in little part,
    Share in thy heaven with Thee.

If I but make the smallest part
    In thy wide heaven's extent,
Or shine but as the farthest star
    In thy great firmament,—

If Thou, who art to me the whole,
    Dost make me part to Thee,
It is enough unto my soul;
    It is my heaven to me.

If I have happiness beside,
    It is engulfed in this;
Or if I suffer, 'tis a wave
    On a deep sea of bliss.

                            J. V. Blake.

148   *All is well.*   L.M.

ASK and receive,—'tis sweetly said;
Yet what to plead for know I not;
For wish is worsted, hope o'ersped,
And aye to thanks returns my thought.
If I would pray, I've nought to say
But this, that God may be God still;
For Him to live is still to give,
And sweeter than my wish his will.

O wealth of life beyond all bound,
Eternity each moment given !
What plummet may the present sound?
Who promises a future heaven?
Or glad, or grieved, oppressed, relieved,
In blackest night, or brightest day,
Still pours the flood of golden good,
And more than heartfull fills me aye.

'All mine is thine,' the sky-soul saith;
'The wealth I am must thou become;
Richer and richer, breath by breath,—
Immortal gain, immortal room.'
And since all his mine also is,
Life's gift outruns my fancies far,
And drowns the dream in larger stream,
As morning drinks the morning star.

D. A. Wasson.

149   *Heaven within.*   7.6.

LORD, when through sin I wander
  So very far from Thee,
I think in some far country
  Thy sinless home must be;
But when with heartfelt sorrow
  I pray Thee to forgive,
Thy pardon is so perfect,
  That in thy heaven I live.

That heaven, Lord, so surrounds me,
  That when I do the right,
The saddest path of duty
  Is lightened by its light;
I know not what its glories
  Before thy throne must be,
But here thy smiling presence
  Is heaven on earth to me.

To love the right and do it
   Is to my heart so sweet,
It makes the path of duty
   A shining golden street;
Give me thy strength, O Father,
   To choose this path each day,
Then heaven within, about me,
   Shall compass all my way.

C. Smith.

150   *Heart and Life.*   S.M.

HELP me, my God, to speak
True words to Thee each day;
Real let my voice be when I praise,
And trustful when I pray.

Thy words are true to me;
Let mine to Thee be true,
The speech of my whole heart and soul
However low and few;

True words of grief for sin,
Of longing to be free,
Of groaning for deliverance,
And likeness, Lord, to Thee;

True words of faith and hope,
Of godly joy and grief.
Lord, I believe, O hear my cry,
Help Thou mine unbelief.

H. Bonar.

151   *Not alone.*   C.M.

YES, Thou art with me, and with Thee
   I cannot be alone,
For joy shall bear me company,
   And peace shall be my own.

The solitude Thou hoverest nigh
  Is peopled all with bliss:
The sandy waste, when Thou art by,
  A verdant landscape is.

There is no night where Thou art seen:
  No light can day afford,
Without thy rays to gild the scene,
  Without thy presence, Lord.

Be with me ever; ever bless,
  And ever guide, and be
In life's decay and death's distress,
  On earth, in heaven, with me.

Sir. J. Bowring.

152 *Visit me with thy salvation.* 6.10.

WILT Thou not visit me?
The plant beside me feels thy gentle dew;
  Each blade of grass I see
From thy deep earth its quickening moisture drew.

Wilt Thou not visit me?
The morning calls on me with cheering tone,
  And every hill and tree
Has but one voice, the voice of Thee alone.

Come, for I need thy love
More than the flower the dew, or grass the rain;
  Come, like thy holy Dove,
And, swift-descending, bid me live again.

Yes, Thou wilt visit me;
Nor plant nor tree thine eye delights so well,
  As when, from sin set free,
Man's spirit comes with thine in peace to dwell.

Jones Very.

153　　　　　*The one prayer.*　　　　　S.M.

ONE gift, my God, I seek,—
To know Thee always near,
To feel thy hand, to see thy face,
Thy blessed voice to hear.

Where'er I go, my God,
O let me find Thee there ;
Where'er I stay, stay Thou with me,
A presence everywhere.

And if Thou bringest peace,
Or if Thou bringest pain,
But come Thyself with all that comes,
And all shall go for gain.

Long listening to thy words,
My voice shall catch thy tone,
And, locked in thine, my hand shall grow
All loving like thine own.

　　　　　　　　　　　　　　B. T.

154　　　　　*For direction.*　　　　　8.8.8.2.7.

LORD of might and Lord of glory,
Humbly do I bow before Thee ;
With my whole heart I adore Thee,
　　　Great Lord ;
Listen to my cry, O Lord.

Passions proud and fierce have ruled me,
Fancies light and vain have fooled me,
But thy training stern hath schooled me ;
　　　Now, Lord,
Take me for thy child, O Lord.

Groping dim and bending lowly,
Mortal vision catcheth slowly
Glimpses of the pure and holy;
    Now, Lord,
Open Thou mine eyes, O Lord.

In the deed that no man knoweth,
Where no praiseful trumpet bloweth,
Where he may not reap who soweth,
    There, Lord,
Let my heart serve Thee, O Lord.

In the work that no gold payeth,
Where he speedeth best who prayeth,
Doeth most who little sayeth,
    There, Lord,
Let me work thy will, O Lord.

J. S. Blackie.

155   *Satisfied.*   C.M.

WHEN hope grows dim and shadows fall,
  And light seems all denied,
I turn unto the One in All,
  Rest, and am satisfied.

On rugged ways and storm-swept heights,
  My spirit may abide,
But sees, through all, love's beacon lights—
  Trusts, and is satisfied.

And through the clearing mists I hear,
  Far up the mountain side,
The call in accents sweet and clear,
  Come, and be satisfied.

Above the cloud-capped mountain tops
  'God's love-lights still abide;
Before that shrine my spirit stops,
  Glad, happy, satisfied.

The shadows far beneath me lie,
  The storm-clouds roll aside,
And in the deep sun-lighted sky
  My soul is satisfied.

When angel hands shall lift the veil,
  Disclosing life's full tide,
Its glory then the stars shall pale;
  Wait, and be satisfied.

                           Louise M. Dunning.

156   *Semper Agens et semper Quietus.*   L.M.

Thou workest on, Eternal God;
No weariness doth Thee oppress;
Yet hast Thou ever thine abode
In awful deeps of quietness.

O endless rest divine that ne'er
Stayeth thy still creating might,
O ceaseless work that may not stir
The stillness of the Infinite!

Alas, we toil, then weary grow,
We mourn repose, a passing guest;
Alas, our fire that burneth low,
Our halting work, our broken rest!

Ah, vainly do our spirits yearn
In peace to dwell, at work to be?
May we not to our Father turn?
May we not, Lord, abide in Thee?

May not thy weary children grow
Strong in thy strength and fully blest ?
May not we restless workers know
Something of thy most perfect rest ?

Father, be ours the soul that strives,
And in thy service wearies not ;
And ours the heavenly rest that gives
The peace divine which passeth thought.

T. H. Gill.

157   *No more sea.*   11.10.

LIFE of our life, and Light of all our seeing,
How shall we rest on any hope but Thee ?
What time our souls, to Thee for refuge fleeing,
Long for the home where there is no more sea.

For still this sea of life, with endless wailing,
Dashes above our heads its blinding spray,
And vanquished hearts, sick with remorse and failing,
Moan like the waves at set of autumn day.

And ever round us swells the insatiate ocean
Of sin and doubt that lures us to our grave ;
When its wild billows, with their mad commotion,
Would sweep us down, then only Thou canst
save.

And deep and dark the fearful gloom unlighted
Of that untried and all-surrounding sea,
On whose bleak shore arriving, lone, benighted,
We fall and lose ourselves at last in Thee.

Yea, in thy life our little lives are ended,
Into thy depths our trembling spirits fall ;
In Thee enfolded, gathered, comprehended,
As holds the sea her waves, Thou hold'st us all.

Eliza Scudder.

158 *Still with Thee.* S.M.

STILL with Thee, O my God,
  I would desire to be ;
By day, by night, at home, abroad,
  I would be still with Thee ;

With Thee, amid the crowd
  That throngs the busy mart,
To hear thy voice, 'mid clamour loud,
  Speak softly to my heart ;

With Thee, when day is done,
  And evening calms the mind ;
The setting as the rising sun
  With Thee my heart would find ;

With Thee when darkness brings
  The signal of repose ;
Calm in the shadow of thy wings
  Mine eyelids I would close ;

With Thee, in Thee, by faith
  Abiding would I be ;
By day, by night, in life, in death,
  I would be still with Thee.
                              J. D. Burns.

159 *Wait on the Lord.* C.M.

YOUNG souls, so strong the race to run,
  And win each height sublime,
Unweary still would ye march on,
  And still exulting climb ?

Walk with the Lord.   Along the road
  Your strength He will renew ;
Wait on the everlasting God,
  And He will wait on you.

Burn with his love.   Your fading fire
  And endless flame will glow;
Life from the Well of Life require,—
  The stream will ever flow.

Ye shall not faint, ye shall not fail,
  Still in the Spirit strong;
Each task divine ye still shall hail,
  And blend the exulting song.

Aspiring eyes ye still shall raise,
  And heights sublime explore;
Like eagles, ye shall sunward gaze,
  Like eagles, heavenward soar.

Your wondrous portion shall be this,
  Your life below, above,—
Eternal youth, eternal bliss,
  And everlasting love.

T. H. Gill.

160   *Waiting.*   S.M.

    Not so in haste, my heart;
      Have faith in God and wait;
    Although He seems to linger long,
      He never comes too late.

    He never comes too late;
      He knoweth what is best;
    Vex not thyself; it is in vain
      Until He cometh, rest.

    Until He cometh, rest,
      Nor grudge the hours that roll;
    The feet that wait for God, 'tis they
      Are soonest at the goal;

Are soonest at the goal
That is not gained by speed ;
Then hold thee still, O restless heart,
For I shall wait his lead.

B. T.

161   *The hope of man.*   L.M.

THE past is dark with sin and shame,
The future dim with doubt and fear,
But, Father, yet we praise thy name,
Whose guardian love is always near.

For man has striven ages long,
With faltering steps to come to Thee,
And in each purpose high and strong
The influence of thy grace could see.

He could not breathe an earnest prayer,
But Thou wast kinder than he dreamed,
As age by age brought hopes more fair,
And nearer still thy kingdom seemed.

But never rose within his breast
A trust so calm and deep as now ;
Shall not the weary find a rest ?
Father, Preserver, answer Thou.

'Tis dark around, 'tis dark above,
But through the shadow streams the sun ;
We cannot doubt thy certain love ;
And man's true aim shall yet be won.

T. W. Higginson.

162   *Faith.*   Irr.

In the bitter waves of woe,
Beaten and tossed about
By the sullen winds that blow
From the desolate shores of doubt.

When the anchors that faith had cast
Are dragging in the gale,
I am quietly holding fast
To the things that cannot fail ;

I know that right is right,
That it is not good to lie,
That love is better than spite,
And a neighbour than a spy ;

I know that passion needs
The leash of a sober mind ;
I know that generous deeds
Some sure reward will find ;

That the rulers must obey,
That the givers shall increase,
That duty lights the way
For the beautiful feet of peace ;

In the darkest night of the year,
When the stars have all gone out,
That courage is better than fear,
That faith is truer than doubt ;

And fierce though the fiends may fight,
And long though the angels hide,
I know that truth and right
Have the universe on their side ;

And that somewhere beyond the stars
Is a love that is better than fate;
When the night unlocks her bars
I shall see Him, and I will wait.

W. Gladden.

163 *Trust.* 8.8.8.4.8.4.

THE child leans on its parent's breast,
Leaves there its cares, and is at rest;
The bird sits singing by his nest,
  And tells aloud
His trust in God, and so is blest
  'Neath every cloud.

He has no store, he sows no seed,
Yet sings aloud and doth not heed;
By flowing stream or grassy mead
  He sings to shame
Men, who forget, in fear of need,
  A Father's name.

The heart that trusts for ever sings,
And feels as light as it had wings;
A well of peace within it springs;
  Come good or ill,
Whate'er to-day, to-morrow brings,
  It is his will.

I. Williams.

164 *The prayers of faith.* 8.8.8.4.

O STRONG, upwelling prayers of faith,
From inmost founts of life ye start,
The spirit's pulse, the vital breath
  Of soul and heart.

From pastoral toil, from traffic's din,
Alone, in crowds, at home, abroad,
Unheard of man, ye enter in
    The ear of God.

Ye brook no forced and measured tasks,
Nor weary rote, nor formal chains ;
The simple heart, that freely asks
    In love, obtains.

For man the living temple is ;
The mercy-seat and cherubim,
And all the holy mysteries
    He bears with him.

And most avails the prayer of love,
Which, wordless, shapes itself in deeds,
And wearies heaven for nought above
    Our common needs ;

Which brings to God's all-perfect will
That trust of his undoubting child,
Whereby all seeming good and ill
    Are reconciled ;

And seeking not for special signs
Of favour, is content to fall
Within the providence which shines
    And rains on all.

                            J. G. Whittier.

165   *Living faith.*   S.M.

WE pray for truth and peace ;
With weary hearts we ask
Some rest in which our souls may cease
From life's perplexing task.

We weep, yet none is found ;
We weep, yet hope grows faint ;
And deeper in its mournful sound
Goes up our wild complaint.

Only to living faith
The promises are shown ;
And by the love that passes death
The rest is won alone.
Be ours the earnest heart,
Be ours the steady will,
To work in silent faith our part ;
For God is working still.

Then newer lights shall rise
Above these clouds of sin,
And heaven's unfolding mysteries
To glad our souls begin.
Our hearts from fear and wrong
Shall win their full release,
With God's own might for ever strong,
And calm with God's own peace.

W. H. Hurlbut.

166   *Returning to God.*   L. M.

To thine eternal arms, O God,
Take us thine erring children in,
From dangerous paths too boldly trod,
From wandering thoughts and dreams of sin.

Thine arms were round our childhood's ways
A guard through helpless years to be ;
O leave not our maturer years,
We still are helpless without Thee.

We trusted hope and pride and strength ;
Our strength proved false, our pride was vain,
Our dreams have faded all at length,—
We come to Thee, O Lord, again.

A guide to trembling steps yet be ;
Give us of thine eternal power ;
So shall our paths all lead to Thee,
And life still smile, like childhood's hour.

T. W. Higginson.

167   *The eternal years.*   C.M.

How shalt thou bear the cross that now
    So dread a weight appears ?
Keep quietly to God, and think
    Upon the Eternal Years.

Brave quiet is the thing for thee,
    Chiding thy faithless fears ;
Learn to be real, from the thought
    Of the Eternal Years.

Bear gently, suffer like a child,
    Nor be ashamed of tears ;
Take up thy cross, and in thy heart
    Sing of the Eternal Years.

Thy cross is quite enough for thee,
    Though little it appears ;
For there is hid in it the weight
    Of the Eternal Years.

He practises all virtue well,
    Who his own cross reveres,
And lives in the familiar thought
    Of the Eternal Years.

F. W. Faber.

168   *Persecuted for righteousness' sake.*   L.M.

Sport of the changeful multitude,
Nor calmly heard, nor understood,
With bonds and scorn and evil will
The world requites its prophets still.

Men followed where the Highest led
For common gifts of daily bread,
And gross of ear, of vision dim,
Owned not the godlike power of Him.

Vain as a dreamer's word to them
His wail above Jerusalem;
And meaningless the watch He kept,
Through which his weak disciples slept.

Yet shrink not then, whoe'er thou art,
For God's great purpose set apart,
Before whose far-discerning eyes,.
The future as the present lies.

Beyond a narrow-bounded age,
Stretches thy prophet heritage,
Thine audience, worlds,—all time to be
The witness of the truth in thee.

J. G. Whittier.

169   *Servants of freedom.*   L.M.

O Freedom, on the bitter blast
The ventures of thy seed we cast,
And trust to warmer sun and rain
To swell the germ, and fill the grain.

It may not be our lot to wield
The sickle in the ripened field,
Nor ours to hear on summer eves
The reaper's song among the sheaves ;

Yet where our duty's task is wrought
In unison with God's great thought,
The near and future blend in one,
And whatsoe'er is willed is done.

Who calls the glorious labour hard ?
Who deems it not its own reward ?
Who, for its trials, counts it less
A cause of praise and thankfulness ?

Be ours the grateful service whence
Comes day by day the recompense,—
The hope, the trust, the purpose stayed,
The fountain and the noon-day shade.

J. G. Whittier.

170   *True freedom.*   7s.

MEN, whose boast it is, that ye
Come of fathers, brave and free,
If there breathe on earth a slave,
Are ye truly free and brave?
If ye do not feel the chain
When it works a brother's pain,
Are ye not base slaves, indeed,
Slaves unworthy to be freed?

Is true freedom but to break
Fetters for our own dear sake,
And with heathen hearts forget
That we owe mankind a debt?

No, true freedom is to share
All the chains our brothers wear,
And with heart and hand to be
Earnest to make others free.

They are slaves who fear to speak
For the fallen and the meek ;
They are slaves, who will not choose
Hatred, scoffing, and abuse
Rather than in silence shrink
From the truth they needs must think ;
They are slaves, who dare not be
In the right with two or three.

J. R. Lowell.

171   *Where is thy God?*   S.M.

WHERE is thy God, my soul?
Is He within thy heart ;
Or ruler of a distant realm
In which thou hast no part?

Where is thy God, my soul ?
Only in stars and sun ;
Or have the holy words of truth
His light in every one?

Where is thy God, my soul?
Confined to Scripture's page ;
Or does his Spirit check and guide
The spirit of each age?

O Ruler of the sky,
Rule Thou within my heart :
O great Adorner of the world,
Thy light of life impart.

Giver of holy words,
  Bestow thy holy power,
And aid me, whether work or thought
  Engage the varying hour.

In Thee have I my help,
  As all my fathers had;
I'll trust Thee when I'm sorrowful,
  And serve Thee when I'm glad.

T. T. Lynch.

172   *Calling.*   12.13.12.10.

FATHER, Thou art calling, calling to us plainly;
  To the spirit comes thy loving message evermore;
Holy One, uplift us, nor for ever vainly
  Stand calling us and waiting at the door.

In the whirling tempest and the storm Thou livest,
  In the rain, and in the sweetness of the after-
    glow;
Summer's golden bounty, winter's snow, Thou givest,
  And blooming meadows where sweet waters flow.

Clearer still and dearer is thy voice appealing,
  Deep within the spirit's secret being speaking
    low:
Enter, O our Father, truth and life revealing;
  From every evil free us as we go.

In Thee living, moving, unto Thee uprearing
  All the hope and joyfulness and trust that fill
    the soul,
Father, we adore Thee, asking nought nor fearing;
  We cannot wander from thy dear control.

J. V. Blake.

173   *Through and through.*   6s.

WE name thy name, O God,
  As our God call on Thee,
Though the dark heart meantime
  Far from thy ways may be.

And we can own thy law,
  And we can sing thy songs,
While this sad inner soul
  To sin and shame belongs.

On us thy love may glow,
  As the pure midday fire
On some foul spot look down;
  And yet the mire be mire.

Then spare us not thy fires,
  The searching light and pain;
Burn out the sin; and, last,
  With thy love heal again.
                    F. T. Palgrave.

174   *The Larger Faith.*   C.M.

WE pray no more, made lowly wise,
  For miracle and sign;
Anoint our eyes to see within
  The common the divine.

'Lo here, lo there,' no more we cry,
  Dividing with our call
The mantle of thy presence, Lord,
  That seamless covers all.

We turn from seeking Thee afar
  And in unwonted ways,
To build from out our daily lives
  The temples of thy praise.

And if thy casual comings, Lord,
   To hearts of old were dear,
What joy shall dwell within the faith
   That feels Thee ever near.

And nobler yet shall duty grow,
   And more shall worship be,
When Thou art found in all our life,
   And all our life in Thee.

F. L. Hosmer.

175   *The secret place of the Most High.*   C.M.

THE Lord is in his Holy Place
   In all things near and far,
Shekinah of the snowflake, He,
   And Glory of the star,
And Secret of the April land
   That stirs the field to flowers,
Whose little tabernacles rise
   To hold Him through the hours.

He hides Himself within the love
   Of those whom we love best;
The smiles and tones that make our homes
   Are shrines by Him possessed;
He tents within the lonely heart
   And shepherds every thought;
We find Him not by seeking long,
   We lose Him not, unsought.

Our art may build its Holy Place,
   Our feet on Sinai stand,
But Holiest of Holy knows
   No tread, no touch of hand;

The listening soul makes Sinai still
  Wherever we may be,
And in the vow, 'Thy will be done,'
  Lies all Gethsemane.

W. C. *Gannett.*

176   *When I awake, I am still with Thee.*   11.10.

STILL, still with Thee, when purple morning
    breaketh,
  When the bird waketh and the shadows flee;
Fairer than morning, lovelier than the daylight,
  Dawns the sweet consciousness, I am with Thee.

Alone with Thee, amid the mystic shadows,
  The solemn hush of nature newly born;
Alone with Thee in breathless adoration,
  In the calm dew and freshness of the morn.

As in the dawning, o'er the waveless ocean,
  The image of the morning star doth rest,
So in this stillness Thou beholdest only
  Thine image in the waters of my breast.

Still, still with Thee, as to each new-born morning,
  A fresh and solemn splendour still is given,
So doth this blessèd consciousness, awaking,
  Breathe, each day, nearness unto Thee and
    heaven.

When sinks the soul, subdued by toil, to slumber,
  Its closing eye looks up to Thee in prayer;
Sweet the repose beneath thy wings o'ershading,
  But sweeter still to wake and find Thee there.

So shall it be at last, in that bright morning
  When the soul waketh and life's shadows flee :
O in that hour, fairer than daylight dawning,
  Shall rise the glorious thought, I am with Thee.

Harriet B. Stowe.

177   *God is Love.*   C.M.

IMMORTAL Love, for ever full,
  For ever flowing free,
For ever shared, for ever whole,
  A never-ebbing sea ;

Our outward lips confess the name
  All other names above ;
But love alone knows whence it came,
  And comprehendeth love.

Blow, winds of God, awake and blow
  The mists of earth away ;
Shine out, O Light divine, and show
  How wide and far we stray.

The letter fails, the systems fall,
  And every symbol wanes :
The Spirit over-brooding all,
  Eternal Love, remains.

J. G. Whittier.

178   *Jesus.*   C M.

HE cometh not a king to reign,
  The world's long hope is dim ;
The weary centuries watch in vain.
  The clouds of heaven for Him.

But warm, sweet, tender, even yet
　　A present help is He;
And faith has still its Olivet,
　　And love its Galilee.

The healing of his seamless dress
　　Is by our beds of pain;
We touch Him in life's throng and press,
　　And we are whole again.

O Lord and Master of us all,
　　Whate'er our name or sign,
We own thy sway, we hear thy call,
　　We test our lives by thine.

J. G. Whittier.

179　　·　　　*Incarnation.*　　　C.M.

O LOVE, O Life, our faith and sight
　　Thy presence maketh one:
As, through transfigured clouds of white,
　　We trace the noon-day Sun,—

So to our mortal eyes subdued,
　　Flesh-veiled, but not concealed,
We know in Thee the fatherhood
　　And heart of God revealed.

We faintly hear, we dimly see,
　　In differing phrase we pray;
But, dim or clear, we own in Thee
　　The Light, the Truth, the Way.

The homage that we render Thee
　　Is still our Father's own;
Nor jealous claim or rivalry
　　Divides the cross and throne.

To do thy will is more than praise,
    As words are less than deeds :
And simple trust can find thy ways
    We miss with chart of creeds.

Our Friend, our Brother, and our Lord,
    What may thy service be ?
Nor name, nor form, nor ritual word,
    But simply following Thee.

.The heart shall ring thy Christmas bells,
    Kind deeds thy altars raise,
Our faith and hope thy canticles,
    And our obedience praise.
               J. G. Whittier.

180   *I am the Way, the Truth, and the Life.*   C.M.

OUR Friend, our Brother, and our Lord,
    What may thy service be?
Nor name, nor form, nor ritual word,
    But simply following Thee.

Thou judgest us; thy purity
    Doth all our lusts condemn;
The love that draws us nearer Thee
    Is hot with wrath to them.

Our thoughts lie open to thy sight;
    And, naked to thy glance,
Our secret sins are in the light
    Of thy pure countenance.

Yet weak and blinded though we be,
    Thou dost our service own;
We bring our varying gifts to Thee,
    And Thou rejectest none.

To Thee our full humanity,
   Its joys and pains, belong;
The wrong of man to man on Thee
   Inflicts a deeper wrong.

Deep strike thy roots, O heavenly Vine,
   Within our earthly sod,
Most human and yet most divine,
   The flower of man and God.

Apart from Thee all gain is loss,
   All labour vainly done;
The solemn shadow of thy cross
   Is better than the sun.

Alone, O Love ineffable,
   Thy saving name is given;
To turn aside from Thee is hell,
   To walk with Thee is heaven.

We faintly hear, we dimly see,
   In differing phrase we pray;
But dim or clear, we own in Thee
   The Light, the Truth, the Way.
                 J. G. Whittier.

181   *Consider the lilies, how they grow.*   7.6.

HE hides within the lily
   A strong and tender care,
That wins the earth-born atoms
   To glory of the air;
He weaves the shining garments
   Unceasingly and still,
Along the quiet waters,
   In niches of the hill.

We linger at the vigil
  With Him who bent the knee
To watch the old-time lilies
  In distant Galilee;
And still the worship deepens
  And quickens into new,
As, brightening down the ages,
  God's secret thrilleth through.

O Toiler of the lily,
  Thy touch is in the Man;
No leaf that dawns to petal
  But hints the angel-plan.
The flower-horizons open;
  The blossom vaster shows;
We hear thy wide worlds echo,—
  See how the lily grows.

Shy yearnings of the savage,
  Unfolding thought by thought,
To holy lives are lifted,
  To visions fair are wrought;
The races rise and cluster,
  And evils fade and fall,
Till chaos blooms to beauty,
  Thy purpose crowning all.

W. C. Gannell.

182   *Heirship.*   7s.

HEIR of all the ages, I,—
  Heir of all that they have wrought,
All their store of emprise high,
  All their wealth of precious thought!

Every golden deed of theirs
  Sheds its lustre on my way;
All their labours, all their prayers,
  Sanctify this present day.

Heir of all that they have earned
  By their passion and their tears;
Heir of all that they have learned
  Through the weary, toiling years;

Heir of all the faith sublime,
  On whose wings they soared to heaven;
Heir of every hope that Time
  To earth's fainting sons hath given;

Aspirations pure and high;
  Strength to do and to endure;
Heir of all the ages, I,—
  Lo, I am no longer poor.
                        Julia C. R. Dorr.

183   *The Word of the Lord abideth for ever.*   8.7.

GOD of ages and of nations,
  Every race, and every time,
Hath received thine inspirations,
  Glimpses of thy truth sublime.
Ever spirits, in rapt vision,
  Passed the heavenly vale within;
Ever hearts, bowed in contrition,
  Found salvation from their sin.

Reason's noble aspiration,
  Truth in growing clearness saw;
Conscience spoke its condemnation,
  Or proclaimed the Eternal Law.

While thine inward revelations
  Told thy saints their prayers were heard,
Prophets to the guilty nations
  Spoke thine everlasting word.

Lord, that word abideth ever;
  Revelation is not sealed;
Answering unto man's endeavour,
  Truth and Right are still revealed.
That which came to ancient sages,
  Greek, Barbarian, Roman, Jew,
Written in the heart's deep pages,
  Shines to-day, for ever new.

S. Longfellow.

184   *Heaven not afar off.*   10s.

FATHER, thy wonders do not singly stand,
  Nor far removed where feet have seldom strayed:
Around us ever lies the enchanted land,
  In marvels rich to thine own sons displayed.

In finding Thee are all things round us found;
  In losing Thee are all things lost beside;
Ears have we, but in vain sweet voices sound,
  And to our eyes the vision is denied.

Open our eyes that we that world may see,
  Open our ears that we thy voice may hear,
And in the spirit-land may ever be,
  And feel thy presence with us always near.

Jones Very.

185   *Love supreme in God.*   L.M.

O SOURCE divine, and Life of all,
  The Fount of being's wondrous sea,
Thy depth would every heart appal,
  That saw not Love supreme in Thee.

We shrink before thy vast abyss,
    Where worlds on worlds eternal brood;
We know Thee truly but in this,
    That Thou bestowest all our good.

And so, 'mid boundless time and space,
    O grant us still in Thee to dwell,
And through the ceaseless web to trace
    Thy presence working all things well.

Nor let Thou life's delightful play
    Thy truth's transcendent vision hide:
Nor strength and gladness lead astray
    From Thee, our nature's only guide.

Bestow on every joyous thrill
    A deeper tone of reverent awe;
Make pure thy children's erring will,
    And teach their hearts to love thy law.
                                    J. Sterling.

186   *Very near.*   L.M.

O SOMETIMES comes to soul and sense
The feeling which is evidence
That very near about us lies
The realm of spirit-mysteries.

The low and dark horizon lifts,
To light the scenic terror shifts;
The breath of a diviner air
Blows down the answer of a prayer.

Then all our sorrow, pain, and doubt
A great compassion clasps about;
And law and goodness, love and force,
Are wedded fast beyond divorce.

Then, Duty leaves to Love its task,
The beggar Self forgets to ask ;
We feel, as flowers the sun and dew,
The One True Life our own renew.

J. G. Whittier.

187   *Old and New.*   L.M.

O SOMETIMES gleams upon our sight,
Through present wrong, the Eternal Right ;
And step by step, since time began,
We see the steady gain of man ;

That all of good the past hath had
Remains to make our own time glad,
Our common, daily life divine,
And every land a Palestine.

We lack but open eye and ear,
To find the Orient's marvels here ;
The still small voice in autumn's hush,
Yon maple wood the burning bush.

For still the new transcends the old,
In signs and tokens manifold ;
Slaves rise up men ; the olive waves,
With roots deep set in battle graves.

Through the harsh noises of our day,
A low, sweet prelude finds its way ;
Through clouds of doubt, and creeds of fear,
A light is breaking calm and clear.

Henceforth my heart shall sigh no more
For olden time and holier shore :
God's love and blessing, then and there,
Are now and here and everywhere.

J. G. Whittier.

188 *Greeting.* L.M.

O LIFE that maketh all things new,
The blooming earth, the thoughts of men,
Our pilgrim feet, wet with thy dew,
In gladness hither turn again.

From hand to hand the greeting flows,
From eye to eye the signals run,
From heart to heart the bright hope glows;
The seekers of the Light are one;

One in the freedom of the Truth,
One in the joy of paths untrod,
One in the soul's perennial youth,
One in the larger thought of God;

The freer step, the fuller breath,
The wide horizon's grander view,
The sense of life that knows no death,
The Life that maketh all things new.
S. Longfellow.

189 *Abide in Me.* 10s.

THAT mystic word of thine, O sovereign Lord,
Is all too pure, too high, too deep for me;
Weary of striving, and with longing faint,
I breathe it back again in prayer to Thee.

Abide in me, I pray, and I in Thee;
From this good hour, O leave me never more;
Then shall the discord cease, the wound be healed,.
The life-long bleeding of the soul be o'er.

Abide in me; o'ershadow by thy love
Each half-formed purpose, and dark thought of
sin;
Quench, ere it rise, each selfish, low desire,
And keep my soul as thine, calm and divine.

As some rare perfume in a vase of clay
  Pervades it with a fragrance not its own,
So, when Thou dwellest in a mortal soul,
  All heaven's own sweetness seems around it
    thrown.

Abide in me; there have been moments blest,
  When I have heard thy voice and felt thy power,
Then evil lost its grasp, and passion hushed
  Owned the divine enchantment of the hour.

These were but seasons, beautiful and rare;
  Abide in me, and they shall ever be;
Fulfil at once thy precept and my prayer—
  Come, and abide in me, and I in Thee.

                              Harriet B. Stowe.

190   *Walk in the Light.*   C.M.

  WALK in the light ! so shalt thou know
    That fellowship of love
  His Spirit only can bestow,
    Who reigns in light above.

  Walk in the light ! and thou shalt find
    Thy heart made truly his,
  Who dwells in cloudless light enshrined,
    In whom no darkness is.

  Walk in the light ! and thou shalt own
    Thy darkness passed away ;
  Because that Light hath on thee shone
    In which is perfect day.

  Walk in the light ! and e'en the tomb
    No fearful shade shall wear ;
  Glory shall chase away its gloom,
    For Christ hath conquered there.

Walk in the light ! and thine shall be
  A path, though thorny, bright ;
For God, by grace, shall dwell in thee,
  And God Himself is Light.

B. Barton.

191   *Listening for God.*   C.M.

I HEAR it often in the dark,
  I hear it in the light,—
Where *is* the voice that calls to me
  With such a quiet might ?
It seems but echo to my thought,
  And yet beyond the stars ;
It seems a heart-beat in a hush,
  And yet the planet jars.

O may it be that far within
  My inmost soul there lies
A *spirit-sky*, that opens with
  Those voices of surprise ?
And can it be, by night and day,
  That firmament serene
Is just the heaven, where God Himself,   ·
  The Father, dwells unseen ?

O God within, so close to me
  That every thought is plain,
Be Judge, be Friend, be Father still,
  And in thy heaven reign.
Thy heaven is mine,—my very soul ;
  Thy words are sweet and strong ;
They fill my inward silences
  With music and with song.

They send me challenges to right,
  And loud rebuke my ill ;
They ring my bells of victory,
  They breathe my ' Peace, be still ;'

They ever seem to say,—'My child,
    Why seek Me so all day;
Now journey inward to thyself,
    And listen by the way.'

W. C. Gannett.

192   *Inspiration.*   7s.

LIFE of Ages, richly poured,
    Love of God, unspent and free,
Flowing in the Prophet's word
    And the People's liberty!

Never was to chosen race
    That unstinted tide confined:
Thine is every time and place,
    Fountain sweet of heart and mind.

Secret of the morning stars,
    Motion of the oldest hours,
Pledge through elemental wars
    Of the coming spirit's powers!

Rolling planet, flaming sun,
    Stand in nobler Man complete;
Prescient laws thine errands run,
    Frame a shrine for Godhead meet.

Homeward led, the wondering eye
    Upward yearned, in joy or awe,
For the Love that waited nigh,
    Guidance of thy guardian Law.

In the touch of earth it thrilled;
    Down from mystic skies it burned;
Right obeyed and passion stilled
    Its eternal gladness earned.

Breathing in the thinker's creed,
　Pulsing in the hero's blood,
Nerving simplest thought and deed,
　Freshening time with truth and good;

Consecrating art and song,
　Holy book and pilgrim track;
Hurling floods of tyrant wrong
　From the sacred limits back,—

Life of Ages, richly poured,
　Love of God, unspent and free,
Flow still in the Prophet's word
　And the People's liberty!

S. Johnson.

193　　　　*Inspiration.*　　　　L.M.

MYSTERIOUS Presence, Source of all,—
The world without, the world within,
Fountian of Life, O hear our call,
And pour thy living waters in.

Thou breathest in the rushing wind,
Thy spirit stirs in leaf and flower;
Nor wilt Thou from the willing mind
Withhold thy light and love and power.

Thy hand unseen to accents clear
Awoke the psalmist's trembling lyre,
And touched the lips of holy seer
With flame from thine own altar fire.

That touch divine still, Lord, impart;
Still give the prophet's burning word;
And vocal in each waiting heart
Let living psalms of praise be heard.

S. C. Beach.

194 *Unfolding.* 7s.

O Eternal Life, whose power
  Gathers ages to a span,
From whose being breaks the flower,
  From whose glory groweth man,
By the whisper of whose breath
Atoms wake that seem but death,
With whose silent-working will
The eternal ages thrill—

Lord of Life, to heaven tower
  Spires of being high and grand,
Till on man Thou lay the power
  That he serve with heart and hand;
Till Thou flood him with thy light
That he see Thee with his sight,
Who art Reason, who art Right,
Majesty of Love and Might.

Not on earth the glory ends;
  In unnumbered worlds it reigns;
From Eternity descends,
  To Eternity remains.
When the things we hear and see
Vanish in life's mystery,
Still, all glories that can be
Wait in thine Infinity.
                    J. V. Blake.

195 *The Blessed Life.* L.M.

O blessèd life ! the heart at rest,
  When all without tumultuous seems,
  That trusts a higher will, and deems
That higher will, made ours, the best.

O blessed life ! the mind that sees—
  Whatever change the years may bring—
  Some good still hid in everything,
And shining through all mysteries.

O blessèd life ! the soul that soars,
  When sense of mortal sight is dim,
  Beyond the sense,—beyond, to Him
Whose love unlocks the heavenly doors.

O blessèd life ! heart, mind, and soul
  From selfish aims and wishes free,
  In all at one with Deity
And loyal to the Lord's control.

O life ! how blessèd ! how divine !
  High life, the earnest of a higher !
  Father, fulfil my deep desire
And let this blessèd life be mine.
W. Tidd Matson.

196   *Rising to God.*   P.M.

MYSTERIOUS Spirit, unto whom
  Is known my sad and earth-bound frame ;
Thou whom my soul, 'midst doubt and gloom,
  Adoreth with a fervent flame ;
Give me the speed of bird or wind,
  Or torrent rushing to the sea,
That soaring upwards I may find
  My resting-place in Thee.

Thoughts of my soul, how swift ye go,
  Swift as the eagle's wing of fire,
Or arrows from the lightning's bow,
  To God, the goal of my desire.

. The weary tempest sleeps at last,
  The torrent in the sea finds rest ;
Let me not always be outcast,
  Lord, take me to thy breast.

My prayer hath pierced to God—The life,
  The resurrection power is mine :
From sin and grief, from pain and strife,
  I rise on wings of love divine ;
Swifter than torrent, tempest, light,
  I fly to my serene abode,
And on the last and holiest height,
  Find rest and joy in God.

S. A. Brooke.
(Founded on a translation from Lamartine by J. G. Whittier.)

197   *Nearer to Thee.*   6.4.6.4.6.6.4.

NEARER, my God, to Thee,
      Nearer to Thee ;
E'en though it be a cross
      That raiseth me,
Still all my song shall be,—
Nearer, my God, to Thee,
      Nearer to Thee.

Though, like the wanderer,
      The sun gone down,
Darkness comes over me,
      My rest a stone,
Yet in my dreams I'd be
Nearer, my God, to Thee,
      Nearer to Thee.

There let the way appear
      Steps unto heaven,
All that Thou sendest me
      In mercy given,

Angels to beckon me
Nearer, my God, to Thee,
    Nearer to Thee.

Then, with my waking thoughts
    Bright with thy praise,
Out of my stony griefs
    Bethel I'll raise;
So by my woes to be
Nearer, my God, to Thee,
    Nearer to Thee.

Or, if on joyful wing,
    Cleaving the sky,
Sun, moon and stars forgot,
    Upwards I fly;
Still all my song shall be,—
Nearer, my God, to Thee,
    Nearer to Thee.

Sarah F. Adams.

198   *A life hidden in God.*   7s.

LET my life be hid in Thee,
    Life of life and Light of light,
Love's illimitable sea,
    Depth of peace, of power the height.

Let my life be hid in Thee
    From vexation and annoy;
Calm in thy tranquillity,
    All my mourning turned to joy.

Let my life be hid in Thee
    When alarms are gathering round,
Covered with thy panoply,
    Safe within thy holy ground.

Let my life be hid in Thee
   When my strength and health shall fail ;
Let thine immortality
   In my dying hour prevail.

Let my life be hid in Thee,
   In the world and yet above ;
Hid in thine eternity,
   In the ocean of thy love.

                          J. B. Clipston.

199   *Life in God.*   7.6.

I READ of many mansions
   Within the house divine ;
I need not go to find them,
   For one of them is mine ;
God lives in mine, and loves me ;
   Who else could bring the day ?
Who spread the sleep upon me ?
   Who give me hands to play ?

And when I say ' Our Father,'
   It seems so far to pray,
To think of heaven up yonder
   I can but turn and say :
' Dear Father, close beside me,
   I feel Thee dimly near,
In every face that loves me,
   In each kind word I hear.'

He's the touch of mother's fingers,
   So full of love and care ;
He's the pleasantness of trying,
   The help inside the prayer.

I do not understand it,
   But so it seems to be,
There always is that Other,
   Whom I but dimly see.
W. C. Gannett.

200   *Life in God.*   11.10

INFINITE Spirit, who art round us ever,
   In whom we float as motes in summer sky,
May neither life nor death the sweet bond sever
   Which binds us to our unseen Friend on high ;—

Unseen, yet not unfelt ; if any thought
   Has raised our minds from earth, a pure desire,
A generous act, a noble purpose brought,
   It is thy breath, O Lord, which fans the fire.

To me, the humblest of thy creatures, kneeling,
   Conscious of weakness, ignorance, sin, and shame,
Give such a force of holy thought and feeling,
   That I may live to glorify thy name ;—

That I may conquer base desire and passion,
   That I may rise o'er selfish thought and will,
O'ercome the world's allurement, threat, and
      fashion,
   Walk humbly, softly, leaning on Thee still.
J. F. Clarke.

201   *The merciful God.*   8.7.8.7.8.8.

THOUGH we long, in sin-wrought blindness,
   From thy gracious paths have strayed,
Cold to Thee and all thy kindness,
   Wilful, reckless, or afraid ;
Through dim clouds that gather round us
Thou hast sought, and Thou hast found us.

Oft from Thee we veil our faces,
　　Children-like, to cheat thine eyes;
Sin, and hope to hide the traces;
　　From ourselves, ourselves disguise;
'Neath the webs enwoven round us
Thy soul-piercing glance has found us.

Sudden, 'midst our idle chorus,
　　O'er our sin thy thunders roll,
Death his signal waves before us,
　　Night and terror take the soul;
Till through double darkness round us
Looks a star—and Thou hast found us.

O most merciful, most holy,
　　Light thy wanderers on their way;
Keep us ever thine, thine wholly,
　　Suffer us no more to stray;
Cloud and storm oft gather round us:
We were lost, but Thou hast found us.

　　　　　　　　　　F. T. Palgrave.

202　　　　　*All things are thine.*　　　　8s.

THOU art, O God, the life and light
　　Of all this wondrous world we see:
Its glow by day, its smile by night,
　　Are but reflections caught from Thee:
Where'er we turn, thy glories shine,
And all things fair and bright are thine.

When day with farewell beam delays
　　Among the opening clouds of even,
And we can almost think we gaze
　　Through golden vistas into heaven,—
Those hues, that make the sun's decline
So soft, so radiant, Lord, are thine.

When night with wings of starry gloom
   O'ershadows all the earth and skies,
Like some dark beauteous bird whose plume
   Is sparkling with unnumbered eyes,—
That sacred gloom, those fires divine,
So grand, so countless, Lord, are thine.

When youthful spring around us breathes,
   Thy Spirit warms her fragrant sigh,
And every flower the summer wreathes
   Is born beneath that kindling eye,—
Where'er we turn, thy glories shine,
And all things fair and bright are thine.

T. Moore.

203   *The Lord is my Shepherd.*   8.6.8.4.

THE God of love my shepherd is,
   My gracious, constant Guide;
I shall not want, for I am his,
   In all supplied.

In his green pastures do I feed,
   And there lie down at will;
He leads me in my thirsty need
   By waters still.

His tenderness restores my soul,
   When sick and faint I roam;
Shows the right path and makes me whole,
   Bearing me home.

Yea, the dark valley when I tread,
   No evil will I fear;
Thy rod and staff dispel my dread;
   I feel Thee near.

Thou spread'st my table 'mid my foes,
   The oil of grace is mine,
My cup with mercy overflows
   And love divine.

Goodness and mercy all my days
   My daily song shall be,
Till heavenly anthems fill with praise
   Eternity.

G. Rawson.

204   *The Lost Sheep.*   Irr.

THERE were ninety and nine that safely lay
   In the shelter of the fold,
But one was out on the hills away,
   Far off from the gates of gold:
Away on the mountains wild and bare,
Away from the tender Shepherd's care.

'Lord, Thou hast here thy ninety and nine;
   Are they not enough for Thee?'
But the Shepherd made answer: 'This of mine
   Has wandered away from Me;
And although the road be rough and steep,
   I go to the desert to find my sheep.'

But none of the ransomed ever knew,
   How deep were the waters crossed;
Nor how dark was the night that the Lord passed
   through,
   Ere He found his sheep that was lost:
Out in the desert He heard its cry—
Sick and helpless and ready to die.

Lord, whence are those blood-drops all the way
  That mark out the mountain's track ? '
' They were shed for one who had gone astray
  Ere the Shepherd could bring him back.'
' Lord, whence are thy hands so rent and torn ? '
' They are pierced to-night by many a thorn.'

And all through the mountains, thunder-riven,
  And up from the rocky steep,
There rose a cry to the gate of heaven,
  ' Rejoice, I have found my sheep ; '
And the angels echoed around the throne,
' Rejoice, for the Lord brings back his own.'

Elizabeth C. Clephane.

205   *The Shepherd.*   L.M.

WHERE dost Thou feed thy favoured sheep ?
  O my Belovèd, tell me where ;
My soul within thy pastures keep,
  And guard me with thy tender care.
Too prone, alas, to turn aside,
  Too prone with alien flocks to stray ;
Be Thou my Shepherd, Thou my Guide,
  And lead me in thy heavenly way.

If thou wouldst know, thou favoured one,
  Where soul-refreshing pastures be ;
Feed on my words of truth alone,
  And walk with those who walk with Me.
I with the contrite spirit dwell :
  The broken heart is mine abode ;
Such spikenard yields a fragrant smell,
  And such are all the saints of God.

R. Pope.

206   *The shadow of a great rock in a weary land.*

THE Shadow of the Rock !
Stay, pilgrim, stay !
Night treads upon the heels of day ;
There is no other resting-place this way.
The Rock is near,
The well is clear,
Rest in the Shadow of the Rock.

The Shadow of the Rock !
Abide, abide !
This Rock moves ever at thy side,
Pausing to welcome thee at eventide.
Ages are laid
Beneath its shade,
Rest in the Shadow of the Rock.

The Shadow of the Rock !
To angel's eyes
This Rock its shadow multiplies,
And at this hour in countless places lies.
One Rock, one shade,
O'er thousands laid,
Rest in the Shadow of the Rock.

The Shadow of the Rock !
To weary feet,
That have been diligent and fleet,
The sleep is deeper and the shade more swe
O weary, rest,
Thou art sore pressed,
Rest in the Shadow of the Rock.

The Shadow of the Rock!
Thy bed is made;
Crowds of tired souls like thine are laid
This night beneath the self-same placid shade.
They who rest here
Wake with heaven near,
Rest in the Shadow of the Rock.

F. W. Faber.

207   *The Lord is my Stay.*   11.10.11.6.

WHEN on my day of life the night is falling,
   And, in the winds from unsunned spaces blown,
I hear far voices out of darkness calling
    My feet to paths unknown;

Thou who hast made my home of life so pleasant,
   Leave not its tenant when its walls decay;
O Love divine, O Helper ever present,
    Be Thou my strength and stay.

Be near me when all else is from me drifting—
   Earth, sky, home's pictures, days of shade and
      shine,
And kindly faces to my own uplifting
    The love which answers mine.

I have but Thee, my Father; let thy Spirit
   Be with me then to comfort and uphold;
No gate of pearl, no branch of palm I merit,
    Nor street of shining gold.

Suffice it if—my good and ill unreckoned,
   And both forgiven through thy abounding
      grace—
I find myself by hands familiar beckoned
    Unto my fitting place;

Some humble door among thy many mansions,
  Some sheltering shade where sin and striving
    cease,
And flows for ever through heaven's green expan-
    sions
      The river of thy peace.

There, from the music round about me stealing,
  I fain would learn the new and holy song,
And find at last, beneath thy trees of healing,
  The life for which I long.
                                J. G. Whittier.

208　　　*The Lord is my Refuge.*　　　8.7.

CALL the Lord thy sure salvation;
  Rest beneath the Almighty's shade;
In his secret habitation
  Dwell, nor ever be dismayed.

There no tumult can alarm thee,
  Thou shalt dread no hidden snare;
Guile nor violence can harm thee,
  In eternal safeguard there.

From the sword at noon-day wasting;
  From the noisome pestilence,
Through the midnight city hasting,
  God shall be thy sure defence.

Fear not thou the deadly quiver,
  Though a thousand arrows fly;
He shall still thy soul deliver
  From his rock of strength on high.

Though the winds and waves are swelling,
  He shall bear thee safe through all;
God Himself shall be thy dwelling,
  Though the very heaven fall.

And when death thy soul deliver
From the peril of the world,
Thou shalt be on high for ever,
Safely in his feathers furled ;

All the trouble and temptation,
Hushed upon the heavenly shore ;
Satisfied with God's salvation,
Crowned with life for evermore.

J. Montgomery and S. A. Brooke.

209　　　*O'er seas of God.*　　　L.M

THE winds that o'er my ocean run
Reach through all worlds beyond the sun ;
Through life and death, through fate, throug
time,
Grand breaths of God they sweep sublime.

A thread of Law runs through my prayer
Stronger than iron cables are ;
And love and longing towards her goal
Are pilots sweet to guide the soul.

O thou, God's mariner, heart of mine,
Spread canvas to the airs divine ;
Spread sail, and let thy Fortune be
Forgotten in thy Destiny.

The wind ahead ?　The wind is free ;
For evermore it favoureth me :
To shores of God still blowing fair,
O'er seas of God my bark doth bear.

For Life must live, and Soul must sail,
And Unseen over Seen prevail ;
And all God's argosies come to shore,
Let ocean smile, or rage, or roar.

D. A. Wasson.

210   *Nature and Man.*   L.M.

WHEN up to nightly skies we gaze,
Where stars pursue their endless ways,
We think we see, from earth's low clod,
The wide and shining house of God.

But could we rise to moon or sun,
Or path where planets duly run,
Still heaven would spread above us far,
And earth remote would seem a star.

This earth with all its dust and tears
Is his, no less than yonder spheres :
And raindrops weak, and grains of sand,
Are stamped by his immediate hand.

The rock, the wave, the little flower,
All fed by streams of living power,
That spring from one almighty will,
Whate'er his thought conceives, fulfil.

And is this all that man can claim ?
Is this our longing's final aim ?
To be like all things round,—no more
Than pebbles cast on Time's grey shore.

Not this our doom, Thou God benign,
Whose rays on us unclouded shine :
Thy breath sustains yon fiery dome ;
But man is most thy favoured home.

We view those halls of painted air,
And own thy presence makes them fair ;
But dearer still to Thee, O Lord,
Is he whose thoughts to thine accord.

J. Sterling.

211 *To be alive!* 10s.

WE wake each morn as if the Maker's grace
  Did us afresh from nothingness derive,
That we might sing, ' How happy is our case,
  How beautiful it is to be alive.'

Lo, all around us his bright servants stand :
  And if with frowning brows for their disguise,
  Yet with such wells of love in their deep eyes,
And so strong rescue hidden in their hands.

And our lives may in glory move along :
  First holy white, and then all good, and fair
  For our dear Lord to see,—the very air
We breathe, self-shaped into a natural song.

And ever towards new heights we still may strive,
  Till, just as any other friend's, we press
  Death's hand ; and, having died, feel none the
    less
How beautiful it is to be alive.

H. S. Sutton.

212 *The Light of Life.* 8s.

SPIRIT of grace, Thou Light of Life
  Amidst the darkness of the dead,
Bright Star, whereby through worldly strife
  The patient pilgrim still is led,
Thou Dayspring in the deepest gloom,
Wildered and dark, to Thee I come.

Pure fire of God, burn out my sin,
  Cleanse all the earthly dross from me ;
Refine my secret heart within,
  The golden streams of love set free ;
Live Thou in me, O Life divine,
Until my deepest love be thine.

O Breath from far Eternity,
    Breathe o'er my soul's unfertile land ;
So shall the pine and myrtle-tree
    Spring up amidst the desert-sand ;
And where thy living water flows,
My heart shall blossom as the rose.

Let me in will and deed and word
    Obey Thee as a little child,
And in thy love abide, O Lord,
    For ever pure and undefiled :
Teach me to work and strive and pray,
And keep me in thy heavenward way.

G. Tersteegen, tr. Emma F. Bevan.

213   *Our Leader.*   10.10.10.10.6.6.

    HE leads us on
By paths we did not know :
Upward He leads us though our steps be slow,
Though oft we faint and falter on the way,
Though storms and darkness oft obscure the day,
    Yet when the clouds are gone,
    We know He leads us on.

    He leads us on
Through all the unquiet years ;
Past all our dreamland hopes, and doubts, and
    fears,
He guides our steps, through all the tangled maze
Of losses, sorrows, and o'er-clouded days
    We know his will is done ;
    And still He leads us on.

And He, at last,
After the weary strife,
After the restless fever we call life,
After the dreariness, the aching pain,
The wayward struggles which have proved in vain,
After our toils are past,
Will give us rest at last.

N. L. Zinzendorf, tr. Jane Borthwick.

214   *The Vow.*   S.M.

GOD of the earnest heart,
The trust assured and still,
Thou who our strength for ever art,
We come to do thy will.

Upon that painful road
By saints serenely trod,
Whereon their hallowing influence flowed,
Would we go forth, O God;

'Gainst doubt and shame and fear
In human hearts to strive,
That all may learn to love and bear,
To conquer self, and live;

To draw thy blessing down,
And bring the wronged redress,
And give this glorious world its crown,
The spirit's Godlikeness.

No dreams from toil to charm,
No trembling on the tongue,—
Lord, in thy rest may we be calm,
Through thy completeness strong.

Thou hearest while we pray;
O deep within us write,
With kindling power, our God, to-day,
Thy word, 'On earth be light.'

S. Johnson.

215   *Providence.*   C.M

GOD moves in a mysterious way
    His wonders to perform;
He plants his footsteps in the sea,
    And rides upon the storm.

Deep in unfathomable mines
    Of never-failing skill,
He treasures up his bright designs,
    And works his sovereign will.

Ye fearful souls, fresh courage take!
    The clouds ye so much dread
Are big with mercy, and shall break
    In blessings on your head.

Judge not the Lord by feeble sense,
    But trust Him for his grace;
Behind a frowning providence
    He hides a smiling face.

His purposes will ripen fast,
    Unfolding every hour;
The bud may have a bitter taste,
    But sweet will be the flower.

Blind unbelief is sure to err,
    And scan his work in vain;
God is his own interpreter,
    And He will make it plain.

W. Cowper.

216 *Help is nigh.* 8.5.8.3.

GOD is near thee, therefore cheer thee ;
  Rest in Him, sad soul ;
He'll defend thee, when around thee
    Billows roll.

Calm thy sadness, look in gladness
  To thy Friend on high ;
Faint and weary pilgrim, cheer thee ;
    Help is nigh.

Mark the sea-bird wildly wheeling
  Through the stormy skies ;
God defends him, God attends him,
    When he cries.

Fare thee onward, through the sunshine,
  Or through wintry blast :
Fear forsake thee, God will take thee
    Home at last.
       Tr. from German.

217 *To the prodigal.* 7s.

BROTHER, hast thou wandered far
  From thy Father's happy home,
With thyself and God at war ?
  Turn thee, brother, homeward come.

Hast thou wasted all the powers
  God for noble uses gave?
Squandered life's most golden hours?
  Turn thee, brother, God can save.

Is a mighty famine now
  In thy heart and in thy soul?
Discontent upon thy brow ?
  Turn thee, God will make thee whole.

He can heal thy bitterest wound,
　He thy gentlest prayer can hear ;
Seek Him, for He may be found ;
　Call upon Him ; He is near.

J. F. Clarke.

218　　　*Father, I have sinned.*　　　7s.

Love for all ; and can it be?
Can I hope it is for me ?
I, who strayed so long ago,
Strayed so far, and fell so low ;

I, the disobedient child,
Wayward, passionate, and wild,
I, who left my Father's home
In forbidden ways to roam ;

I, who spurned his loving hold,
I, who would not be controlled,
I, who would not hear his call,
I, the wilful prodigal ;

I, who wasted and misspent
Every talent He had lent,
I, who sinned again, again,
Giving every passion rein.

To my Father can I go ?
At his feet myself I'll throw ;
In his house there yet may be
Place, a servant's place, for me.

See, my Father waiting stands ;
See, He reaches out his hands ;
God is love : I know, I see
There is love for me, e'en me.

S. Longfellow.

219 *Our Refuge.* 8.8.6.

O GOD, Thou art my fortress high,
My refuge when the storm is nigh,
   My joy, my hope divine ;
Descend in power upon my life,
Through change and stillness, pain and strife,
   Preserve me wholly thine.

Since fear and doubt are round my way,
And past desires upon me prey,
   Be gracious to my soul :
Let me forget the sinful years,
Bring the deep love that casts out fears,
   The hopes that life control.

Kindle in me thy righteous fire
Till I have only one desire—
   The love of Holy Love :
Till sin and grief I shall forget,
And all my soul with freedom set
   To gain thy home above.

This path of life to me display,
And lead me in Thyself the way,
   Till all thy grace is given :
Then to thy righteousness unite,
And bear me through the spheres of light,
   To brighter light in heaven.

                C. Wesley and S. A. Brooke.

220 *At the fountain.* C.M.

O GOD, unseen, but ever near,
   Our blessèd rest art Thou ;
And we, in love that hath no fear,
   Take refuge with Thee now.

All soiled with dust our pilgrim feet,
   And weary with the way;
We seek thy shelter from the heat
   And burden of life's day.

O welcome in the wilderness
   The shadow of thy love;
The stream that springs our thirst to bless,
   The manna from above.

Awhile beside the fount we stay
   And eat this bread of thine,
Then go rejoicing on our way,
   Renewed with strength divine.

S. Longfellow.

221   *The soul's prophecy.*   7s.

ALL before us lies the way;
   Give the past unto the wind.
All before us is the day;
   Night and darkness are behind.

Eden, with its angels bold,
   Love, and flowers, and purity,
Is not ancient story told,
   But a glowing prophecy.

In the spirit's perfect air,
   In the passions tame and kind,
Innocence from selfish care,
   Truest Eden we shall find.

When the soul to sin hath died,
   True and beautiful, and sound,
Then all earth is sanctified,
   Upsprings Paradise around.

Then shall come the Eden days,
　　Guardian watch from seraph eyes,
Angels on the beauteous rays,
　　Voices from the opening skies.

From this spirit-land, afar
　　All disturbing force shall flee ;
Stir, nor toil, nor sin shall mar
　　Its immortal unity.

Miss Clapp.

222　　　　*The love of God.*　　　　8s.

My God, why dost Thou longer stay ?
　　I thirst to know Thee as Thou art ;
Weary and faint with long delay !
　　When wilt Thou come within my heart,
From sin and sorrow set me free,
And satisfy my soul with Thee?

Come, O Thou universal good,
　　Balm of the wounded conscience, come,
The hungry, dying spirit's food,
　　The weary, wandering pilgrims home,
Haven to take the shipwrecked in,
My everlasting rest from sin.

Come, O my comfort, O my way,
　　My strength and health, my shield and rest ;
Still lead me lest I go astray,
　　And bear me on thy gentle breast ;
And if I wander in the wild,
Seek and forgive thy sinful child.

O grant that nothing in my heart
　　May dwell, but thy pure love alone,
Let all strange fires from me depart,
　　And wandering passion be unknown.
Thy deeper love drive out all love
I may not keep with Thee above.

In suffering, be thy love my peace,
  In weakness, be thy love my power ;
And when the storms of life shall cease,
  My Father, in that lonely hour,
In tenderness eternal rise,
And light my soul to Paradise.

C. Wesley.

223　　　　*If any comfort of love.*　　　　8s.

I HAVE no comfort but thy love ;
  Without it, life is death to me ;
Joyless through all its joys I move,
  Hopeless through all its misery ;
Yet, trusting Thee, I daily prove
The blessèd comfort of thy love.

Thou art the Rock on which I stand,
  When round me rages life's rough sea,
Mine anchor, and my sheltering strand,
  The haven where my soul would be :
Daily I feel, and nightly prove
The blessèd comfort of thy love.

O lift me higher, nearer Thee,
  And as I rise more pure and meet,
O let my soul's humility
  Make me lie lower at thy feet ;
Less trusting self the more I prove
The blessèd comfort of thy love.

Grateful my songs arise to Thee,
  With morning's dawn and evening's fall ;
For Thou hast ever been to me
  My light, my life, mine all in all :
My day is night, if Thou remove ;
Give me all comfort in thy love.

J. S. B. Monsell.

224   *The Voyage of Life.*   S.M.

O GOD, whose love is near,
  Although it seem to stay,
Be with us through our voyage here,
  And smooth the ocean way.

Though on a foreign sea,
  We sail not far from home ;
And nearer to the port of peace
  We every moment come.

When loud the surges rise,
  And calms delay to be,
The storm is blest and kind the waves
  That drive us nearer Thee.

And when the winds are hushed,
  And on the deep is peace,
And we behold the land where lies
  Our haven of release :

With soft and gentle winds
  O waft us smooth along;
While fastened deep within the veil,
  Hope is our anchor strong.

Wait till all tempests flee,
  Wait thy appointed hour ;
Wait till the Master of thy soul
  Reveal his love with power.

Tarry his leisure then,
  Although He seem to stay ;
For heaven's harbourage with Him
  All storms shall over pay.

                     A. M. Toplady and S. A. Brooke.

LONG did I toil, and knew no earthly rest;
   Far did I rove, and found no certain home;
At last I sought them in his sheltering breast
   Who opes his arms, and bids the weary come;
With Him I found a home, a rest divine;
And I since then am his, and He is mine.

Yes, He is mine, and nought of earthly things,
   Not all the charms of pleasure, wealth, or power,
The fame of heroes, or the pomp of kings,
   Could tempt me to forego his love an hour;
'Go, worthless world,' I cry, 'with all that's thine,
Go, I my Father's am, and He is mine.'

The good I have is from his stores supplied;
   The ill is only what He deems the best;
He for my friend, I'm rich with nought beside,
   And poor without Him, though of all possessed;
Changes may come: I take, or I resign;
Content while I am his, while He is mine.

Whate'er may change, in Him no change is seen,
   A glorious sun, that wanes not nor declines;
Above the clouds and storm He walks serene,
   And sweetly on his people's darkness shines:
All may depart; I fret not, nor repine,
While I my Father's am, while He is mine.

He stays me falling, lifts me up when down,
   Reclaims me wandering, guards from every foe,
Plants on my worthless brow the victor's crown,
   Which, in return, before his feet I throw;
Grieved that I cannot better grace his shrine
Who deigns to own me his, as He is mine.

While here, alas, I know but half his love,
  But half discern Him, and but half adore,
But when I meet Him in the realms above,
  I hope to love Him better, praise Him more ;
And feel, and tell amid the choir divine,
How fully I am his, and He is mine.

J. Quarles and H. F. Lyte.

226   *God is love.*   8s.

LET all men know, that all men move
Under a canopy of love,
As broad as the blue sky above ;

That doubt and trouble, fear and pain,
And anguish, all are shadows vain ;
That death itself shall not remain ;

That weary deserts we may tread,
A dreary labyrinth we may thread,
Through dark ways underground be led.

Yet, if we will our Guide obey,
The dreariest path, the darkest way,
Shall issue out in heavenly day ;

And we on divers shores now cast,
Shall meet, our perilous voyage past,
All in our Father's house at last.

Whate'er befall, 'tis true that love,
Blessing, not cursing, rules above,
And that in it we live and move.

Despite of all that seems at strife
With blessing, all with curses rife,
This faith is blessing, this is life.

Archbishop Trench,

227   *The fulness of Divine love.*   8.8.6.

O LOVE divine, how sweet Thou art;
When shall I find my willing heart
    All taken up by Thee?
I thirst, I faint, I die to prove
The greatness of redeeming love,
    The love of God to me.

Stronger his love than death or hell;
Its riches are unsearchable;
    The first-born sons of light
Desire in vain its depths to see;
They cannot reach the mystery,
    The length, and breadth, and height.

Jesus, Thou know'st the love of God;
O that it now were shed abroad
    In this poor stony heart:
For love I sigh, for love I pine;
This only portion, Lord, be mine,
    Be mine this better part.

For ever would I take my seat
With Mary at the Master's feet;
    Be this my happy choice;
My only care, delight, and bliss,
My joy, my heaven on earth, be this,
    To hear the bridegroom's voice.
                   C. Wesley.

228   *God is love.*   8.7.

GOD is love: his mercy brightens
    All the path in which we rove;
Bliss He wakes, and woe He lightens:
    God is wisdom, God is love.

Chance and change are busy ever;
  Man decays, and ages move;
But his mercy waneth never;
  God is wisdom, God is love.

E'en the hour that darkest seemeth
  Will his changeless goodness prove;
From the gloom his brightness streameth:
  God is wisdom, God is love.

He with earthly cares entwineth
  Hope and comfort from above;
Everywhere his glory shineth;
  God is wisdom, God is love.

Sir J. Bowring.

229   *The love of God.*   8.7.

SOULS of men, why will ye scatter
  Like a crowd of frightened sheep?
Foolish hearts, why will ye wander
  From a love so true and deep?

Was there ever kindest shepherd,
  Half so gentle, half so sweet,
As the Father who would have us
  Come and gather round his feet?

There's a wideness in God's mercy
  Like the wideness of the sea;
There's a kindness in his justice
  Which is more than liberty.

There is no place where earth's sorrows
  Are more felt than up in heaven;
There is no place where earth's failings
  Have such kindly judgment given.

There is grace enough for thousands
    Of new worlds as great as this;
There is room for fresh creations
    In that upper home of bliss.

For the love of God is broader
    Than the measures of man's mind;
And the heart of the Eternal
    Is most wonderfully kind.

If our love were but more simple,
    We should take Him at his word;
And our lives would be all sunshine
    In the sweetness of our Lord.

F. W. Faber.

230   *God is love.*   8.8.8.4.

WE cannot always trace the way
    Where Thou, our gracious Lord, dost move,
But we can always surely say
    That Thou art love.

When fear its gloomy cloud will fling
    O'er earth,—our souls to heaven above,
As to their sanctuary, spring;
    For Thou art love.

When mystery shrouds our darkened path,
    We'll check our dread, our doubts reprove;
In this our soul sweet comfort hath,
    That Thou art love.

Yes, Thou art love; and truth like this
    Can every gloomy thought remove,
And turn all tears, all woes to bliss;
    Our God is love.

Sir J. Bowring.

13

231 *He careth for us.* 8.7.

Yes, for me, for me He careth,
　With a father's tender care ;
Yes, with me, with me He shareth
　Every burden, every fear.

Yes, o'er me, o'er me He watcheth,
　Ceaseless watcheth, night and day ;
Yes, e'en me, e'en me He snatcheth
　From the perils of the way.

Yes, in me abroad He sheddeth
　Joys unearthly, love and light ;
And to cover me He spreadeth
　His paternal wing of might.

Yes, in me, in me He dwelleth ;
　I in Him, and He in me :
And my empty soul He filleth,
　Here and through eternity.

H. Bonar.

232 *God is good.* L.M.

Yes, God is good: in earth and sky,
　From ocean depths and spreading wood,
Ten thousand voices seem to cry,
　God made us all, and God is good.

The sun that keeps his trackless way,
　And downward pours his golden flood,
Night's sparkling hosts, all seem to say
　In accents clear, that God is good.

We hear it in the rushing breeze ;
　The hills that have for ages stood,
The echoing sky and roaring seas,
　All swell the chorus, God is good.

The merry birds prolong the strain,
  Their song with every spring renewed;
And balmy air and falling rain,
  Each softly whisper, God is good.

Yes, God is good, all nature says,
  By God's own hand with speech endued;
And man, in louder notes of praise,
  Should sing for joy that God is good.

For all thy gifts we bless Thee, Lord,
  But chiefly for our heavenly food;
Thy pardoning grace, thy quickening word,
  These prompt our song that God is good.
                    Eliza Follen and J. H. Gurney.

233   *Prayer-answer.*   S.M.

  At first I prayed for Light:—
  Could I but see the way,
How gladly, swiftly would I walk
  To everlasting day.

  And next I prayed for Strength :—
  That I might tread the road
With firm, unfaltering feet, and win
  The heaven's serene abode.

  And then I asked for Faith :—
  Could I but trust my God,
I'd live enfolded in his peace,
  Though foes were all abroad.

  But now I pray for Love:
  Deep love to God and man ;
A living love that will not fail,
  However dark his plan ;—

And Light and Strength and Faith
Are opening everywhere:
God only waited for me till
I prayed the larger prayer. .

Mrs. E. D. Cheney.

234   *Prayer for aid.*   10.10.10.10.6.

WE ask not that our path be always bright,
But for thine aid to walk therein aright;
That Thou, O Lord, through all its devious way,
Wilt give us strength sufficient to our day,
  For this, for this we pray.

Not for the fleeting joys that earth bestows,
Not for exemption from its many woes;
But that, come joy or woe, come good or ill,
With childlike faith we trust thy guidance still,
  And do thy holy will.

Teach us, dear Lord, to find the latent good,
That sorrow yields when rightly understood;
And for the frequent joy that crowns our days,
Help us, with grateful hearts, our hymns to raise
  Of thankfulness and praise.

Thou knowest all our needs, and wilt supply;
No veil of darkness hides us from thine eye;
Nor vainly from the depths on Thee we call;
Thy tender love, that breaks·the tempter's thrall,
  Folds and encircles all.

Through sorrow and through loss, by toil and
  prayer,
Saints won the starry crowns which now they wear,
And by the bitter ministry of pain,
Grievous and harsh, but O not felt in vain,
  Found their eternal gain.

If it be ours, like them, to suffer loss, ·
Give grace, as unto them, to bear our cross,
Till, victors over each besetting sin,
We, too, thy perfect peace shall enter in,
     And crowns of glory win.
               W. H. Burleigh.

235   *Seeking God.*   8s.

THOU hidden love of God, whose height,
  Whose depth unfathomed, no man knows,
I see from far thy beauteous light,
  Inly I sigh for thy repose;
My heart is pained, nor can it be
At rest, till it finds rest in Thee.

Is there a thing beneath the sun
  That strives with Thee my heart to share?
Ah, tear it thence, and reign alone,
  The Lord of every motion there;
Then shall my heart from earth be free,
When it hath found repose in Thee.

O Love, thy sovereign aid impart,
  To save me from low-thoughted care;
Chase this self-will through all my heart,
  Through all its hidden mazes there;
Make me thy loving child, that I
Ceaseless may 'Abba, Father,' cry.

Each moment draw from earth away
  My heart, that lowly waits thy call;
Speak to my inmost soul, and say,
  'I am thy love, thy God, thy all;'
To feel thy power, to hear thy voice,
To know thy truth, be all my choice.
     P. Gerhardt and G. Tersteegen, tr. J. Wesley.

236 *Seeking.* 7s.

THIRSTING for a living spring,
  Seeking for a higher home,
Resting where our souls must cling,
  Trusting, hoping, Lord, we come.

Glorious hopes our spirit fill,
  When we feel that Thou art near :
Father, then our fears are still,
  Then the soul's bright end is clear.

Life's hard conflict we would win,
  Read the meaning of life's frown ;
Change the thorn-bound wreath of sin
  For the spirit's starry crown.

Make us beautiful within
  By thy spirit's holy light :
Guard us when our faith burns dim,
  Father of all love and might.

F. P. Appleton.

237 *Hear Thou from heaven.* 7.5.8.8.

WHEN the weary, seeking rest,
  To thy goodness flee ;
When the heavy-laden cast
  All their load on Thee ;
When the troubled, seeking peace,
  On thy name shall call ;
When the sinner, seeking life,
  At thy feet shall fall :
Hear then, in love, O Lord, the cry,
In heaven thy dwelling-place on high.

When the worldling, sick at heart,
   Lifts his soul above;
When the prodigal looks back
   To his Father's love;
When the proud man, in his pride,
   Stoops to seek thy face;
When the burdened brings his guilt
   To thy throne of grace:
Hear then, in love, O Lord, the cry,
In heaven thy dwelling-place on high.

When the stranger asks a home,
   All his toils to end;
When the hungry craveth food,
   And the poor a friend;
When the sailor on the wave
   Bows the suppliant knee:
When the soldier on the field
   Lifts his heart to Thee:
Hear then, in love, O Lord, the cry,
In heaven thy dwelling-place on high.

When the man of toil and care
   In the city crowd;
When the shepherd on the moor
   Names the name of God;
When the learnèd and the high,
   Tired of earthly fame,
Upon higher joys intent,
   Name the blessèd name:
Hear then, in love, O Lord, the cry,
In heaven thy dwelling-place on high.

When the child, with grave fresh lip,
   Youth or maiden fair;
When the agèd, weak and grey,
   Seek thy face in prayer;

When the widow weeps to Thee,
  Sad and lone and low;
When the orphan brings to Thee
  All his orphan-woe:
Hear then, in love, O Lord, the cry,
In heaven thy dwelling-place on high.

When creation, in her pangs,
  Heaves her heavy groan;
When thy Salem's exiled sons
  Breathe their bitter moan;
When thy waiting, weeping Church,
  Looking for a home,
Sendeth up her silent sigh,
  Come, O Father, come:
Hear then, in love, O Lord, the cry,
In heaven thy dwelling-place on high.

H. Bonar.

238   *Out of self.*   7s.

WHAT Thou wilt, O Father, give;
All is gain that I receive;
Let the lowliest task be mine,
Grateful, so the work be thine.

Let me find the humblest place
In the shadow of thy grace;
Let me find in thine employ
Peace, that dearer is than joy.

If there be some weaker one,
Give me strength to help him on;
If a blinder soul there be,
Let me guide him nearer Thee.

Make my mortal dreams come true
With the work I fain would do ;
Clothe with life the weak intent,
Let me be the thing I meant ;

Out of self to love be led,
And to heaven acclimated,
Until all things sweet and good
Seem my natural habitude.

J. G. Whittier.

239   *Shield thy servants.*   7s.

GRACIOUS Father, hear our prayer,
Leave us not, lest we despair ;
Let thine arm our safeguard be,
Hear the prayer we raise to Thee :
    God of power, and God of might,
    Shield thy servants in the fight.

Soldiers of the cross, we stand,
Armed for battle by thine hand ;
Rock of strength, to Thee we fly ;
Hide us in adversity.
    God of power, and God of might,
    Shield thy servants in the fight.

Lasting are thy mercies, Lord,
Truth eternal is thy word ;
Justice is thy dazzling throne,
Yet Thou reign'st by love alone.
    God of power, and God of might,
    Shield thy servants in the fight.

Let the glorious heavens sing,
Hallelujah to our King;
Earth and seas, repeat the word,
Men and angels praise the Lord.
    O Defender of the right,
    Shield thy servants in the fight.

C. Wesley and S. A. Brooke.

240   *Aspiration.*   8.7.

God eternal, changing never,
    Of our hearts the strength and stay;
We would be thine own for ever,
    Climb, though weak, the heavenly way;
        Ever nearer,
    To thy pure and perfect day.

May we not draw forth new treasure,
    From thy wisdom's boundless store?
Tak'st Thou not, blest Spirit, pleasure,
    On each age thy breath to pour?
        Strong and holy,
    Com'st Thou not, as heretofore?

By each gift of our receiving
    From thy witnesses divine,
By the radiance of achieving
    Which on us from Christ doth shine,
        Hear us, hear us,
    God Almighty, help us on.

Make our own a nobler story,
    Than was ever writ before;
Stay not then, show forth thy glory
    In our aftercomers more.
        Love eternal,
    Fuller grace incessant pour.

T. H. Gill.

241   *Confession.*   11.11.11.5.

FROM the recesses of a lowly spirit
My humble prayer ascends ; O Father, hear it ;
Upsoaring on the wings of fear and meekness,
       Forgive its weakness.

I know, I feel, how mean and how unworthy
The trembling sacrifice I pour before Thee ;
What can I offer in thy presence holy,
       But sin and folly ?

For in thy sight, who every bosom viewest,
Cold are our warmest vows, and vain our truest ;
Thoughts of a hurrying hour—our lips repeat
    them—
       Our hearts forget them.

We see thy hand ; it leads us, it supports us ;
We hear thy voice ; it counsels and it courts us ;
And then we turn away, and still thy kindness
       Pardons our blindness.

O how long-suffering, Lord, but Thou delightest
To win with love the wandering : Thou invitest,
By smiles of mercy, not by frowns or terrors,
       Man from his errors.

Who can resist thy gentle call, appealing
To every generous thought and grateful feeling ?
Thy voice paternal, whispering, watching ever ?
       O let *me* never.

Father and Saviour, plant within my bosom
The seeds of holiness, and bid them blossom
In fragrance, and in beauty bright and vernal,
       And spring eternal.

             Sir J. Bowring.

Treasures.

LET me count my treasures,
  All my soul holds dear,
Given me by dark spirits
  Whom I used to fear.

Through long days of anguish
  And sad nights, did Pain
Forge my shield, Endurance,
  Bright and free from stain.

Doubt, in misty caverns,
  'Mid dark horrors sought,
Till my peerless jewel
  Faith to me she brought.

Sorrow, that I wearied
  Should remain so long,
Wreathed my starry glory,
  The bright crown of Song.

Strife, that racked my spirit,
  Without hope or rest,
Left the blooming flower,
  Patience, on my breast.

Suffering, that I dreaded,
  Ignorant of her charms,
Laid the fair child, Pity,
  Smiling, in my arms.

So I count my treasures,
  Stored in days long past,
And I thank the givers,
  Whom I know at last.

Adelaide A. Procter.

243   *For Divine Strength.*   11.10.

FATHER, in thy mysterious presence kneeling,
  Fain would our souls feel all thy kindling love;
For we are weak, and need some deep revealing
  Of Trust and Strength and Calmness from
    above.

Lord, we have wandered forth through doubt and
  sorrow,
  And Thou hast made each step an onward one;
And we will ever trust each unknown morrow,—
  Thou wilt sustain us till its work is done.

In the heart's depths a peace serene and holy
  Abides; and when pain seems to have its will,
Or we despair, O may that peace rise slowly,
  Stronger than agony, and we be still.

Now, Father, now, in thy dear presence kneeling,
  Our spirits yearn to feel thy kindling love:
Now make us strong, we need thy deep revealing
  Of Trust and Strength and Calmness from
    above.

                         S. Johnson.

244   *The Prayer of Life.*   8 7.

FATHER, hear the prayer we offer:
  Not for ease that prayer shall be;
But for strength, that we may ever
  Live our lives courageously.

Not for ever in green pastures
  Do we ask our way to be;
But the steep and rugged pathway
  May we tread rejoicingly.

Not for ever by still waters
  Would we idly quiet stay;
But would smite the living fountains
  From the rocks along our way.

Be our strength in hours of weakness;
  In our wanderings, be our guide;
Through endeavour, failure, danger,
  Father, be Thou at our side.

Anon.

245   *Strive, Wait, and Pray.*   Irr.

STRIVE; yet I do not promise
  The prize you dream of to-day
Will not fade when you think to grasp it,
  And melt in your hand away;
But another and holier treasure,
  You would now perchance disdain,
Will come when your toil is over,
  And pay you for all your pain.

Wait; yet I do not tell you
  The hour you long for now,
Will not come with its radiance vanished,
  And a shadow upon its brow;
Yet far through the misty future,
  With a crown of starry light,
An hour of joy you know not
  Is winging her silent flight.

Pray; though the gift you ask for
  May never comfort your fears,
May never repay your pleading,
  Yet pray, and with hopeful tears;

An answer, not that you long for,
But diviner, will come one day,
Your eyes are too dim to see it,
Yet strive, and wait, and pray.

Adelaide A. Procter.

246   *The Unity of the Spirit.*   10s.

ETERNAL Ruler of the ceaseless round
Of circling planets singing on their way,
Guide of the nations from the night profound
Into the glory of the perfect day,
Rule in our hearts that we may ever be
Guided and strengthened and upheld by Thee.

We are of Thee, the children of thy love,
The brothers of thy well-belovèd Son;
Descend, O Holy Spirit, like a dove,
Into our hearts that we may be as one,—
As one with Thee, to whom we ever tend;
As one with Him, our Brother and our Friend.

We would be one in hatred of all wrong,
One in our love of all things sweet and fair,
One with the joy that breaketh into song,
One with the grief that trembles into prayer,
One in the power that makes thy children free
To follow truth, and thus to follow Thee.

O clothe us with thy heavenly armour, Lord,
Thy trusty shield, thy sword of love divine.
Our inspiration be thy constant word;
We ask no victories that are not thine.
Give or withhold, let pain or pleasure be,
Enough to know that we are serving Thee.

J. W. Chadwick.

247　*I will not let Thee go except Thou bless me.*　　8s.

COME, O Thou Traveller unknown,
　　Whom still I hold, but cannot see ;
My company before is gone,
　　And I am left alone with Thee ;
With Thee all night I mean to stay,
And wrestle till the break of day.

I need not tell Thee who I am,
　　My misery and sin declare ;
Thyself hast called me by my name,
　　Look on thy hands and read it there ;
But who, I ask Thee, who art Thou ?　　•
Tell me thy name, and tell me now.

Wilt thou not yet to me reveal
　　Thy new, unutterable name ?
Tell me, I still beseech Thee, tell ;
　　To know it now resolved I am ;
Wrestling, I will not let Thee go,
Till I thy name, thy nature know.

Yield to me now, for I am weak,
　　But confident in self-despair ;
Speak to my heart, in blessings speak,
　　Be conquered by my instant prayer ;
Speak, or Thou never hence shalt move,
And tell me if.thy name is Love.

My prayer hath power with God ; the grace
　　Unspeakable I now receive ;
Through faith I see Thee face to face,
　　I see Thee face to face, and live ;
In vain I have not wept and strove ;
Thy nature and thy name is Love.

'Tis Love, 'tis Love, Thou lovest me;
   I hear thy whisper in my heart;
The morning breaks, the shadows flee,
   Pure, universal Love Thou art;
To me, to all, thy mercies move;
Thy nature and thy name is Love.

                           C. Wesley.

248   *Faith and love.*   L.M.

No human eyes thy face may see;
   No human thought thy form may know;
But all creation dwells in Thee,
   And thy great life through all doth flow;

And yet, O strange and wondrous thought!
   Thou art a God who hearest prayer,
And every heart with sorrow fraught
   To seek thy present aid may dare.

And though most weak our efforts seem
   Into one creed these thoughts to bind,
And vain the intellectual dream,
   To see and know the Eternal Mind;

Yet Thou wilt turn them not aside,
   Who cannot solve thy life divine,
But would give up all reason's pride
   To know their hearts approved by thine.

So though we faint on life's dark hill,
   And thought grow weak and knowledge flee
Yet faith shall teach us courage still,
   And love shall guide us on to Thee.

                        T. W. Higginson.

249 *Step by step.* 8.7.

NOT so fearful, doubting pilgrim,
  Though the darkness round thee close,
Though the future glooms foreboding,
  Threatening all thy soul's repose.

'Tis not in this life vouchsafed us
  All our way to see before ;
Clears the path as we go forward,
  Step by step, and nothing more.

Noble ones have gone before thee ;
  Fear not, while thine eyes may greet,
Leading on, their faithful footprints ;
  In them strive to set thy feet.

Wait not for the noonday brightness :
  Haste thee through the morning gray ;
Lo, the eastern glow before thee,
  Broadening, brightening ray by ray.

Thus, the just one's day beginneth :
  First, the streak of dawn is given ;
Earth sees but the early morning,
  Cloudless noon is found in heaven.

M. J. Savage.

250 *The dearer trust.* C.M.

MY God, I rather look to Thee
  Than to my fancy fond,
And wait, till Thou reveal to me
  That fair and far Beyond.

I seek not of thy Eden-land
  The forms and hues to know,
What trees in mystic order stand,
  What strange, sweet waters flow ;

What duties fill the heavenly day, .
Or converse glad and kind ;
Or how along each shining way
The bright processions wind.

O sweeter far to trust in Thee
While all is yet unknown,
And through the death-dark cheerily
To walk with Thee alone.

In Thee, my powers, my treasures live ;
To Thee my life must tend ;
Giving Thyself, Thou all dost give,
O soul-sufficing Friend.

Eliza Scudder.

251　　　*Remember me.*　　　C. M.

O THOU from whom all goodness flows,
I lift my heart to Thee ;
In all my sorrows, conflicts, woes,
Good Lord, remember me !

When on my aching, burdened heart,
My sins lie heavily,
Thy pardon grant, thy peace impart,
Good Lord, remember me !

When trials sore obstruct my way,
And ills I cannot flee,
Then let my strength be as my day ;
Good Lord, remember me !

If worn with pain, disease, and grief,
This feeble frame should be,
Grant patience, rest, and kind relief
Good Lord, remember me !

And O when in the hour of death
I bow to thy decree,
To Thee I give my parting breath ;
Good Lord, remember me !

T. Haweis.

252 *The inner calm.* C.M.

CALM me, my God, and keep me calm,
While these hot breezes blow ;
Be like the night-dew's cooling balm
Upon earth's fevered brow.

Yes, keep me calm, though loud and rude
The sounds my ear that greet,
Calm in the closet's solitude,
Calm in the bustling street ;

Calm in my hour of buoyant health,
Calm in my hour of pain ;
Calm in my poverty or wealth,
Calm in my loss or gain ;

Calm in the sufferance of wrong,
Like Him who bore my shame ;
Calm 'mid the threatening, taunting throng
Who hate thy holy name ;

Calm as the ray of sun or star,
Which storms assail in vain ;
Moving unruffled through earth's war,
The eternal calm to gain.

H. Bonar.

253 *The pure and peaceful mind.* 8.6.8.8.6.

DEAR Lord and Father of mankind,
　Forgive our feverish ways ;
Reclothe us in our rightful mind ;
In purer lives thy service find,
　In deeper reverence, praise.

O Sabbath rest by Galilee !
　O calm of hills above !
Where Jesus knelt to share with Thee
The silence of eternity,
　Interpreted by love !

With that deep hush subduing all
　Our words and works that drown
The tender whisper of thy call,
As noiseless let thy blessing fall
　As fell thy manna down.

Drop thy still dews of quietness,
　Till all our strivings cease :
Take from our souls the strain and stress ;
And let our ordered lives confess
　The beauty of thy peace.

Breathe through the pulses of desire
　Thy coolness and thy balm ;
Let sense be dumb—its heats expire ;
Speak through the earthquake, wind, and fire,
　O still small voice of calm.

　　　　　　　　　　J. G. Whittier.

254　　　*Peace.*　　10.4.10.4.10.10.

IMMORTAL Love, within whose righteous will
　Is always peace ;
O pity me, storm-tossed on waves of ill ;
　Let passion cease ;

Come down in power within my heart to reign,
For I am weak, and struggle has been vain.

The days are gone, when far and wide my will
 Drove me astray;
And now I fain would climb the arduous hill,
 That narrow way
Which leads through mist and rocks to thine abode;
Toiling for man, and Thee, Almighty God.

Whate'er of pain thy loving hand allot
 I gladly bear;
Only, O Lord, let peace be not forgot,
 Nor yet thy care,
Freedom from storms, and wild desires within,
Peace from the fierce oppression of my sin.

So may I, far away, when evening falls
 On life and love,
Arrive at last the holy, happy halls,
 With Thee above;
Wounded yet healed, sin-laden yet forgiven,
And sure that goodness is my only heaven.

S. A. Brooke.

255   *The repose of faith.*   7s.

HAPPY soul, that free from harms,
Rests within his Shepherd's arms,
Who his quiet shall molest?
Who shall violate his rest?

Like a long-forgotten child,
I have wandered on the wild;
Lost myself in vain desires,
Torn with thorns, and burned with fires.

Lonely with the self I hate,
By my will made desolate,
Sick of sin, out-wearied, cold,
I would rest within thy fold.

Father, seek thy wandering sheep ;
Bring me back, and lead, and keep ;
Take on Thee my every care ;
Bear me, on thy bosom bear.

Let me know my Shepherd's voice ;
More and more in Thee rejoice ;
More and more of Thee receive,
Ever in thy Spirit live ;—

Live, till all the love I know,
I can find in Thee below ;
Till I hear thy gracious voice,
'Come up higher, and rejoice.'

Then from sin and death set free,
Shepherded, O Lord, by Thee,
I shall join the flock above,
Where the fold is perfect Love.

C. Wesley and S. A. Brooke.

256 *Peace.* L.M.

In quiet hours the tranquil soul
Reflects the beauty of the sky ;
No passions rise or billows roll,
And only God and heaven are nigh.

The tides of being ebb and flow,
Creating peace without alloy ;
A sacred happiness we know,
Too high for mirth, too deep for joy.

Like birds that slumber on the sea,
Unconscious where the current runs,
We rest on God's infinity
Of bliss, that circles stars and suns.

His perfect peace has swept from sight
The narrow bounds of time and space,
And looking up with still delight
We catch the glory of his face.

Augusta Larned.

257 *The calm of the soul.* 11.10.

WHEN winds are raging o'er the upper ocean,
And billows wild contend with angry roar,
'Tis said, far down beneath the wild commotion,
That peaceful stillness reigneth evermore. .

Far, far beneath, the noise of tempests dieth,
And silver waves chime ever peacefully ;
And no rude storm, how fierce soe'er it flieth,
Disturbs the sabbath of that deeper sea.

So to the heart that knows Thee, Love Eternal,
There is a temple, sacred evermore ;
And all the babble of life's angry voices
Dies in hushed stillness at its peaceful door.

Far, far away, the roar of passion dieth,
And loving thoughts rise calm and peacefully ;
And no rude storm, how fierce soe'er it flieth,
Disturbs the soul that dwells, O Lord, in Thee.

O Rest of rests, O Peace serene, eternal,
Thou ever livest, and Thou changest not ;
And in the secret of thy presence dwelleth
Fulness of joy, both now and evermore.

Harriet B. Stowe.

258 *The Peace of God.* C.M.

WE bless Thee for thy peace, O God,
  Deep as the unfathomed sea,
Which falls like sunshine on the road
  Of those who trust in Thee.

·We ask not, Father, for repose
  Which comes from outward rest,
If we may have through all life's woes
  Thy peace within our breast ;

That peace which suffers and is strong,
  Trusts where it cannot see,
Deems not the trial-way too long,
  But leaves the end with Thee ;

That peace which flows serene and deep,
  A river in the soul,
Whose banks a living verdure keep,
  God's sunshine o'er the whole.

O Father, give our hearts this peace,
  Whate'er may outward be,
Till all life's discipline shall cease,
  And we go home to Thee.

Anon.

259 *Rest.* C.M.

O THAT Thou would'st the heavens rend,
  And comfort me with light ;
In love and holiness descend,
  And scatter all my night.

Consume my sin, my death dispel,
  Bid feebleness depart,
Be stronger than my selfish will,
  And greater than my heart.

Then, when my sin has found defeat,
  And Thou hast all my soul,
Lead me to pastures soft, where sweet
  The healing waters roll,

That I may rest awhile, before
  I take my work again ;
And hear, from forth the eternal shore,
  The requiem of pain.

S. A. Brooke.

260 *The broken shield.* 10s.

O SEND me not away ; for I would drink,
  E'en I, the weakest, at the fount of life ;
Chide not my steps, that venture near the brink,
  Weary and fainting from the deadly strife.

Went I not forth undaunted and alone,
  Strong in the majesty of human might ?
Lo, I return, all wounded and forlorn,
  My dream of glory lost in shades of night.

Was I not girded for the battle-field ?
  Bore I not helm of pride and glittering sword?
Behold the fragments of my broken shield,
  And give to me thy heavenly armour, Lord.

Anon.

261 *Service.* C.M.

ETERNAL Life, whose love divine
  Enfolds us each and all,
We know no other truth than thine,
  We heed no other call.

O may we serve in thought and deed
    Thy kingdom yet to be,
Till Truth and Righteousness and Love
    Shall lead all souls to Thee.

Emma E. Marean.

262   *In thy light shall we see light.*   S.M.

TEACH me, my God and King,
    In all things Thee to see ;
And what I do in anything,
    To do it as for Thee.

A man that looks on glass,
    On it may stay his eye ;
Or if he pleaseth, through it pass,
    And then the heaven espy.

All may of Thee partake :
    Nothing can be so mean,
Which with this tincture, *for thy sake,*
    Will not grow bright and clean.

A servant with this clause
    Makes drudgery divine ;
Who sweeps a room, as for thy laws,
    Makes that and the action fine.

This is the famous stone
    That turneth all to gold :
For that which God doth touch and own
    Cannot for less be told.

G. Herbert.

263 *In thy light shall we see light.* L.M.

O GRANT us light, that we may know
    The wisdom Thou alone canst give;
That truth may guide where'er we go,
    And virtue bless where'er we live.

O grant us light, that we may see
    Where error lurks in human lore,
And turn our doubting minds to Thee,
    And love thy simple word the more.

O grant us light, that we may learn
    How dead is life from Thee apart;
How sure is joy for all who turn
    To Thee an undivided heart.

O grant us life, in grief and pain,
    To lift our burdened hearts above,
And count the very cross a gain,
    And bless our Father's hidden love.

O grant us light, when soon or late
    All earthly scenes shall pass away,
In Thee to find the open gate
    To deathless home and endless day.

                           L. Tuttiett.

264 *Lead Thou me on.* 10.4.10.4.10.10.4.

LEAD, kindly Light, amid the encircling gloom
    Lead Thou me on:
The night is dark, and I am far from home,
    Lead Thou me on.
Keep Thou my feet; I do not ask to see
The distant scene; one step enough for me.

I was not ever thus, nor prayed that Thou
    Shouldst lead me on ;
I loved to choose and see my path ; but now
    Lead Thou me on.
I loved the garish day, and, spite of fears,
Pride ruled my will : remember not past years.

So long thy power hath blest me, sure it still
    Will lead me on,
O'er moor and fen, o'er crag and torrent, till
    The night is gone,
And with the morn those angel faces smile,
Which I have loved long since, and lost awhile.

Cardinal Newman.

265   *All for God.*   7s.

TAKE my life, and let it be
Consecrated, Lord, to Thee ;
Take my moments and my days,
Let them flow in ceaseless praise.

Take my hands, and let them move
At the impulse of thy love ;
Take my feet, and let them be
Swift and beautiful for Thee.

Take my voice, and let me sing
Always, only for my King ;
Take my lips, and let them be
Filled with messages from Thee.

Take my silver and my gold,
Not a mite would I withhold ;
Take my intellect, and use
Every power as Thou shalt choose.

Take my will, and make it thine;
It shall be no longer mine:
Take my heart, it is thine own;
It shall be thy royal throne.

Take my love; my Lord, I pour
At thy feet, its treasure-store;
Take myself, and I will be
Ever, only, all for Thee.

Frances R. Havergal.

266 *O send out thy Light and thy Truth.* S. M.

O EVERLASTING Light,
Giver of dawn and day,
Dispeller of the ancient night
In which creation lay!

O everlasting Health,
Flow through life's inmost springs;
The heart's best bliss, the soul's best wealth,
What life thy presence brings.

O everlasting Truth,
The soul of all that's true,
Sure guide alike of age and youth,
Lead me and teach me too.

O everlasting Might,
My broken life repair;
Nerve thou my will, and clear my sight,
Give strength to do and bear.

O everlasting Love,
Wellspring of grace and peace;
Pour down thy fulness from above,
Bid doubt and trouble cease.

H. Bonar.

267   *The Reformers.*   C.M.

O PURE Reformers, not in vain
   Your trust in human kind;
The good which bloodshed could not gain,
   Your peaceful zeal shall find.

The truths ye urge are borne abroad
   By every wind and tide;
The voice of nature and of God
   Speaks out upon your side.

The weapons which your hands have found
   Are those which heaven hath wrought,
Light, Truth, and Love; your battle-ground,
   The free, broad field of Thought.

O may no selfish purpose break
   The beauty of your plan,
No lie from throne or altar shake
   Your steady faith in man.

Press on, and, if we may not share
   The glory of your fight,
We'll ask at least, in earnest prayer,
   God's blessing on the Right.
              J. G. Whittier.

268   *The Right must win.*   C.M.

O IT is hard to work for God,
   To rise and take his part
Upon this battle-field of earth,
   And not sometimes lose heart.

He hides Himself so wondrously,
   As though there were no God;
He is least seen when all the powers
   Of ill are most abroad.

Workmen of God, O lose not heart,
    But learn what God is like;
And in the darkest battle-field
    Thou shalt know where to strike.

Thrice blest is he to whom is given
    The instinct that can tell
That God is on the field when He
    Is most invisible.

Blest too is he who can divine
    Where real right doth lie,
And dares to take the side that seems
    Wrong to man's blindfold eye.

God's glory is a wondrous thing,
    Most strange in all its ways;
And, of all things on earth, least like
    What men agree to praise.

Muse on his justice, downcast soul,
    Muse, and take better heart;
Back with thine angel to the field,
    And bravely do thy part.

For right is right, since God is God;
    And right the day must win;
To doubt would be disloyalty,
    To falter would be sin.

F. W. Faber.

269   *Watchman, what of the night ?*   L.M.

OUT of the dark the circling sphere
    Is rounding onward to the light;
We see not yet the full day here,
    But we do see the paling night.

And Hope, that lights her fadeless fires,
  And Faith, that shines, a heavenly will,
And Love, that courage re-inspires,—
  These stars have been above us still.

O sentinels, whose tread we heard
  Through long hours when we could not see,
Pause now; exchange with cheer the word,
  The unchanging watchword, Liberty.

Look backward, how much has been won;
  Look round, how much is yet to win;
The watches of the night are done;
  The watches of the day begin.

O Thou, whose mighty patience holds
  The night and day alike in view,
Thy will our dearest hope enfolds:
  O keep us steadfast, patient, true.
                                    S. Longfellow.

270   *Even me.*   8.7.8.7.3.

LORD, I hear of showers of blessing
  Thou art scattering full and free,
Showers, the thirsty land refreshing;
  Let some drops now fall on me,
                    Even me.

Pass me not, O God, my Father,
  Sinful though my heart may be;
Thou mightst leave me, but the rather
  Let thy mercy light on me,
                    Even me.

Pass me not, O gracious Father,
  Let me live and cling to Thee;
I am longing for thy favour;
  Whilst thou'rt calling, O call me,
                    Even me.

15

Have I long in sin been sleeping?
　Long been slighting, grieving Thee?
Has the world my heart been keeping?
　O forgive and rescue me,
　　　　　　Even me.

Love of God, so pure and changeless,
　Love of God, so rich and free,
Love of God, so strong and boundless,
　Magnify thy love in me,
　　　　　　Even me.

Elizabeth Codner.

271　　　　*Our Creed.*　　　　8.7.

WE believe in Human Kindness
　Large amid the sons of men,
Nobler far in willing blindness
　Than in censure's keenest ken.
We believe in Self-Denial,
　And its secret throb of joy ;
In the Love that lives through trial,
　Dying not, though death destroy.

We believe in dreams of Duty,
　Warning us to self-control,
Foregleams of the glorious beauty
　That shall yet transform the soul :
In the godlike wreck of nature
　Sin doth in the sinner leave,
That he may regain the stature
　He hath lost,—we do believe.

We believe in Love renewing
　All that sin hath swept away,
Leaven-like its work pursuing
　Night by night and day by day ;

In the power of its remoulding,
  In the grace of its reprieve,
In the glory of beholding
  Its perfection,—we believe.

We believe in Love Eternal,
  Fixed in God's unchanging will,
That beneath the deep infernal,
  Hath a depth that's deeper still;
In its patience, its endurance
  To forbear and to retrieve,
In the large and full assurance
  Of its triumph,—we believe.

From ' Good Words.'

272   *Coming of God's Kingdom.*   8.7.

How shall come thy kingdom holy,
  In which all the earth is blest,
That shall lift on high the lowly,
  And to weary souls give rest?
Not with trumpet call of legions ·
  Bursting through the upper sky,
Waking earth through all its regions
  With their heaven-descending cry:

Not with dash or sudden sally,
  Swooping down with rushing wing;
But as, creeping up a valley,
  Come the grasses in the spring:
First one blade and then another,
  Still advancing are they seen,
Rank on rank, each by its brother,
  Till each inch of ground is green.

Through the weary days of sowing,
  Burning sun, and drenching shower,
Day by day, so slowly growing,
  Comes the waited harvest hour:

So the kingdom cometh ever,
　Though it seem so far away;
Each bright thought and true endeavour
　Hastens on the blessed day.
M. J. Savage.

273　　　　　　• *Thy kingdom come.*　　　　　7s.

FATHER, let thy kingdom come,
　Let it come with living power;
Speak at length the final word,
　Usher in the triumph hour.

As it came in days of old,
　In the deepest hearts of men,
When thy martyrs died for Thee,
　Let it come, O God, again.

Tyrant thrones and idol shrines,
　Let them from their place be hurled;
Enter on thy better reign,
　Wear the crown of this poor world.

O what long, sad years have gone
　Since thy Church was taught this prayer;
O what eyes have watched and wept
　For the dawning everywhere.

Break, triumphant day of God,
　Break at last, our hearts to cheer;
Throbbing souls and holy songs
　Wait to hail thy dawning here.

Empires, temples, sceptres, thrones,
　May they all for God be won;
And, in every human heart,
　Father, let thy kingdom come.
J. P. Hopps.

274   *Home Missions.*   L.M.

Look from thy sphere of endless day,
    O God of mercy and of might;
In pity look on those who stray
    Benighted, in this land of light.

In peopled vale, in lonely glen,
    In crowded mart, by stream or sea,
How many of the sons of men
    Hear not the message sent from Thee.

Send forth thy heralds, Lord, to call
    The thoughtless young, the hardened old,
A scattered homeless flock, till all
    Be gathered to thy peaceful fold.

Send them thy mighty word to speak,
    Till faith shall dawn, and doubt depart,
To awe the bold, to stay the weak,
    And bind and heal the broken heart.

Then all these wastes, a dreary scene,
    That make us sadden as we gaze,
Shall grow, with living waters, green,
    And lift to heaven the voice of praise.
                    W. C. Bryant.

275   *The Church's Work.*   S.M.

Thou, whose glad summer yields
    Fit increase of the spring,
In faith we sow these living fields,
    Bless Thou the harvesting.

Thy Church must lead aright
    Life's work, left all undone,
Till founded fast in love and light,
    Earth home to heaven be won.

Grant, then, thy servants, Lord,
   Fresh strength from hour to hour ;
Through speech and deed the living word
   Find utterance with power,

To keep the child's faith bright,
   To strengthen manhood's truth,
And set the age-dimmed eye alight
   With heaven's eternal youth ;

That in the time's stern strife,
   With saints we speed reform,
Unresting in the calm of life,
   Unshrinking in the storm.

S. Johnson.

276   *He knows.*   8.8.8.2.

HE knows the bitter, weary way,
The endless striving day by day,
The souls that weep, the souls that pray
         He knows !

He knows how hard the fight hath been,
The clouds that came our lives between,
The wounds the world hath never seen
         He knows !

He knows when faint and worn we sink,
How deep the pain, how near the brink
Of dark despair we pause and shrink ;
         He knows !

He knows ! O thought so full of bliss !
For though on earth our joy we miss,
We still can bear it, feeling this,
         He knows !

He knows ! O heart, take up thy cross
And know earth's treasures are but dross,
And he will prove as gain our loss ;
    He knows !
Marian L. Morris.

277   *Thou knowest.*   11.10.11.10.10.10.

THOU knowest, Lord, the weariness and sorrow
  Of each sad heart that comes to Thee for rest ;
Cares of to-day, and burdens for to-morrow,
  Blessings implored, and sins to be confessed ;
  We come before Thee at thy gracious word,
  And lay them at thy feet : Thou knowest, Lord.

Thou knowest all the past : how long and blindly
  On the dark mountains the lost wanderer strayed ;
How the good Shepherd followed, and how kindly
  He bore it home, upon his shoulders laid ;
  And healed the bleeding wounds and soothed
    the pāin,
  And brought back life, and hope, and strength
    again.

Thou knowest all the present ; each temptation,
  Each toilsome duty, each foreboding fear ;
All to each one assigned of tribulation,
  Or to belovèd ones, than self more dear ;
  All pensive memories, as we journey on,
  Longings for vanished smiles and voices gone.

Thou knowest all the future ; gleams of gladness
  By stormy clouds too quickly overcast ;
Hours of sweet fellowship and parting sadness, .
  And the dark river to be crossed at last ;
  O what could hope and confidence afford
  To tread that path ; but this, Thou knowest, Lord.
Jane Borthwick.

278 *Weary.* 8.8.8.6.

TO-DAY, beneath thy chastening eye,
I crave alone for peace and rest;
Submissive in thy hand to lie,
And feel that it is best.

A marvel seems the Universe;
A miracle our life and death;
A mystery which I cannot pierce,
Around, above, beneath.

And now my spirit sighs for home,
And longs for light whereby to see,
And, like a weary child, would come,
O Father, unto Thee.

Though oft, like letters traced on sand,
My weak resolves have passed away,
In mercy lend thy helping hand
Unto my prayer to-day.

J. G. Whittier.

279 *Choose Thou my path.* 6s.

THY way, not mine, O Lord,
However dark it be:
Lead me by thine own hand,
Choose out the path for me.

Smooth let it be or rough,
It will be still the best;
Winding or straight, it leads
Right onward to thy rest.

I dare not choose my lot,
I would not, if I might;
Choose Thou for me, my God,
So shall I walk aright.

My cup of life and love,
  With joy or sorrow fill :
As best to Thee may seem,
  Choose Thou my good and ill.

Choose Thou for me my friends,
  My sickness or my health ;
Choose Thou my cares for me,
  My poverty or wealth.

Not mine, not mine the choice
  In things or great or small ;
Be Thou my Guide, my Strength,
  My Wisdom, and my All.

                  H. Bonar.

280   *The might of faith.*   11.10.

WE will not weep ; for God is standing by us,
  And tears will blind us to the blessèd sight :
We will not doubt : if darkness still doth try us,
  Our souls have promise of serenest light.

We will not faint ; if heavy burdens bind us,
  They press no harder than our souls can bear,
The thorniest way is lying still behind us,
  We shall be braver for the past despair.

O not in doubt shall be our journey's ending,
  Sin with its fears shall leave us at the last,
All its best hopes in glad fulfilment blending,
  Life shall be with us when the Death is past.

Help us, O Father, when the world is pressing
  On our frail hearts, that faint without their
    friend ;
Help us, O Father, let thy constant blessing
  Strengthen our weakness, till the joyful end.

                W. H. Hurlbut.

281   *The morning cometh.*   C.M.

WE wait in faith, in prayer we wait,
   Until the happy hour
When God shall ope the morning gate,
   By his almighty power.

We wait in faith, and turn our face
   To where the day-light springs,
Till He shall come earth's gloom to chase,
   With healing on his wings.

And even now amid the gray,
   The east is brightening fast,
And kindling to that perfect day
   Which never shall be past.

We wait in faith, we wait in prayer,
   Till that blest day shall shine,
When earth shall fruits of Eden bear,
   And all, O God, be thine.

O guide us till our night is done,
   Until, from shore to shore,
Thou, Lord, our everlasting Sun,
   Art shining evermore.
        Imitated from J. M. Neale, by S. Longfellow.

282   *The enduring gift.*   C.M.

WE read upon the lettered page
   Words so divinely bright
That evermore, from age to age,
   They burn with living light.

They tell the deathless spirit's power,
   So strong, so grandly free,
O'erlooking from its peaceful tower
   The restless, stormy sea.

O happy soul, to win the fight,
   For ever then to rest
Upon such calm and lofty height,
   Serene and self-possessed !

So weary ones in vales below
   With longing hearts complain,
And think their lives have all of woe
   And others all of gain.

But know those heights have valleys deep
   That brave heart sometimes fears ;
The joyful have their times to weep ;
   Long vigils mark the years.

Though loyal souls, through suffering meek,
   The mount of vision gain,
Whence thrilling words their raptures speak,
   No soul can there remain.

'Tis earnest struggle all the way,
   Yet seek to know God's will,
Though joy and rapture may not stay,
   Deep peace abideth still.

Eliza M. Hickok.

283   *Led.*   8.6.

SWEET is the solace of thy love,
   My heavenly Friend, to me,
While through the hidden way of faith
   I journey home with Thee,
Learning by quiet thankfulness
   As a dear child to be.

Though from the shadow of thy peace
　My feet would often stray,
Thy mercy follows all my steps,
　And will not turn away;
Yea, Thou wilt comfort me at last,
　As none beneath Thee may.

Oft, in a dark and lonely place,
　I hush my hastened breath,
To hear the comfortable words
　Thy loving Spirit saith;
And feel my safety in thy hand
　From every kind of death.

O there is nothing in the world
　To weigh against thy will;
E'en the dark times I dread the most
　Thy covenant fulfil;
And when the pleasant morning dawns,
　I find Thee with me still.

Then in the secret of my soul,
　Though hosts my peace invade,
Through many a waste and weary land
　My lonely way be made,
Thou, even Thou, wilt comfort me;
　I need not be afraid.

Still in the solitary place
　I would awhile abide,
Till with the solace of thy love
　My heart be satisfied,
And all my hopes of happiness
　Stay calmly at thy side.

Anna L. Waring.

284 *Trust.* 11.10.11.6.

STILL will we trust, though earth seem dark and
 dreary
 And the heart faint beneath his chastening rod ;
Though rough and steep our pathway, worn and
 weary,
  Still will we trust in God.

Our eyes see dimly till by faith anointed,
 And our blind choosing brings us grief and
 pain,
Through Him alone, who hath our way appointed,
  We find our peace again.

Choose for us, God, nor let our weak preferring
 Cheat us of good Thou hast for us designed ;
Choose for us, God ; thy wisdom is unerring,
  And we are fools and blind.

So from the sky the night shall furl her shadows,
 And day pour gladness through her golden
 gates ;
Our rough path lead to flower-enamelled meadows,
  Where joy our coming waits.

Let us press on, in patient self-denial,
 Accept the hardship, shrink not from the loss :
Our portion lies beyond the hour of trial,
  Our crown beyond the cross.

W. H. Burleigh.

285 *Through Peace to Light.* 10.4.

I DO not ask, O Lord, that life may be
  A pleasant road ;
I do not ask that Thou wouldst take from me
  Aught of its load :

I do not ask that flowers should always spring
    Beneath my feet :
I know too well the poison and the sting
    Of things too sweet.

For one thing only, Lord, dear Lord, I plead :
    Lead me aright,
Though strength should falter, and though heart
    should bleed,
    Through Peace to Light.

I do not ask, O Lord, that Thou shouldst shed
    Full radiance here ;
Give but a ray of peace, that I may tread
    Without a fear.

I do not ask my cross to understand,
    My way to see ;
Better in darkness just to feel thy hand,
    And follow Thee.

Joy is like restless day ; but peace divine
    Like quiet night.
Lead me, O Lord, till perfect day shall shine,
    Through Peace to Light.

Adelaide A. Procter.

286   *Made perfect through suffering.*   L.M.

I BLESS Thee, Lord, for sorrows sent
    To break my dream of human power ;
For now my shallow cistern's spent,
    I find thy founts, and thirst no more.

I take thy hand, and fears grow still ;
    Behold thy face, and doubts remove ;
Who would not yield his wavering will
    To perfect Truth and boundless Love ?

That Love this restless soul doth teach
   The strength of thine eternal calm;
And tune its sad and broken speech
   To join, on earth, the angels' psalm.

O be it patient in thy hands,
   And drawn, through each mysterious hour,
To service of thy pure commands,
   The narrow way to Love and Power.

S. Johnson.

287   *Trust in Him at all times.*   8.6.

   Go not far from me, O my God,
      Whom all my times obey;
   Take from me any thing Thou wilt,
      But go not Thou away;
   And let the storm that does thy work
      Deal with me as it may.

   On thy compassion I repose
      In weakness and distress:
   I will not ask for greater ease,
      Lest I should love Thee less.
   O 'tis a blessed thing for me
      To need thy tenderness.

   When I am feeble as a child,
      And flesh and heart give way,
   Then on thy everlasting strength
      With passive trust I stay,
   And the rough wind becomes a song,
      The darkness shines like day.

Deep unto deep may call, but I
  With peaceful heart can say,
Thy loving-kindness hath a charge
  No waves can take away :
Then let the storm that speeds me home
  Deal with me as it may.
Anna L. Waring.

288   *The eternal goodness.*   C.M.

I LONG for household voices gone,
  For vanished smiles I long ;
But God hath led my dear ones on,
  And He can do no wrong.

I know not what the future hath
  Of marvel or surprise,
Assured alone that life and death
  His mercy underlies.

And if my heart and flesh are weak
  To bear an untried pain,
The bruisèd reed He will not break
  But strengthen and sustain.

And so beside the Silent Sea
  I wait the muffled oar ;
No harm from Him can come to me
  On ocean or on shore.

I know not where his islands lift
  Their fronded palms in air ;
I only know I cannot drift
  Beyond his love and care.

O Thou, my God, by whom are seen
  Thy creatures as they be,
Forgive me, if too close I lean
  My human heart on Thee.
J. G. Whittier.

289   *The eternal goodness.*   C.M.

FIRM, in the maddening maze of things,
    And tossed by storm and flood,
To one fixed state my spirit clings,—
    I know that God is good.

Not mine to look where cherubim
    And seraphs may not see,
But nothing can be good in Him
    Which evil is in me.

The wrong that pains my soul below
    I dare not throne above ;
·I know not of his hate, I know
    His goodness and his love.

And Thou, O Lord, by whom are seen
    Thy creatures as they be,
Forgive me, if too close I lean
    My human heart on Thee.
                        J. G. Whittier.

290   *The Soldiers of the Cross.*   L.M.

THOU Lord of Hosts, whose guiding hand
    Hast brought us here before thy face ;
Our spirits wait for thy command,
    Our silent hearts implore thy peace.

Our spirits lay their noblest powers,
    As offerings, on thy holy shrine ;
Thine was the strength that nourished ours ;
    The soldiers of the Cross are thine.

While watching on our arms at night,
    We saw thine angels round us move ;
We heard thy call, we felt thy light,
    And followed, trusting to thy love.

And now with hymn and prayer we stand,
  To give our strength to Thee, great God;
We would redeem thy holy land,
  That land which sin so long has trod.

Send us where'er Thou wilt, O Lord,
  Through rugged toil and wearying fight;
Thy conquering love shall be our sword,
  And faith in Thee our truest might.

Send down thy constant aid, we pray;
  Be thy pure angels with us still;
Thy Truth, be that our firmest stay;
  Our only rest, to do thy will.

O. B. Frothingham.

291   *Father, to Thee.*   11.10.

FATHER, to Thee we look in all our sorrow,
  Thou art the fountain whence our healing flows;
Dark though the night, joy cometh with the
    morrow;
  Safely they rest who on thy love repose.

When fond hopes fail, and skies are dark before us,
  When the vain cares that vex our life increase,—
Comes with its calm the thought that Thou art o'er
    us,
  And we grow quiet, folded in thy peace.

Nought shall affright us on thy goodness leaning,
  Low in the heart faith singeth still her song;
Chastened by pain we learn life's deeper meaning,
  And in our weakness Thou dost make us strong.

Patient, O heart, though heavy be thy sorrows,
  Be not cast down, disquieted in vain ;
Yet shalt thou praise Him when these darkened
    furrows,
  Where now he ploweth, wave with golden grain.

F. L. Hosmer.

292　　　　*My times are in thy hands.*　　　　8.6.

FATHER, I know that all my life
  Is portioned out for me :
The changes that will surely come
  I do not fear to see.
I ask Thee for a present mind,
  Intent on pleasing Thee.

I ask Thee for a thoughtful love,
  Through constant watching wise,
To meet the glad with joyful smiles,
  And wipe the weeping eyes ;
A heart at leisure from itself,
  To soothe and sympathize.

I would not have the restless will
  That hurries to and fro,
Seeking for some great thing to do,
  Or secret thing to know :
I would be treated as a child,
  And guided where I go.

Wherever in the world I am,
  In whatsoe'er estate,
I have a fellowship with hearts
  To keep and cultivate ;
A work of lowly love to do
  For Him on whom I wait.

I ask Thee for the daily strength
   To none that ask denied ;
A mind to blend with outward life,
   While keeping at thy side ;
Content to fill a little space,
   If Thou be glorified.

Briers beset my every path,
   That call for patient care ;
There is a cross in every lot,
   An earnest need for prayer :
But lowly hearts that lean on Thee
   Are happy everywhere.

In service which thy love appoints
   There are no bonds for me ;
My secret heart is taught the truth
   That makes thy children free :
A life of self-renouncing love
   Is one of liberty.

Anna L. Waring.

293   *I am so weak.*   S.M.

FATHER, I am so weak,
   Let me thy presence feel,
Take now my tired hands in thine,
   And bless me as I kneel.

Renew my failing strength,
   And teach me how to rise,
And, bearing all my heavy load,
   To seek thy bluer skies.

Let me not wait nor stay,
   Nor to the past return,
But kindle still my fainting heart
   With zeal anew to burn,

Till I shall see thy love
In every cross I bear ;
And, keeping close my hands in thine,
Shall trust Thee everywhere.

Miss J. F. McCaine.

294   *Trust in God.*   S.M.

COMMIT thou all thy griefs
And ways into his hands ;
To his sure truth and tender care
Who earth and heaven commands ;
Who points the clouds their course,
Whom winds and seas obey ;
He shall direct thy wandering feet,
And shepherd all thy way.

Give to the winds thy fears ;
Hope and be undismayed :
God hears thy sighs and counts thy tears,
God shall lift up thy head.
Through waves, through clouds, and storms,
He gently clears thy way :
Abide his will ; and weary night
Shall end in joyous day.

He everywhere hath sway,
And all things serve his might :
His every act pure blessing is ;
His path, unsullied light.
When He makes bare his arm,
What shall his work withstand ?
When God his people's cause defends,
What man shall stay his hand ?

Thou seest our weakness, Lord ;
Our hearts are known to Thee ;
O lift Thou up the trembling hands ;
Confirm the feeble knee :

So shall our life and death
Thy steadfast truth declare,
And all eternity proclaim
Thy love and guardian care.

P. Gerhardt, tr. J. Wesley.

295   *Until the day break.*   10s.

DARK is the sky that overhangs my soul,
The mists are thick that through the valley roll,
But as I tread, I cheer my heart and say,
When the day breaks, the shadows flee away.

I bear the lamp my Master gave to me,
Burning and shining must it ever be,
And I must tend it till the night decay,
Till the day break, and shadows flee away.

God maketh all things good unto his own,
For them in every darkness light is sown;
He will make good the gloom of this my day,
Till that day break, and shadows flee away.

He will be near me in the awful hour
When the last foe shall come in blackest power;
And He will hear me when at last I pray,
'Let the day break, the shadows flee away.'

In Him, my God, my Glory, I will trust,—
Awake and sing, O dwellers in the dust,—
Who shall come, will come, and will not delay;
His day will break, those shadows flee away.

S. J. Stone·

296 *All as God wills.* C.M.

ALL as God wills, who wisely heeds
   To give or to withhold,
And knoweth more of all my needs
   Than all my prayers have told.

Enough, that blessings undeserved
   Have marked my erring track;
That, wheresoe'er my feet have swerved,
   Thy chastening turned me back;

That more and more a Providence
   Of love is understood,
Making the springs of time and sense
   Bright with eternal good;

That death seems but a covered way
   Which opens into light,
Wherein no blinded child can stray
   Beyond the Father's sight;

That care and trial seem at last,
   Through memory's sunset air,
Like mountain-ranges overpast,
   In purple distance fair; .

That all the jarring notes of life
   Seem blending in a psalm,
And all the angles of its strife
   Slow rounding into calm.

And so the shadows fall apart,
   And so the west winds play;
And all the windows of my heart
   I open to the day.

J. G. Whittier.

297 *My psalm.* C.M.

No longer forward or behind
    I look in hope or fear,
But, grateful, take the good I find,
    God's blessing now and here.

I plough no more a desert land,
    To harvest weed and tare;
The manna dropping from God's hand
    Rebukes my painful care.

I break my pilgrim staff, I lay
    Aside the toiling oar;
The angel sought so far away
    I welcome at my door.

And all the jarring notes of life
    Seem blending in a psalm,
And all the angles of its strife
    Slow rounding into calm.

And so the shadows fall apart,
    And so the west winds play;
And all the windows of my heart
    I open to the day.
J. G. Whittier.

298 *Trust.* 6.5.

PURER yet, and purer,
    I would be in mind,
Dearer yet, and dearer
    Every duty find;
Hoping still, and trusting
    God without a fear,
Patiently believing
    He will make all clear.

Calmer yet, and calmer
  In the hours of pain,
Surer yet and surer
  Peace at last to gain ;
Suffering still and doing,
  To his will resigned,
And to God subduing
  Heart and will and mind.

Higher yet and higher
  Out of clouds and night,
Nearer yet and nearer
  Rising to the light,—
Light serene and holy,
  Where my soul may rest,
Purified and lowly,
  Sanctified and blest.

Swifter yet and swifter·
  Ever onward run,
Firmer yet and firmer
  Step as I go on ;
Oft these earnest longings
  Swell within my breast,
Yet their inner meaning
  Ne'er can be expressed.
           J. W. von Goethe, tr. Anon.

299   *Through unknown paths.*   C.M.

O THOU who art of all that is
  Beginning both and end,
We follow Thee through unknown paths,
  Since all to Thee must tend :
Thy judgments are a mighty deep
  Beyond all fathom-line ;
Our wisdom is the childlike heart,
  Our strength, to trust in thine.

We bless Thee for the skies above,
    And for the earth beneath,
For hopes that blossom here below
    And wither not with death;
But most we bless Thee for Thyself,
    O heavenly Light within,
Whose dayspring in our hearts dispels
    The darkness of our sin.

Be Thou in joy our deeper joy,
    Our comfort when distressed;
Be Thou by day our strength for toil,
    And Thou by night our rest.
And when these earthly dwellings fail
    And Time's last hour is come,
Be Thou, O God, our dwelling-place
    And our eternal home.

F. L. Hosmer.

300   *Trust in God.*   L.M.

O LOVE divine, that stoop'st to share
    Our sharpest pang, our bitterest tear,
On Thee we cast each earth-born care;
    We smile at pain while Thou art near.

Though long the weary way we tread,
    And sorrow crown each lingering year,
No path we shun, no darkness dread,
    Our hearts still whispering, 'Thou art near.'

When drooping pleasure turns to grief,
    And trembling faith is changed to fear,
The murmuring wind, the quivering leaf,
    Shall softly tell us Thou art near.

On Thee we cast our burdening woe,
  O Love divine, for ever dear,
Content to suffer, while we know,
  Living or dying, Thou art near.

O. W. Holmes.

301   *Blessed are they that mourn.*   L.M.

O DEEM not they are blest alone
  Whose lives a peaceful tenor keep ;
The Power who pities man has shown
  A blessing for the eyes that weep.

The light of smiles shall fill again
  The lids that overflow with tears,
And weary hours of woe and pain
  Are promises of happier years.

There is a day of sunny rest,
  For every dark and troubled night ;
And grief may bide an evening guest,
  But joy shall come with early light.

And thou, who o'er thy friend's low bier,
  Sheddest the bitter drops like rain,
Hope that a brighter, happier sphere,
  Will give him to thy arms again.

Nor let the good man's trust depart,
  Though life its common gifts deny,
Though with a pierced and broken heart,
  And spurned of men, he goes to die.

For God has marked each sorrowing hour
  And numbered every secret tear ;
And heaven's long age of love and power
  Grows out of all we suffer here.

W. C. Bryant.

302 *Love.* 11.10.

HE whom the Master loved has truly spoken :—
  The holier worship, which God deigns to bless,
Restores the lost, binds up the spirit-broken,
  And feeds the widow and the fatherless.

O brother man, fold to thy heart thy brother ;
  For where love dwells the peace of God is there ;
To worship rightly is to love each other ;
  Each smile a hymn, each kindly deed a prayer.

Follow with reverent steps the great example
  Of Him whose holy work was doing good :
So shall the wide earth seem our Father's temple,
  Each loving life a psalm of gratitude.

Then shall all shackles fall ; the stormy clangour
  Of wild war-music o'er the earth shall cease ;
Love shall tread out the baleful fire of anger,
  And in its ashes plant the tree of peace.
                                    J. G. Whittier.

303 *Our light afflictions.* 7.6.

    O HAPPY band of pilgrims,
      If onward ye will tread
    With Jesus as your Fellow
    . To Jesus as your Head.

    O happy if ye labour
      As Jesus did for men :
    O happy if ye hunger
      As Jesus hungered then.

    The Cross that Jesus carried
      Ye carry in his love :
    The crown that Jesus weareth
      Ye too shall wear above.

The faith by which ye see Him,
  The hope in which ye yearn,
The love that through all troubles
  To hear his voice will turn,

The trials that beset you,
  The sorrows ye endure,
The manifold temptations
  That death alone can cure,

What are they but his jewels
  Of right celestial worth?
What are they but the ladder
  Set up to heaven on earth?

O happy band of pilgrims,
  Look upward to the skies,
Where such a light affliction
  Shall win so great a prize.
          Joseph of the Studium, tr. J. M. Neale.

304   *Looking unto God.*   8.6.8.6.8.8.

I LOOK to Thee in every need,
  And never look in vain;
I feel thy strong and tender love,
  And all is well again:
The thought of Thee is mightier far
Than sin and pain and sorrow are.

Discouraged in the work of life,
  Disheartened by its load,
Shamed by its failures or its fears,
  I sink beside the road;
But let me only think of Thee,
And then new heart springs up in me.

Thy calmness bends serene above,
    My restlessness to still;
Around me flows thy quickening life,
    To nerve my faltering will;
Thy presence fills my solitude;
Thy providence turns all to good.

Embosomed deep in thy dear love,
    Held in thy law, I stand;
Thy hand in all things I behold,
    And all things in thy hand;
Thou leadest me by unsought ways,
And turn'st my mourning into praise.

S. Longfellow.

305   *Thy will be done.*   8.8.8.4.

My God, my Father, while I stray,
Far from my home on life's rough way,
O teach me from my heart to say,
        'Thy Will be done.'

Though dark my path, and sad my lot,
Let me be still and murmur not,
Or breathe the prayer divinely taught,
        'Thy Will be done.'

If thou should'st call me to resign
What most I prize, it ne'er was mine;
I only yield Thee what is thine;
        'Thy Will be done.'

E'en if again I ne'er should see
The friend more dear than life to me,
Ere long we both shall be with Thee;
        'Thy Will be done.'

Should pining sickness waste away
My life in premature decay,
My Father, still I strive to say,
      ' Thy Will be done.'

Let but my fainting heart be blest
With thy sweet Spirit for its guest,
My God, to Thee I leave the rest ;
      ' Thy Will be done.'

Renew my will from day to day,
Blend it with thine, and take away
All that now makes it hard to say,
      ' Thy Will be done.'

Then when on earth I breathe no more
The prayer oft mixed with tears before,
I'll sing upon a happier shore,
      ' Thy Will be done.'

Charlotte Elliott.

306   *Passing understanding.*   7s.

MANY things in life there are
Past our understanding far,
And the humblest flower that grows
Hides a secret no man knows.

All unread by outer sense
Lies the soul's experience ;
Mysteries around us rise,
We, the deeper mysteries.

Who hath scales to weigh the love
That from heart to heart doth move,
The divine unrest within,
Or the keen remorse for sin ?

Who can map those tracks of light
Where the fancy wings its flight,
Or to outer vision trace
Thought's mysterious dwelling-place?

Who can sound the silent sea
Where, with sealèd orders, we
Voyage from birth's forgotten shore
Toward the unknown land before?

While we may so little scan
Of thy vast creation's plan,
Teach us, O our God, to be
Humble in our walk with Thee.

May we trust, through ill and good,
Thine unchanging Fatherhood,
And our highest wisdom find
In the reverent heart and mind.

Clearer vision shall be ours,
Larger wisdom, ampler powers,
And the meaning yet appear
Of what passes knowledge here.

F. L. Hosmer.

307　　　　　*Resignation.*　　　　　C.M.

In trouble and in grief, O God,
　Thy smile hath cheered my way,
And joy hath budded from each thorn
　That round my footsteps lay.

The hours of pain have yielded good,
　Which prosperous days refused,
As herbs, though scentless when entire,
　Perfume the air when bruised.

The oak strikes deeper as its boughs
  By furious blasts are driven,
So life's vicissitudes the more
  Have fixed my heart in heaven.

All-gracious Lord, whate'er my lot
  At other times may be,
I'll welcome still the heaviest grief
  That brings me near to Thee.

  R. P. (Pope ?)

308   *A Psalm of trust.*   C.M.

I LITTLE see, I little know,
  Yet can I fear no ill :
He who hath guided me till now
  Will be my leader still.

No burden yet was on me laid
  Of trouble or of care,
But He my trembling step hath stayed,
  And given me strength to bear.

I came not hither of my will
  Or wisdom of mine own :
That higher Power upholds me still,
  And still must bear me on.

I knew not of this wondrous earth,
  Nor dreamed what blessings lay
Beyond the gates of human birth
  To glad my future way.

And what beyond this life may be
  As little I divine,
What love may wait to welcome me,
  What fellowships be mine.

I know not what beyond may lie,
  But look, in humble faith,
Into a larger life to die
  And find new birth in death.

He will not leave my soul forlorn ;
  I still must find Him true,
Whose mercies have been new each morn
  And every evening new.

Upon his providence I lean,
  As lean in faith I must :
·The lesson of my life hath been
  A heart of grateful trust.

And so my onward way I fare
  With happy heart and calm,
And mingle with my daily care
  The music of my psalm.

F. L. Hosmer.

309 *Safe to the land.* 8.4.

I KNOW not if the dark or bright
  Shall be my lot ;
If that wherein my hopes delight
  Be best or not.

It may be mine to drag for years
  Toil's heavy chain ;
Or day and night my meat be tears
  On bed of pain.

Dear faces may surround my hearth
  With smiles and glee ;
Or I may dwell alone, and mirth
  Be strange to me.

My bark is wafted to the strand
    By breath divine,
And on the helm there rests a hand
    Other than mine.

How can I fear the storm to sail,
    With Him on board ?
Above the raging of the gale
    I hear my Lord.

He holds me when the billows smite ;
    I shall not fall.
If sharp, 'tis short ; if long, 'tis light ;
    He tempers all.

Safe to the land, safe to the land,
    The end is this ;
And then with Him go, hand in hand,
    Far into bliss.

Dean Alford.

310   *Our refuge.*   7s.

Jesu, Lover of my soul,
    Let me to thy bosom fly,
While the gathering waters roll,
    While the tempest still is high :
Hide me, O my Saviour, hide,
    Till the storm of life be past ;
Safe into the haven guide,
    O receive my soul at last.

Other refuge have I none ;
    Hangs my helpless soul on Thee ;
Leave, O leave me not alone,
    Still support and comfort me.

All my trust on Thee is stayed,
  All my help from Thee I bring;
Cover my defenceless head
  With the shadow of thy wing.

Plenteous grace with Thee is found,
  Grace to cleanse from every sin;
Let the healing streams abound;
  Make and keep me pure within;
Thou of life the fountain art;
  Freely let me take of Thee;
Spring Thou up within my heart,
  Rise to all eternity.

                           C. Wesley.

311   *Christianity.*   L.M.

O FAIREST-BORN of Love and Light,
  Yet bending brow and eye severe
On all which pains the holy sight,
  Or wounds the pure and perfect ear,

Beneath thy broad, impartial eye,
  How fade the lines of caste and birth;
How equal in their sufferings lie
  The groaning multitudes of earth;

Still to a stricken brother true,
  Whatever clime hath nurtured him;
As stooped to heal the wounded Jew
  The worshipper of Gerizim.

In holy words which cannot die,
  In thoughts which angels leaned to know,
Christ gave thy message from on high,
  Thy mission to a world of woe.

That voice's echo hath not died ;
  From the blue lake of Galilee,
From Tabor's lonely mountain-side,
  It calls a struggling world to thee.

J. G. Whittier.

312   *Things temporal and eternal.*   C.M.

THE roseate hues of early dawn,
  The brightness of the day,
The crimson of the sunset sky,
  How fast they fade away.
O for the pearly gates of heaven,
  O for the golden floor,
O for the Sun of Righteousness
  That setteth nevermore.

The lark that soared so high at dawn
  On weary wing lies low,
The flowers so fragrant all day long
  Are dead or folded now.
O for the songs that never cease
  Where saints to angels call,
O for the tree of life that stands
  By the pure river's fall.

O'er the dull ocean broods the night,
  And all the strand is dark,
Save where a line of broken foam
  Lies at low water mark.
O for the land that needs no light,
  Where never night shall be ;
O for the quiet home in heaven,
  Where there is no more sea.

The highest hopes we cherish here,
  How fast they tire and faint ;
How many a spot defiles the robe
  That wraps an earthly saint.

O for a heart that never sins,
  O for a soul washed white,
O for a voice to praise our King,
  Nor weary day nor night.

Here faith is ours and heavenly hope,
  And grace to lead us higher ;
But there are perfectness and peace,
  Beyond our best desire.
O guard us, Lord, by love and power,
  Throughout the evil day ;
Grant that we fall not from thy grace,
  Nor cast our crown away.

Mrs. C. F. Alexander.

313   *The soul.*   7s.

WHAT is this that stirs within,
Loving goodness, hating sin,
Always craving to be blest,
Finding here below no rest ?

What is it ? and whither, whence
This unsleeping, secret sense,
Longing for its rest and food
In some hidden, untried good ?

'Tis the Soul,—mysterious name ;
Him it seeks from whom it came.
While I muse, I feel the fire
Burning on, and mounting higher.

Onward, upward, to thy throne,
O Thou Infinite, Unknown,
Still it presseth, till it see
Thee in all, and all in Thee.

W. H. Furness.

314   *Patience.*   8.8.8.6.

SHALL we grow weary in our watch,
  And murmur at the long delay,
Impatient of our Father's time,
  And his appointed way?

When harassed sore with passion's cry,
  Or overcome with sorrow's sleep,
We find it hard within our hearts
  The watch of life to keep.

O Thou, who in the garden's shade
  Did'st wake thy weary ones again
When, slumbering at that fearful hour,
  They all forgot thy pain,—

Bend o'er us now, as over them,
  And set our sleep-bound spirits free,
That we be faithful through the watch
  Our souls shall keep with Thee.

J. G. Whittier.
Ver. 2, S. A. Brooke.

315   *Patience.*   8s.

To weary hearts, to mourning homes,
God's meekest angel gently comes :
No power has he to banish pain,
Or give us back our lost again ;
And yet, in kindest love, our dear
And heavenly Father sends him here.

There's quiet in that angel's glance,
There's rest in his still countenance:
He mocks no grief with idle cheer,
Nor wounds with words the mourner's ear :
What ills and woes he may not cure,
He kindly trains us to endure.

Angel of patience sent to calm
Our feverish brows with cooling palm;
To lay the storms of hope and fear,
And reconcile life's smile and tear;
The throbs of wounded hearts to still,
And make our own our Father's will.

O thou who mournest on the way,
With longings for the close of day;
He walks with thee, that angel kind,
And gently whispers, ' Be resigned,
Bear up, bear up, the end shall tell,
The dear Lord ordereth all things well.'

From the German, tr. J. G. Whittier.

316　　　*Friendship in God.*　　　　10s.

'TIS a beautiful world which God has made,
Where the sunlight blends with the evening shade,
Where, 'midst the rough tumult of earthly things,
Is heard the soft moving of angels' wings,
And the Lord shall watch between me and thee,
And his pardoning Love shall our refuge be.

But our sins have made sad this world so fair;
They have brought us sorrow and pain and care;
Where always some weary head bends to die,
And ever the world seems to say, 'Good-bye:'
And the Lord shall watch between me and thee,
And his pardoning Love shall our refuge be.

Through the shades of night we feel God's hand
To be leading us to a better Land,
Where weary souls rest in a peace untold,
And walk in the Light through the gates of gold:
And the Lord shall watch between me and thee
And his pardoning Love shall our refuge be.

And to-day is the old, old story told,
How our souls may reach those bright streets of
    gold,
Where Love is the sun that shall ever shine,
And all that is his shall be callèd mine :
And the Lord shall watch between me and thee,
And his pardoning Love shall our refuge be.

And beside the still waters God shall lead,
To the pastures green his own flock to feed,
Where tears and where sorrow are never known,
Where death finds no place by the sunlit Throne :
And the Lord shall watch between me and thee,
And his pardoning Love shall our refuge be.
E. Husband.

317   *Duty.*   7s.

THOU, whose name is blazoned forth
    On our banner's gleaming fold,
Freedom, all thy sacred worth
    Never yet has half been told.

But to-day we sing of one
    Older, graver far than thou ;
With the seal of time begun
    Stamped upon her awful brow.

She is Duty : in her hand
    Is a sceptre heaven-brought ;
Hers the accent of command,
    Hers the dreadful, mystic *Ought.*

But her bondage is so sweet,
    And her burdens make us strong :
Wings they seem to weary feet,
    Laughter to our lips, and song.

Wheresoever **she may** lead,
 Freshly burdened every day,
Freedom, make us free to speed
 In her ever brightening way.
J. W. Chadwick.

318   *Thinking no evil.*   C.M.

O GOD, whose thoughts are brightest light,
 Whose love runs always clear,
To whose kind wisdom sinning souls
 Amidst their sins are dear ;

Sweeten my bitter-thoughted heart
 With charity like thine,
Till self shall be the only spot
 On earth which does not shine.

Hard-heartedness dwells not with souls
 Round whom thine arms are drawn ;
And dark thoughts fade away in grace,
 Like cloud-spots in the dawn.

When we ourselves least kindly are,
 We deem the world unkind ;
Dark hearts, in flowers where honey lies,
 Only the poison find.

But they have caught the way of God,
 To whom self lies displayed
In such clear vision as to cast
 O'er others' faults a shade.

All bitterness is from ourselves,
 All sweetness is from Thee ;
Dear God, for evermore be Thou
 Fountain and fire in me.
F. W. Faber.

319 *Hope.* C.M.

THE world may change from old to new,
From new to old again ;
Yet hope and heaven, for ever true,
Within man's heart remain.

The dreams that bless the weary soul,
The struggles of the strong,
Are steps towards some happy goal,
The story of hope's song.

Hope leads the child to plant the flower,
The man to sow the seed ;
Nor leaves fulfilment to her hour,
But prompts again to deed :

And ere upon the old man's dust
The grass is seen to wave,
We look, through falling tears, to trust
Hope's sunshine on the grave.

O no, it is no flattering lure,
No fancy weak or fond,
When hope would bid us rest secure
Of better life beyond.

Nor love, nor shame, nor grief, nor sin,
Her promise may gainsay ;
The voice divine hath spoke within,
And God did ne'er betray.

*Paraphrased from J. C. F. von Schiller,
by Sarah F. Adams.*

320 *Hope on.* 8.7.4.4.7.

HOPE on, hope on, the golden days
Are not as yet a-dawning,
The mists of night
Precede the light,
And usher in the morning.

Hope on, hope on, though black the clouds,
Black shadows intertwining,
    Yet calm and still,
    O'er heath and hill,
The stars will soon be shining.

Hope on, hope on, through frost and snow,
Through trouble, toil, and sorrow ;
    Through wind and rain,
    And tears and pain,
The sun shall pierce to-morrow.

Hope on, hope on, though friends be few,
And dark the way before thee,
    A God of love
    From heaven above
Shall shed his radiance o'er thee.

G. Thring.

321   *Integer vitæ.*   7s.

PURE in heart and free of sin,
Upright in thy daily path,
Fair without and true within,
Free from anger, safe from wrath.

Mighty in thy silent power
Of great virtue over wrong,
Beautifying every hour
By thy bearing, brave and strong ;

By thy mercy to the weak,
By thy justice to the low,
By thy grace unto the meek,
By thy kindness to thy foe.

Thou art free from passion's rage,
Thou art free from envy's sting,
Thou canst others' griefs assuage,
Canst to others comfort bring.

Peace and rest are in thy soul,
Bringing joy into thy life,
Outward storms around thee roll,
But they bring no inward strife.

And a sinner, tired and worn,
Weary of his life, at length
Findeth in thy words new hope,
Findeth courage in thy strength.

Florence T. Griswold.

322 *Independence.* L.M.

How happy is he born or taught,
  Who serveth not another's will;
Whose armour is his honest thought,
  And simple truth his highest skill;

Whose passions not his masters are;
  Whose soul is still prepared for death,
Not tied unto the world with care
  Of prince's ear or vulgar breath;

Who God doth late and early pray
  More of his grace than goods to lend;
And walks with man, from day to day,
  As with a brother and a friend.

This man is freed from servile bands
  Of hope to rise, or fear to fall;
Lord of himself, though not of lands,
  And having nothing, yet hath all.

Sir H. Wotton.

323 *Words.* S.M.

A FITLY spoken word,
   It hath mysterious powers ;
Its far-off echoes shall be heard
   Ringing through future hours.

An honest, truthful word,
   It has a tongue of flame ;
On wings of wind it flies abroad,
   And wins a heavenly fame.

A wise and holy word,
   It falls as doth the dew ;
A sweet refreshment to afford,
   And virtue's strength renew.

A gentle, gracious word,
   'Tis music in the heart ;
Thrilling its very inmost chord,
   Till tears unbidden start.

Speak thou, then, lovingly,
   Out of a Christ-like soul ;
Thy words a blessèd balm shall be,
   To make the sin-sick whole.

Speak, for the love of God,
   Speak, for the love of man ;
The words of truth love sends abroad,
   Shall never be in vain.
                  G. B. Bubier.

324 *To Truth.* 7.6.

O STAR of Truth, down shining,
   Through clouds of doubt and fear,
I ask but 'neath your guidance
   My pathway may appear.

However long the journey,
   How hard soe'er it be,
Though I be lone and weary,
   Lead on, I'll follow thee.

I know thy blessed radiance
   Can never lead astray,
However ancient custom
   May tread some other way.
E'en if through untrod deserts,
   Or over trackless sea,
Though I be lone and weary,
   Lead on, I'll follow thee.

The bleeding feet of martyrs
   Thy toilsome road have trod ;
But fires of human passion
   May light the way to God.
Then, though my feet should falter,
   While I thy beams can see,
Though I be lone and weary,
   Lead on, I'll follow thee.

Though loving friends forsake me,
   Or plead with me in tears ;
Though angry foes may threaten,
   To shake my soul with fears ;
Still to my high allegiance
   I must not faithless be :
Through life or death, forever
   Lead on, I'll follow thee.

M. J. Savage.

325   . *Truth.*   C.M.

O GOD of Truth, whose living Word
   Upholds whate'er hath breath,
Look down on thy creation, Lord,
   Enslaved by sin and death.

Set up thy standard, Lord, that we
   Who claim a heavenly birth,
May march with Thee to smite the lies
   That vex thy groaning earth.

Ah, would we join that blest array,
   And follow in the might
Of Him the Faithful and the True,
   In raiment clean and white !

We fight for truth, *we* fight for God,
   Poor slaves of lies and sin !
He who would fight for Thee on earth
   Must first be true within.

Then, God of Truth, for whom we long,
   Thou who wilt hear our prayer,
Do thine own battle in our hearts,
   And slay the falsehood there.

Still smite, still burn, till nought is left
   But God's own truth and love ;
Then, Lord, as morning dew come down,
   Rest on us from above.

Yea, come ; then, tried as in the fire,
   From every lie set free,
Thy perfect truth shall dwell in us,
   And we shall live in Thee.

                             T. Hughes.

326   *Steadfastness.*   7s.

God of Truth, thy sons should be
Firmly grounded upon Thee,
Ever on the rock abide,
High above the changing tide.

Theirs is the unwavering mind,
No more tossed with every wind;
No more doth their stablished heart
From the living God depart.

Father, strengthen Thou my will;
With thine own steadfastness fill;
Rooted, grounded, may I be,
Fixed in thy stability.

Henceforth may I nobly stand;
Build no longer on the sand;
But defy temptation's shock,
Firmly founded on the rock.

Imitated from C. Wesley,
by S. Longfellow.

327　　　*Loyalty to Truth.*　　　C.M.

WHEN courage fails, and faith burns low,
And men are timid grown,
Hold fast thy loyalty, and know
That Truth still moveth on.

For unseen messengers she hath
To work her will and ways,
And even human scorn and wrath
God turneth to her praise.

She can both meek and lordly be,
In heavenly might secure;
With her is pledge of victory,
And patience to endure.

The race is not unto the swift,
The battle to the strong,
When dawn her judgment-days that sift
The claims of right and wrong.

And more than thou canst do for Truth
   Can she on thee confer,
If thou, O heart, but give thy youth
   And manhood unto her.

For she can make thee inly bright,
   Thy self-love purge away,
And lead thee in the path whose light
   Shines to the perfect day.

Who follow her, though men deride,
   In her strength shall be strong,
Shall see their shame become their pride,
   And share her triumph-song.
                      F. L. Hosmer.

328   *The choice.*   8.7.

ONCE to every man and nation
   Comes the moment to decide,
In the strife of Truth with Falsehood,
   For the good or evil side;
Some great cause, God's new Messiah,
   Offers each the bloom or blight,
And the choice goes by forever
   'Twixt that darkness and that light.

Then to side with Truth is noble,
   When we share her wretched crust,
Ere her cause bring fame and profit,
   And 'tis prosperous to be just;
Then it is the brave man chooses,
   While the coward stands aside,
Till the multitude make virtue
   Of the faith they had denied.

Though the cause of Evil prosper,
    Yet 'tis Truth alone is strong;
Though her portion be the scaffold,
    And upon the throne be Wrong,
Yet that scaffold sways the future,
    And, behind the dim unknown,
Standeth God within the Shadow,
    Keeping watch above his own.

J. R. Lowell.

329   *Come, labour on.*   4.10.10.10.4.

COME, labour on:
Who dares stand idle on the harvest plain,
While all around him waves the golden grain,
And every servant hears the Master say,
    'Go, work to-day'?

Come, labour on:
The labourers are few, the field is wide;
New stations must be filled, and blanks supplied:
From voices distant far, or near at home,
    The call is 'Come.'

Come, labour on:
The enemy is watching, night and day,
To sow the tares, to snatch the seed away:
While we in sleep our duty have forgot,
    He slumbereth not.

Come, labour on:
Away with gloomy doubt and faithless fear,
No arm so weak but may do service here;
By hands the feeblest can our God fulfil
    His righteous will,

Come, labour on :
No time for rest, till glows the western sky,
While the long shadows o'er our pathway lie,
And a glad sound comes with the setting sun,
  'Servants, well done.'

Come, labour on :
The toil is pleasant and the harvest sure ;
Blessed are those who to the end endure ;
How full their joy, how deep their rest shall be,
  O Lord, with Thee.
Jane Borthwick.

330   *Work.*   C.M.

THE toil of brain, or heart, or hand,
  Is man's appointed lot ;
He who God's call can understand,
  Will work and murmur not.

Toil is no thorny crown of pain,
  Bound round man's brow for sin ;
True souls, from it, all strength may gain,
  High manliness may win.

O God, who workest hitherto,
  Working in all we see,
Fain would we be, and bear, and do,
  As best it pleaseth Thee.

Where'er Thou sendest we will go,
  Nor any question ask,
And what Thou biddest we will do,
  Whatever be the task.

Our skill of hand, and strength of limb,
   Are not our own, but thine ;
We link them to the work of Him
   Who made all life Divine.

Our Brother-Friend, thy holy Son,
   Shared all our lot and strife ;
And nobly will our work be done,
   If moulded by his life.

                      T. W. Freckelton.

331   *Work.*   7s.

   WITHOUT haste and without rest :
   Bind the motto to thy breast,
   Bear it with thee as a spell ;
   Storm or sunshine, guard it well ;
   Heed not flowers that round thee bloom ;
   Bear it onward to the tomb.

   Haste not—let no thoughtless deed
   Mar the spirit's steady speed ;
   Ponder well and know the fight,
   Onward then with all thy might ;
   Haste not—years can ne'er atone
   For one reckless action done.

   Rest not—life is sweeping by,
   Do and dare before you die ;
   Something worthy and sublime
   Leave behind to conquer time :
   Glorious 'tis to live for aye,
   When these forms have passed away.

Haste not—rest not, calm in strife ;
Meekly bear the storms of life ;
Duty be thy polar guide,
Do the right whate'er betide ;
Haste not, rest not ; conflicts past,
God shall crown thy work at last.

J. W. von Goethe, tr. C. C. Cox.

332　　　　　*Work.*　　　　　8.7.

WORK, it is thy highest mission,
　Work, all blessing centres there,
Work for culture, for the vision
　Of the True, and Good, and Fair.

'Tis of knowledge the condition,
　Opening still new fields beyond ;
'Tis of thought the full fruition ;
　'Tis of love the perfect bond.

Work, by labour comes the unsealing
　Of the thoughts that in thee burn ;
Comes in action the revealing
　Of the truths thou hast to learn.

Work in helping, loving union
　With thy brethren of mankind ;
With the foremost hold communion,
　Succour those who toil behind.

For true work can never perish,
　And thy followers in the way
For thy works thy name shall cherish :
　Work, while it is called to-day.

F. M. White.

333   *Behold, the fields are white.*   C.M.

O STILL, in accents sweet and strong,
    Sounds forth the ancient word,—
' More reapers for white harvest fields,
    More labourers for the Lord.'

We hear the call ; in dreams no more
    In selfish ease we lie,
But, girded for our Father's work,
    Go forth beneath his sky.

Where prophets' word, and martyrs' blood,
    And prayers of saints were sown ;
We, to their labours entering in,
    Would reap where they have strewn.

O Thou, whose call our hearts has stirred
    To do Thy will, we come ;
Thrust in our sickles at thy word,
    And bear our harvest home.

S. Longfellow.

334   *Love thy neighbour.*   7.6.

O LORD, Thou art not fickle,
    Our hope is not in vain,
The harvest for the sickle
    Will ripen yet again.

But though enough be given
    For all the world to eat,
Sin with thy love has striven,
    Its bounty to defeat.

Were men to one another
    As kind as God to all,
Then no man on his brother
    For help would vainly call.

On none for idle wasting
   Would honest labour frown;
And none, to riches hasting,
   Would tread his neighbour down.

No man enough possesses
   Until he has to spare;
Possession no man blesses
   While self is all his care.

For blessings on our labour,
   O, then, in hope we pray,
When love unto our neighbour
   Is ripening every day.

T. T. Lynch.

335   *Living for others.*   L.M.

THY task may well seem over hard,
Who scatterest in a thankless soil
Thy life as seed, with no reward
Save that which duty gives to toil.

Not wholly is thy heart resigned
To heaven's benign and just decree,
Which, linking thee with all thy kind,
Transmits their joys and griefs to thee.

Break off that sacred chain, and turn
Back on thyself thy love and care;
Be thou thine own mean idol, burn
Faith, hope, and trust, thy children, there.

Released from that fraternal law
Which shares the common bale and bliss,
No sadder lot could folly draw,
Or sin provoke from fate, than this.

The meal unshared is food unblest ;
Thou hoard'st in vain what love shall spend
Self-ease is pain, thy only rest
Is labour for a worthy end ;—

A toil that gains with what it yields,
And scatters to its own increase,
And hears, while sowing outward fields,
The harvest-song of inward peace.

J. G. Whittier.

336 *What I live for.* P.M.

I LIVE for those who love me,
  For those I know are true,
For the heaven that smiles above me,
  And awaits my spirit too ;
For all human ties that bind me,
For the task by God assigned me,
For the bright hopes left behind me
  And the good that I can do.

I live to learn their story
  Who've suffered for my sake,
To emulate their glory,
  And follow in their wake ;
Bards, martyrs, patriots, sages,
The noble of all ages,
Whose deeds crowd history's pages,
  And Time's great volume make.

I live to hail that season
  By gifted minds foretold ;
When men shall live by reason,
  And not alone by gold ;

When **man** to **man** united,
And every wrong thing righted,
The whole world shall be lighted,
  As Eden was of old.

I live to hold communion
  With all that is divine,
To feel there is a union
  'Twixt Nature's heart and mine ;
To profit by affliction,
Reap truths from fields of fiction,
Grow wiser from conviction,
  Fulfil each great design.

I live for those who love me,
  For those who know me true,
For the heaven that smiles above me,
  And awaits my spirit too ;
For the wrong that needs resistance,
For the cause that lacks assistance,
For the future in the distance,
  And the good that I can do.

G. L. Banks.

337   *The best prayer.*   8.6.

HE prayeth well, who loveth well,
  Both man and bird and beast ;
He prayeth best, who loveth best
  All things both great and small,
For the dear God who loveth us
He made and loveth all.

S. T. Coleridge.

338   *The true life.*   L.M.

HE liveth long who liveth well ;
  All else is being flung away ;
He liveth longest who can tell
  Of true things truly done each day.

Waste not thy being ; bac'₁ to Him,
　Who freely gave it, freely give,
Else is that being but a dream,
　'Tis but to *be*, and not to *live*.

Be wise, and use thy wisdom well ;
　Who wisdom *speaks* must *live* it too ;
He is the wisest who can tell ;
　How first he *lived*, then *spoke*, the true.

Be what thou seemest ; live thy creed ;
　Hold up to earth the torch divine ;
Be what thou prayest to be made ;
　Let the great Master's steps be thine.

Fill up each hour with what will last ;
　Buy up the moments as they go ;
The life above, when this is past,
　Is the ripe fruit of life below.

Sow truth, if thou the true wouldst reap ;
　Who sows the false shall reap the vain ;
Erect and sound thy conscience keep,
　From hollow words and deeds refrain.

Sow love, and taste its fruitage pure ;
　Sow peace, and reap its harvest bright ;
Sow sunbeams on the rock and moor,
　And find a harvest-home of light.
H. Bonar.

339　　　*The Voice of the Soul.*　　8.7.8.5.

HAST thou, 'midst life's empty noises,
　Heard the solemn steps of Time,
And the low, mysterious voices
　Of another clime ?

Early hath life's mighty question
   Thrilled within thy heart of youth,
With a deep and strong beseeching,—
   What, and where, is Truth?

Not to ease and aimless quiet
   Doth the inward answer tend;
But to works of love and duty,
   As our being's end;

Not to idle dreams and trances,
   Folded hands and solemn tone;
But to faith, in daily striving
   And performance shown;

Earnest toil and strong endeavour
   Of a spirit which within
Wrestles with familiar evil
   And besetting sin;

And without, with tireless vigour,
   Steady heart, and purpose strong,
In the power of Truth assaileth
   Every form of wrong.
                J. G. Whittier.

340   *On the Lord's side.*   C.M.

God's trumpet wakes the slumbering world:
   Now, each man to his post;
The red-cross banner is unfurled;
   Who joins the glorious host?

He who, in fealty to the Truth,
   And counting all the cost,
Doth consecrate his generous youth,—
   He joins the noble host.

He who, no anger on his tongue,
  Nor any idle boast,
Bears steadfast witness against wrong,—
  He joins the sacred host.

He who, with calm, undaunted will,
  Ne'er counts the battle lost,
But, though defeated, battles still,—
  He joins the faithful host.

He who is ready for the cross,
  The cause despised loves most,
And shuns not pain or shame or loss,—
  He joins the martyr host.

S. Longfellow.

341   *The day.*   Irr.

ROUTINE of duties,
  Commonplace cares,—
Angels disguised,
  Entertained unawares;—

Sweet human fellowships
  Kindred and near,
Drawing the soul from
  Its self atmosphere;

The book's friendly company,
  Leading along
To fields of new knowledge
  And uplands of song;

In-shinings of nature,
  Morning's red bars,
Waysides in beauty,
  Night with its stars;

The nearer communion
In silence apart,
When thought blooms to prayer,
And song fills the heart,

While the things unseen
Grow more and more real,
And life deepens and broadens
Toward larger ideal :—

How many the blessings
Each day has to give
The soul that is seeking
Truly to live.

F. L. Hosmer.

342   *Faith and Work.*   8.5.

EVERY day hath toil and trouble,
Every heart hath care :
Meekly bear thine own full measure,
And thy brother's share.
Fear not, shrink not, though the burden
Heavy to thee prove :
God shall fill thy mouth with gladness,
And thy heart with love.

Patiently enduring ever,
Let thy spirit be
Bound by links that cannot sever,
To humanity.
Labour, wait, thy Master perished
Ere his task was done :
Count not lost thy fleeting moments ;
Life hath but begun.

Labour, wait, though midnight shadows
    Gather round thee here,
And the storm above thee lowering
    Fill thy heart with fear;
Wait in hope; the morning dawneth
    When the night is gone,
And a peaceful rest awaits thee
    When thy work is done.

J. Bailey.

343   *Trust in God and do the right.*   8.7.

COURAGE, brother; do not stumble
    Though thy path be dark as night;
There's a star to guide the humble:
    'Trust in God, and do the right.'
Though the road be long and dreary,
    And its ending out of sight:
Foot it bravely—strong or weary:
    'Trust in God, and do the right.'

Trust no party, church, or faction,
    Trust no leaders in the fight,
But in every word and action
    'Trust in God, and do the right.'
Some will hate thee, some will love thee,
    Some will flatter, some will slight;
Cease from man, and look above thee:
    'Trust in God, and do the right.'

Trust no forms of guilty passion,
    Fiends can look like angels bright;
Trust no custom, school, or fashion,
    'Trust in God, and do the right.'
Simple rule and safest guiding,
    Inward peace and inward light,
Star upon our path abiding,
    'Trust in God, and do the right.'

N. Macleod.

344   *Watch and pray.*   7.7.7.3.

' CHRISTIAN, seek not yet repose,'
Hear thy loving Master say ;
Thou art in the midst of foes ;
    ' Watch and pray.'

Gird thy heavenly armour on,
Wear it ever night and day ;
Stand, till evil days be done ;
    ' Watch and pray.'

Hear the victors who o'ercame ;
Still they mark each warrior's way ;
All with one sweet voice exclaim,
    ' Watch and pray.'

Hear, above all, hear thy Lord,
Him thou lovest to obey ;
Hide within thy heart his word,
    ' Watch and pray.'

Watch, as if on that alone
Hung the issue of the day ;
Pray, till sin be overthrown ;
    ' Watch and pray.'
              Charlotte Elliott.

345   *The Builders.*   7s.

ALL are architects of fate,
Working in these walls of Time :
Some with massive deeds and great,
Some with ornaments of rhyme.

Nothing useless is or low :
Each thing in its place is best ;
And what seems but idle show
Strengthens and supports the rest.

For the structure that we raise,
Time is with materials filled :
Our to-days and yesterdays
Are the blocks with which we build.

Build to-day, then, strong and sure,
With a firm and ample base ;
And ascending and secure
Shall to-morrow find its place.

H. W. Longfellow.

346　　　　　*Beauty and Duty.*　　　　　8.7.

ALL around us, fair with flowers,
　　Fields of beauty sleeping lie ;
All around us clarion voices
　　Call to duty stern and high.

Thankfully we will rejoice in
　　All the beauty God has given ;
But beware it does not win us
　　From the work ordained of heaven.

Following every voice of mercy
　　With a trusting, loving heart,
Let us in life's earnest labour
　　Still be sure to do our part.

Now, to-day, and not to-morrow,
　　Let us work with all our might,
Lest the wretched faint and perish
　　In the coming stormy night ;

Now, to-day, and not to-morrow,
　　Lest, before to-morrow's sun, 　.
We too, mournfully departing,
　　Shall have left our work undone.

Anon.

347   *One by one.*   8.7.

ONE by one the sands are flowing,
   One by one the moments fall :
Some are coming, some are going ;
   Do not strive to grasp them all.

One by one thy duties wait thee ;
   Let thy whole strength go to each :
Let no future dreams elate thee ;
   Learn thou first what these can teach.

One by one, bright gifts from heaven,
   Joys are lent thee here below :
Take them readily when given ;
   Ready, too, to let them go.

One by one thy griefs shall meet thee ;
   Do not fear an armèd band :
One will fade as others greet thee ;
   Shadows passing through the land.

Do not.look at life's long sorrow ;
   See how small each moment's pain ;
God will help thee for to-morrow,
   So each day begin again.

Every hour that fleets so slowly
   Has its task to do or bear ;
Luminous the crown, and holy,
   When each gem is set with care.

Do not linger with regretting,
   Or for passing hours despond ;
Nor, the daily toil forgetting,
   Look too eagerly beyond.

Hours are golden links, God's token,
  Reaching heaven; but one by one
Take them, lest the chain be broken
  Ere the pilgrimage be done.
Adelaide A. Procter.

348   *From strength to strength.*   8.8.6.

Lord God, by whom all change is wrought,
By whom new things to light are brought,
  In whom no change is known,
Whate'er Thou dost, whate'er Thou art,
Thy children still in Thee have part;
  Still, still, Thou art our own.

Spirit, who makest all things new,
Thou leadest onward; we pursue
  The heavenly march sublime.
In thy renewing fire we glow,
And still from strength to strength we go,
  From height to height we climb.

Darkness and dread we leave behind;
New light, new glory still we find,
  New realms divine possess;
New births of good, new conquests bring,
Until triumphant we shall sing
  In perfect Holiness.
T. H. Gill.

349   *The race that is set before us.*   8.8.6.

Oft, as we run the weary way,
That leads through shadows unto day,
  With trial sore amazed,
We deem our sorrows are unknown,
Our battle joined and fought alone,
  Our victory unpraised.

Faithless and blind, who cannot trace
The witnesses who watch our race,
   Beyond the sense's ken;
The mighty cloud of all who died
With faithful rapture, humble pride,
   For love of God and Man:

Who, from the battlements above,
Follow our course with eager love,
   And cheer our contest on;
Who cry at every faithful blow,
Struck at the old usurping foe,
   'Servant of God, well done.'.

And One, the conqueror of death,
Captain and perfecter of faith,
   Who, for the joy of love,
Endured the cross, despised the shame,
Awakes us in the battle flame,
   And waits for us above.

Therefore with patience run the race,
With joy and confidence and grace,
   With cheerful hope and power;
Cast off the sin that checks our speed,
The weights that faith and love impede,
   Withstand the evil hour.

For heaven is round us as we move,
Our days are compassed with its love,
   Its light is on our road:
And when the knell of death is rung,
Loud Hallelujahs shall be sung
   To welcome us to God.

S. A. Brooke.

350 *A Psalm of Life.* 8.7.

TELL me not in mournful numbers,
   Life is but an empty dream;
For the soul is dead that slumbers,
   And things are not what they seem.

Life is real, life is earnest,
   And the grave is not its goal;
' Dust thou art, to dust returnest,'
   Was not spoken of the soul.

Not enjoyment, and not sorrow,
   Is our destined end or way;
But to act that each to-morrow
   Find us farther than to-day.

Art is long, and Time is fleeting,
   And our hearts, though stout and brave,
Still, like muffled drums, are beating
   Funeral marches to the grave.

Lives of great men all remind us
   We can make our lives sublime;
And, departing, leave behind us
   Footprints on the sands of time;

Footprints that, perhaps, another,
   Sailing o'er life's solemn main,
A forlorn and shipwrecked brother,
   Seeing, shall take heart again.

Let us, then, be up and doing,
   With a heart for any fate;
Still achieving, still pursuing,
   Learn to labour and to wait.

                        H. W. Longfellow.

351 *A purpose in life.* 8.7.

LIVE for something ; be not idle ;
  Look about thee for employ ;
Sit not down to useless dreaming,—
  Labour is the sweetest joy.
Folded hands are ever weary,
  Selfish hearts are never gay.
Life for thee hath many duties :
  Active be, then, while you may.

Scatter blessings in your pathway,
  Gentle words and cheering smiles :
Better far than gold and silver
  Are their grief-dispelling wiles.
As the pleasant sunshine falleth
  Ever on the grateful earth,
So let sympathy and kindness
  Gladden well the darkened hearth.

Hearts that are oppressed and weary,
  Drop the tear of sympathy ;
Whisper words of hope and comfort ;
  Give, and thy reward shall be
Joy unto thy soul returning
  From this perfect fountain-head.
Freely, as thou freely givest,
  Shall the grateful light be shed.

Anon.

352 *The Christian warfare.* 7s.

ONWARD, Christians, onward go ;
Join the war, and face the foe ;
Faint not ; much doth yet remain,
Dreary is the long campaign.

Shrink not, Christians : will ye yield?
Will ye quit the painful field?
Will ye flee in danger's hour?
Know ye not your Captain's power?

Let your drooping hearts be glad ;
March, in heavenly armour clad ;
Fight, nor think the battle long ;
Victory soon shall tune your song.

Let not sorrow dim your eye ;
Soon shall every tear be dry ;
Let not woe your course impede ;
Great your strength, if great your need.

Onward, then, to battle move ;
More than conquerors ye shall prove :
Though opposed by many a foe,
Christian soldiers, onward go.

H. K. White and Frances S. Colquhoun.

353　　　　*The march of life.*　　　　L.M.

SILENT like men in solemn haste,
Girded wayfarers of the waste,
We press along the narrow road
That leads to life, to truth, to God.

We fling aside the weight, the sin,
Resolved the victory to win :
We know the peril, but our eyes
Rest on the splendour of the prize.

No idling now, no wasteful sleep,
From Christian toil our limbs to keep,
No shrinking from the desperate fight,
No thought of yielding or of flight ;

No love of present gain or ease,
No seeking man or self to please ;
With the brave heart and steady eye,
We onward march to victory.

What though with weariness oppressed ?
'Tis but a little, and we rest ;
Finished the toil—the race is run ;
The battle fought—the field is won.

H. Bonar.

354.   *The conflict of life.*   8.7.

ONWARD, onward, though the region
  Where thou art be drear and lone ;
God hath set a guardian legion
  Very near thee,—press thou on.

Upward, upward !   Their Hosanna
  Rolleth o'er thee, ' God is Love ;'
All around thy red-cross banner
  Streams the radiance from above.

By the thorn-road, and none other,
  Is the mount of vision won ;
Tread it without shrinking, brother ;
  Jesus trod it,—press thou on.

By thy trustful, calm endeavour,
  Guiding, cheering, like the sun,
Earth-bound hearts thou shalt deliver ;
  O for their sake, press thou on.

Be this world the wiser, stronger,
  For thy life of pain and peace ;
While it needs thee, O no longer
  Pray thou for thy quick release ;

Pray thou, undisheartened, rather,
    That thou be a faithful son ;
By the prayer of Jesus,—'Father,
    Not my will, but thine, be done.'

S. Johnson.

355   *Onward, upward.*   8.7.

ONWARD ! upward ! Christian soldier,
    Turn not back nor sheath thy sword ;
Let its blade be sharp for conquest,
    In the battle for the Lord.
From the great white throne eternal
    God Himself is looking down ;
He it is who now commands thee,
    'Take the cross and win the crown.'

Onward ! doing and enduring,
    With the Lord who lived for thee ;
Face the foe, and meet with daring
    Danger whatso'er it be ;
From the battlements of glory,
    Holy ones are looking down ;
Thou canst almost hear them crying,
    'On ! let no one take thy crown.'

Onward ! till thy course be finished,
    Like the ransomed ones before ;
Keep the faith through persecution,
    Never give the battle o'er ;
Onward ! upward ! till victorious
    Thou shalt lay thine armour down,
And thy loving Father bid thee
    At his hand receive thy crown,

AWAKE our souls, away our fears,
Let every trembling thought be gone ;
Awake, and run the heavenly race,
And put a cheerful courage on.

True, 'tis a straight and thorny road,
And mortal spirits tire and faint ;
But we rest on the mighty God,
Who feeds the strength of every saint.

From Him, the everflowing spring,
Our souls shall drink inspiring truth,
Till from the caves of death we rise,
All glorious in immortal youth.

Then, as an eagle cleaves the air,
We'll mount with joy the heavenly height,
And, perfect in his love, possess
Life in the fulness of his light.

Almighty God, thy matchless power
Is ever new and ever young,
And firm endures, while endless years
Their everlasting circles run.

I. Watts and S. A. Brooke.

PRESS on, press on, ye sons of light,
Untiring in your holy fight,
Still treading each temptation down,
And battling for a brighter crown.

Press on, press on, through toil and woe,
With calm resolve to triumph, go ;
And make each dark and threatening ill
Yield but a higher glory still.

Press on, press on ; still look in faith
To Him who conquereth sin and death ;
Then shall ye hear his word, ' Well done.'
True to the last, press on, press on.

W. Gaskell.

358   *The Church Universal.*   C.M.

ONE holy Church of God appears
  Through every age and race,
Unwasted by the lapse of years,
  Unchanged by changing place.

From oldest time, on farthest shores,
  Beneath the pine or palm,
One Unseen Presence she adores,
  With silence or with psalm.

Her priests are all God's faithful sons,
  To serve the world raised up ;
The pure in heart her baptized ones ;
  Love, her communion-cup.

The truth is her prophetic gift,
  The soul her sacred page ;
And feet on mercy's errands swift
  Do make her pilgrimage.

O living Church, thine errand speed ;
  Fulfil thy task sublime ;
With bread of life earth's hunger feed ;
  Redeem the evil time.

S. Longfellow.

359 *For behold, the kingdom of God is within you.*   6s.

O THOU not made with hands,
　Not throned above the skies,
Nor walled with shining walls,
　Nor framed with stones of price,
More bright than gold or gem,
God's own Jerusalem :

Where'er the gentle heart
　Finds courage from above ;
Where'er the heart forsook
　Warms with the breath of love ;
Where faith bids fear depart,
City of God, thou art.

Thou art where'er the proud
　In humbleness melts down ;
Where self itself yields up ;
　Where martyrs win their crown ;
Where faithful souls possess
Themselves in perfect peace.

Where in life's common ways
　With cheerful feet we go ;
Where in his steps we tread
　Who trod the way of woe ;
Where He is in the heart,
City of God, thou art.

Not throned above the skies
　Nor golden-walled afar,
But where Christ's two or three
　In his name gathered are ;
Be in the midst of them,
God's own Jerusalem.

F. T. Palgrave,

360   *The city of God.*   C.M.

In Thee my powers, my treasures, live ;
    To Thee my life must tend ;
Giving Thyself, Thou all dost give,
    O soul-sufficing Friend.

And wherefore should I seek above
    The City in the sky,
Since firm in faith, and deep in love,
    Its broad foundations lie ?

Since in a life of peace and prayer,
    Nor known on earth nor praised,
By humblest toil, by ceaseless care,
    Its holy towers are raised.

Where pain the soul hath purified,
    And penitence hath shriven,
And truth is crowned and glorified,
    There, only there, is heaven.
                        Eliza Scudder.

361   *The city of God.*   C.M.

City of God, how broad and far
    Outspread thy walls sublime ;
The true thy chartered freemen are,
    Of every age and clime.

One holy church, one army strong,
    One steadfast high intent,
One faith and work, one hope and song,
    One King Omnipotent !

How purely hath thy speech come down
    From man's primeval youth ;
And slow and vast thine empire grown
    Of Freedom, Love, and Truth.

The watch-fires gleam from night to **night,**
    With never-fainting ray;
Thy towers uprise, serene and bright,
    To meet the dawning day.

In vain the surges' angry shock,
    In vain the drifting sands;
Unharmed, upon the Eternal Rock,
    The Eternal City stands.

S. Johnson.

362   *The city of light.*   8.7.

HAVE you heard the Golden City
    Mentioned in the legends old?
Everlasting light shines o'er it,
    Wondrous tales of it are told.

Only righteous men and women
    Dwell within its gleaming wall,
Wrong is banished from its borders,
    Justice reigns supreme o'er all.

Do you ask: Where is that City,
    Where the perfect Right doth reign?
I must answer, I must tell you
    That you seek its site in vain.

You may roam o'er hill and valley,
    You may pass o'er land and sea,
You may search the wide earth over—
    'Tis a City yet to be.

We are builders of that City,
    All our joys and all our groans
Help to rear its shining ramparts,
    All our lives are building-stones.

Some can do but humblest service,
  Hew rough stones or break the soil,
While the few alone may gather
  Joy and honour from their toil;

While the few may plan the arches,
  And the fluted columns fair,
And immortal thought embody,
  And immortal beauty there.

But if humble or exalted,
  All are called to task divine,
All but aid alike to carry
  Forward one sublime design.

What that plan may be, we know not;
  How the seat of Justice high,
How the city of our vision
  Will appear to mortal eye—

That no mortal eye can picture,
  That no mortal tongue can tell,
We can barely dream the glories
  Of the Future's citadel.

But for it we still must labour,
  For its sake bear pain and grief,
In it find the end of living
  And the anchor of belief.

But a few brief years we labour,
  Soon our earthly day is o'er,
Other builders take our places,
  And 'our place knows us no more.'

But the work that we have builded,
  Oft with bleeding hands and tears,
And in error and in anguish,
  Will not perish with our years.

It will be at last made perfect
In the universal plan,
It will help to crown the labours
Of the toiling hosts of man.

It will last and shine transfigured
In the final reign of Right,
It will merge into the splendours
Of the City of the Light.

F. Adler.

363   *Praise.*   6.5.

On our way rejoicing,
As we homeward move,
Hearken to our praises,
O Thou God of love.
Is there grief or sadness?
Thine it cannot be.
Is our sky beclouded?
Clouds are not from Thee.
On our way rejoicing,
As we homeward move,
Hearken to our praises,
O Thou God of love.

If with honest-hearted
Love for God and man,
Day by day Thou find us
Doing what we can—
Thou who giv'st the seed time
Wilt give large increase,
Crown the head with blessings,
Fill the heart with peace.
On our way rejoicing, &c.

On our way rejoicing
  Gladly let us go;
Conquered hath our Leader,
  Vanquished is our foe;
Loving cheer around us,
  Cheerful love within,
Faith's good battle fighting,
  Victory we shall win.
     On our way rejoicing, &c.

Unto God our Father
  Joyful songs we sing;
For his many mercies
  Thankful hearts we bring.
God the Eternal Goodness
  Bow we and adore,
On our way rejoicing
  Now and evermore.
     On our way rejoicing, &c.
          J. S. B. Monsell.

364   *Processional Hymn.*   S.M.

REJOICE, ye pure in heart,
  Rejoice, give thanks, and sing;
Your festal banner wave on high,
  The cross of Christ your King.

Bright youth and snow-crowned age,
  Strong men and maidens meek,
Raise high your free exulting song,
  God's wondrous praises speak.

Yes, onward, onward still,
  With hymn, and chant, and song,
Through gate, and porch, and columned aisle,
  The hallowed pathways throng.

With ordered feet pass on ;
Bid thoughts of evil cease.
Ye may not bring the strife of tongues
Within the house of peace.

With all the angel choirs,
With all the saints on earth,
Pour out the strains of joy and bliss,
True rapture, noblest mirth.

Your clear Hosannas raise,
And Hallelujahs loud,
Whilst answering echoes upward float,
Like wreaths of incense-cloud.

With voice as full and strong   .
As ocean's surging praise,
Send forth the hymns our fathers loved,
The psalms of ancient days.

Yes, on, through life's long path,
Still chanting as ye go,
From youth to age, by night and day,
In gladness and in woe.

Still lift your standard high,
Still march in firm array,
As warriors through the darkness toil,
Till dawns the golden day.

At last the march shall end,
The wearied ones shall rest,
The pilgrims find their Father's house,
Jerusalem the blest.

Then on, ye pure in heart,
Rejoice, give thanks, and sing,
Your festal banner wave on high,
The cross of Christ your King.

Dean Plumptre.

5   *To the only wise God, our Saviour.*   6.5.

SAVIOUR, blessèd Saviour,
Listen while we sing,
Hearts and voices raising
Praises to our King ;
All we have we offer,
All we hope to be,
Body, soul, and spirit,—
All we yield to Thee.

Great and ever greater
Are thy mercies here,
True and everlasting
Are the glories there,—
Where no pain nor sorrow,
Toil, nor care, is known ;
Where the angel legions
Circle round thy throne.

Dark and ever darker
Was the wintry past,
Now a ray of gladness
O'er our path is cast ;
Every day that passeth,
Every hour that flies,
Tells of love unfeignèd,
Love that never dies.

Clearer still and clearer
Dawns the light from heaven,
In our sadness bringing
News of sin forgiven ;

Life has lost its shadows,
  Pure the light within ;
Thou hast shed thy radiance
  On a world of sin.

Brighter still and brighter
  Glows the western sun,
Shedding all its gladness
  O'er our work that's done ;
Time will soon be over,
  Toil and sorrow past,
May we, blessèd Saviour,
  Find a rest at last.

Higher then, and higher,
  Bear the ransomed soul,
Earthly toils forgotten,
  Saviour, to its goal ;
Where in joys unthought of
  Saints with angels sing,
Never weary, raising
  Praises to their King.

G. Thring.

366   *The Pilgrims' March.*   8.7.

THROUGH the night of doubt and sorrow,
  Onward goes the pilgrim band,
Singing songs of expectation,
  Marching to the Promised Land.

Clear before us through the darkness
  Gleams and burns the guiding Light ;
Brother clasps the hand of brother,
  Stepping fearless through the night.

One the Light of God's own Presence
O'er his ransomed people shed,
Chasing far the gloom and terror,
Brightening all the path we tread :

One the object of our journey,
One the faith which never tires,
One the earnest looking forward,
One the hope our God inspires :

One the strain that lips of thousands
Lift as from the heart of one ;
One the conflict, one the peril,
One the march in God begun :

One the gladness of rejoicing
On the far eternal shore,
Where the One Almighty Father
Reigns in love for evermore.

Onward therefore, pilgrim brothers,
Onward with the Cross our aid ;
Bear its shame, and fight its battle,
Till we rest beneath its shade.

Soon shall come the great awaking,
Soon the rending of the tomb ;
Then the scattering of all shadows,
And the end of toil and gloom.
B. S. Ingemann, tr. S. Baring Gould.

367   *Eternity.*   7s.

O THE clanging bells of time ;
Night and day they never cease ;
We are wearied with their chime,
For they do not bring us peace ;

And we hush our breath to hear,
   And we strain our eyes to see
If thy shores are drawing near,
   Eternity, eternity.

O the clanging bells of time,
   How their changes rise and fall;
But in undertone sublime,
   Sounding clearly through them all,
Is a voice that must be heard,
   As our moments onward flee,
And it speaketh aye one word,
   Eternity, eternity.

O the clanging bells of time,
   To their voices loud and low,
In a long, unresting line,
   We are marching to and fro;
And we yearn for sight or sound
   Of the life that is to be,
For thy breath doth wrap us round,
   Eternity, eternity.

O the clanging bells of time;
   Soon their notes will all be dumb;
And in joy and peace sublime
   We shall feel the silence come;
And our souls their thirst will slake,
   And our eyes the King will see,
When thy glorious morn shall break,
   Eternity, eternity.

Mrs. E. H. Gates.

368   *Teach us to number our days.*   7.6.

O GOD, the Rock of Ages,
   Who evermore hast been,
What time the tempest rages,
   Our dwelling-place serene:

Before thy first creations,
  O Lord, the same as now,
To endless generations
  The Everlasting Thou !

Our years are like the shadows
  On sunny hills that lie,
Or grasses in the meadows
  That blossom but to die :
A sleep, a dream, a story
  By strangers quickly told,
An unremaining glory
  Of things that soon are old.

O Thou, who canst not slumber,
  Whose light grows never pale,
Teach us aright to number
  Our years before they fail.
On us thy mercy lighten,
  On us thy goodness rest,
And let thy Spirit brighten
  The hearts Thyself hast blest.

Lord, crown our faith's endeavour
  With beauty and with grace,
Till, clothed in light for ever,
  We see Thee face to face :
A joy no language measures ;
  A fountain brimming o'er ;
An endless flow of pleasures ;
  An ocean without shore.
                    Bishop E. H. Bickersteth.

369   *For ever with the Lord.*   S.M.

' For ever with the Lord ! '
  Amen ; so let it be ;
Life from the dead is in that word,
  'Tis immortality.

Here in the body pent,
Absent from Him I roam,
Yet nightly pitch my moving tent
A day's march nearer home.

My Father's house on high,
Home of my soul, how near
At times to faith's foreseeing eye
Thy golden gates appear :
Ah, then my spirit faints
To reach the land I love,
The bright inheritance of saints,
Jerusalem above.

I hear at morn and even,
At noon and midnight hour,
The choral harmonies of heaven
Earth's Babel-tongues o'erpower.
And then I feel that He,
Remembered or forgot,
The Lord, is never far from me,
Though I perceive Him not.

' For ever with the Lord ! '
Father, if 'tis thy will,
The promise of that faithful word
Even here to me fulfil.
Be thou at my right hand,
Then can I never fail ;
Uphold Thou me, and I shall stand,
Fight, and I must prevail.

So when my latest breath
Shall rend the veil in twain,
By death I shall escape from death,
And life eternal gain.

Knowing as I am known,
How shall I love that word,
And oft repeat before the throne,
'For ever with the Lord.'

J. Montgomery.

370 *He turneth the shadow of death into morning.*   7.6.

Now slowly, slowly darkening,
   The evening hours roll on,
And soon behind the cloud-land
   Will sink my setting sun.

Around my path life's mysteries
   Their deepening shadows throw,
And as I gaze and ponder,
   They dark and darker grow.

Yet still amid the darkness
   I feel the light is near ;
And in the awful silence
   God's voice I seem to hear :

But hear it as the thunder,
   Or murmuring of the sea ;
The secret it is telling,
   It tells it not to me.

Yet hark, a voice above me,
   Which says, 'Wait, trust, and pray :
The night will soon be over ;
   And light will come with day.'

Amen, the light and darkness
   Are both alike to Thee :
Then to thy waiting servant
   Alike they both shall be.

That great unending future,
  I cannot pierce its shroud,
But I nothing doubt, nor tremble ;
  God's bow is on the cloud.

To Him I yield my spirit ;
  On Him I lay my load ;
Fear ends with death ; beyond it
  I nothing see but God.

Thus moving towards the darkness,
  I calmly wait his call,
Seeing and fearing nothing,
  Hoping and trusting all.

S. Greg.

371   *I will wait till my change come.*   8.7.

ONLY waiting, till the shadows
  Are a little longer grown ;
Only waiting, till the glimmer
  Of the day's last beam is flown ;
Till the light of earth is faded
  From the heart once full of day ;
Till the stars of heaven are breaking
  Through the twilight soft and gray.

Only waiting, till the reapers
  Have the last sheaf gathered home ;
For the summer-time is faded,
  And the autumn winds have come.
Quickly, reapers,—gather quickly
  These last ripe hours of my heart ;
For the bloom of life is withered,
  And I hasten to depart.

Only waiting, till the shadows
    Are a little longer grown;
Only waiting, till the glimmer
    Of the day's last beam is flown.
Then, from out the gathered darkness
    Holy, deathless stars shall rise,
By whose light my soul shall gladly
    Tread its pathway to the skies.

Frances L. Mace.

372   *The end of life.*   Irr.

ONE sweetly solemn thought
    Comes to me o'er and o'er;
I am nearer home to-day
    Than I ever have been before;

Nearer my Father's house,
    Where the many mansions be;
Nearer the great white throne,
    Nearer the crystal sea;

Nearer the bound of life,
    Where we lay our burdens down;
Nearer leaving the cross,
    Nearer gaining the crown.

But lying darkly between,
    Winding down through the night,
Is the silent, unknown stream,
    That leads at last to the light.

O, if my mortal feet
    Have almost gained the brink;
If it be I am nearer home
    Even to-day than I think;

Father, perfect my trust ;
   Let my spirit feel in death
That her feet are firmly set
   On the rock of a living faith.

Phœbe Cary.

373   *Heaven is our home.*   6.4.6.4.6.6.6.4.

WE are but pilgrims here,
   Heaven is our home ;
Travelling through deserts drear,
   Heaven is our home.
Danger and sorrow stand
   Round us on every hand,
Heaven is our fatherland,
   Heaven is our home.

What though the tempests rage ?
   Heaven is our home ;
Short is our pilgrimage,
   Heaven is our home.
Time's wild and wintry blast
   Soon will be overpast,
We shall reach home at last ;
   Heaven is our home.

Lord, may we murmur not,
   Heaven is our home,—
Whate'er our earthly lot,
   Heaven is our home.
Grant us at last to stand
   There at thine own right hand,
In thy blest fatherland ;
   Heaven is our home.

T. R. Taylor.

374   *No continuing city.*   7.6.

BRIEF life is here our portion ;
  Brief sorrow, short-lived care ;
The life that knows no ending,
  The tearless life, is there.

O happy retribution ;
  Short toil, eternal rest ;
For mortals and for sinners
  A mansion with the blest.

And now we fight the battle,
  But then shall wear the crown
Of full and everlasting
  And passionless renown.

There grief is turned to pleasure,
  And martyrdom hath peace,
And from our vain desire,
  God giveth us release.

The morning shall awaken,
  The shadows shall decay,
And each true-hearted servant
  Shall shine as doth the day.

And God, our King and Portion,
  In fulness of his grace,
Shall we behold for ever,
  And worship face to face.

O sweet and blessèd country,
  The home of God's elect ;
O sweet and blessèd country,
  That eager hearts expect ;

Where they who with their Leader,
 Have conquered in the strife,
For ever and for ever
 Are clad with robes of life.
Bernard of Cluny, tr. J. M. Neale.

375   *Here and there.*   8.7.

HERE is the sorrow, the sighing,
 Here are the cloud and the night ;
Here is the sickness, the dying,—
 There are the life and the light.

Here is the fading, the wasting,
 The foe that so watchfully waits ;
There are the hills everlasting,
 The city with beautiful gates.

Here are the locks growing hoary,
 The glass with the vanishing sands ;
There are the crown and the glory,
 The house that is made not with hands.

Here is the longing, the vision,
 The hopes that so swiftly remove ;
There is the blessed fruition,
 The feast, and the fulness of love.

Here are the heart-strings a-tremble,
 And here is the chastening rod ;
There is the song and the cymbal,
 And there is our Father and God.
Alice Cary.

376   *The heavenly Jerusalem.*   C.M.

JERUSALEM, my happy home,
 When shall I come to thee ?
When shall my labours have an end ?
 Thy joys when shall I see ?

O happy harbour of the saints,
    O sweet and pleasant soil,
In thee no sorrow may be found,
    No death, no care, nor toil.

We that are here in banishment
    Our vigil still must keep;
Must stand and wait, and often long
    These tears no more to weep.

But blessèd are the pure in heart
    That find their home in thee,
Where weary spirits are at rest
    In God eternally.

Why should I shrink at pain and woe,
    Or feel, at death, dismay?
I've Canaan's goodly land in view,
    And realms of endless day.

Apostles, martyrs, prophets there,
    In holy converse stand:
And soon the sons of God below
    Will join the glorious band.

Jerusalem, my happy home,
    My soul still longs for thee;
Then shall my labours have an end,
    When I thy joys shall see.

Latin of the 9th Century, altered in the 16th; tr. Anon, 1616.

377   *Heaven.*   L.M.

WHAT is that goal of human hope,
    That heaven, where every soul is blest?
'Tis light for those who darkly grope;
    To weary ones, 'tis perfect rest;

To young and eager souls, a place
   Where high deeds may be grandly wrought ;
To those who mourn some absent face,
   'Tis where the lost ones may be sought.

It is a land where each may find
   That which in vain he sought for here ;
Where every element is kind,
   And summer reigns the live-long year.

Is there a country such as this ?
   Some glad day thou shalt know, O soul ;
Hope whispers of the perfect bliss,
   And points her finger toward the goal.

                                M. J. Savage.

378   *Heaven.*   s.m.

THERE is no night in heaven :—
   In that blest world above
Work never can bring weariness,
   For work itself is love.

There is no grief in heaven :—
   There all is perfect day ;
There tears are 'mid those former things,
   Which all have passed away.

There is no sin in heaven :—
   Amid that blessèd throng,
All-holy is their spotless robe,
   All-holy is their song.

There is no death in heaven :—
   For they who gain that shore
Have won their immortality,
   And they can die no more.

O Father, be our Guide,
And lead us safely on,
Till night, and grief, and sin, and death
Are past, and heaven is won.

F. M. Knollis.

379　　　*Jerusalem, the Golden.*　　　7.6.

JERUSALEM, the golden,
　With milk and honey blest,
Beneath thy contemplation
　Sink heart and voice opprest.
I know not, O I know not
　What joys await us there,
What radiancy of glory,
　What bliss beyond compare.

They stand, those halls of Zion,
　All jubilant with song,
And bright with many an angel
　And all the martyr throng.
There is the throne of glory ;
　And there, from care released,
The shout of them that triumph,
　The song of them that feast.

And they who, strong and faithful,
　Have conquered in the fight,
For ever and for ever
　Are clad in robes of white.
O land that sees no sorrow,
　O state that fears no strife,
O royal land of flowers,
　O realm and home of life !

Bernard of Cluny, tr. J. M. Neale.

380 *Heaven.* 7.7.7.4.

In this world, the Isle of dreams,
While we sit by sorrow's streams,
Tears and terrors are our themes,
Sad reciting.

But when once from hence we fly,
More and more approaching nigh
Unto young Eternity
There uniting;

In that whiter Island where
Things are ever more sincere;
Candor here, and lustre there,
All delighting;

There no monstrous fancies shall
Out of hell a horror call,
To create, or cause at all
Dread affrighting.

There in calm and cooling sleep
We our eyes shall never steep;
But eternal watch shall keep,
There attending

Pleasures such as shall pursue
Me immortalized, and you;
And fresh joys, as never too
Have an ending.
R. Herrick.

381 *Heaven.* 6.4.

My song and city is
Jerusalem on high;
My prayer and praise and bliss,
My refuge when I die.

O world of grace
When shall I see
God's glorious face
In purity.

O sweet and fair alone,
  The court of God most high,
The Heaven of Heavens, the throne
  Of Truth and Majesty.
      Awake, mine eyes,
      To see those skies,
      Where love and light
      Are infinite.

No sun by day is there,
  No moon by silent night:
The Lord God shineth fair,
  And is the city's light.
      Through golden streets,
      Life's river fleets:
      And from the throne,
      Love streams alone.

The stranger homeward bends,
  And sigheth for his rest:
My home is there, my friends
  Dwell in that quiet nest;
      Where each pure soul
      In long white stole,
      And palms in hand,
      Do ravished stand.

No tears from weary eyes,
  Drop in that holy quire:
But Death itself there dies,
  In Love's supreme desire.

So in a ring,
The praises sing
Of God alone,
Who fills the throne.

There all temptations cease,
    And frailties have an end,
And I shall rest in peace
    With God, my heavenly Friend.
        O happy place,
        Where all have grace,
        And garlands stored
        For their reward.

Lord God, on Thee I cry,
    Outwearied with delay :
My palace is on high ;
    Disclose its heavenly day,
        Where all men raise
        Thy glorious praise,
        And angels then
        Loud sing, Amen.

*Latin, tr. J. M. Neale, alt. S. A. Brooke,
partly from R. Herrick.*

382   *The strains of heaven.*   11.10.

HARK, hark, my soul ; angelic songs are swelling
    O'er earth's green fields and ocean's wave-beat
        shore :
How sweet the truth those blessèd strains are tell-
        ing
    Of that new life when sin shall be no more.
    Angels of Jesus, angels of light,
Singing to welcome the pilgrims of the night.

Onward we go, for still we hear them singing
  ' Come, weary souls, for Jesus bids you come,'
And through the dark, its echoes sweetly ringing,
  The music of the Gospel leads us home.
  Angels of Jesus, angels of light,
Singing to welcome the pilgrims of the night.

Far, far away, like bells at evening pealing,
  The voice of Jesus sounds o'er land and sea ;
And laden souls, by thousands meekly stealing,
  Kind Shepherd, turn their weary steps to Thee.
  Angels of Jesus, angels of light,
Singing to welcome the pilgrims of the night.

Rest comes at length ; though life be long and
    dreary,
  The day must dawn, and darksome night be past :
All journeys end in welcomes to the weary,
  And heaven, the heart's true home, will come at
    last.
  Angels of Jesus, angels of light,
Singing to welcome the pilgrims of the night.

Angels, sing on, your faithful watches keeping ;
  Sing us sweet fragments of the songs above ;
Till morning's joy shall end the night of weeping,
  And life's long shadows break in cloudless love.
  Angels of Jesus, angels of light,
Singing to welcome the pilgrims of the night.
                              F. W. Faber.

383   *The land beyond the sea.*   6.6.8.10.6.6.

  THE land beyond the sea !
  When will life's task be o'er ?
When shall we reach that soft blue shore,
O'er the dark strait whose billows foam and roar ?
  When shall we come to thee,
  Calm land beyond the sea ?

The land beyond the sea !
How close it often seems,
When flushed with evening's peaceful gleams :
The wistful heart looks o'er the strait and dreams ;
It longs to fly to thee,
Calm land beyond the sea.

The land beyond the sea !
Sometimes across the strait,
Like a drawbridge to a castle gate,
The slanting sunbeams lie, and seem to wait
For us to pass to thee,
Calm land beyond the sea.

The land beyond the sea !
When will our toil be done ?
Slow-footed years, more swiftly run
Into the gold of that unsetting sun :
Home-sick we are for thee,
Calm land beyond the sea !

The land beyond the sea !
Why fadest thou in light ?
Why art thou better seen towards night ?
Dear land, look always plain, look always bright,
That we may gaze on thee,
Calm land beyond the sea.

F. W. Faber.

384   *The eternal home.*   10.6.

ALONE, to land alone upon that shore !
With no one sight that we have seen before,—
Things of a different hue,
And sounds all strange and new,
No forms of earth our fancies to arrange,—
But to begin alone that mighty change !

Alone, to land alone upon that shore !
Knowing so well we can return no more ;
  No voice or face of friend,
  None with us to attend
Our disembarking on that awful strand,—
But to arrive alone in such a land !

Alone ? no, God hath been there long before,
Eternally hath waited on that shore
  For us who were to come
  To our eternal home :
O is He not tne life-long friend we know
More privately than any friend below ?

Alone ? the God we trust is on that shore,
The Faithful One whom we have trusted more
  In trials and in woes
  Than we have trusted those
On whom we leaned most in our earthly strife :
O we shall trust Him more in that new life.

So not alone we land upon that shore ;
'Twill be as though we had been there before ;
  We shall meet more we know
  Than we can meet below,
And find our rest like some returning dove,
Our home at once with the Eternal Love.
       F. W. Faber.

385   *The paths of Death.*   8.6.8.8.6.

How pleasant are thy paths, O Death !
  Like the bright slanting west,
Thou leadest down into the glow,
Where all those heaven-bound sunsets go,
  Ever from toil to rest.

How pleasant are thy paths, O Death !
  Thither where sorrows cease,
To a new life, to an old past,
Softly and silently we haste,
  Into a land of peace.

How pleasant are thy paths, O Death !
  E'en children after play
Lie down, without the least alarm,
And sleep, in thy maternal arm,
  Their little life away.

How pleasant are thy paths, O Death !
  The old, the very old
Smile when their slumbrous eye grows dim ;
Smile when they feel thee touch each limb ;
  Their age was not less cold.,

How pleasant are thy paths, O Death !
  Straight to our Father's home ;
All loss were gain that gained us this,—
The sight of God, that single bliss
  Of the grand world to come.

                   F. W. Faber.

386   *Not lost, but gone before.*   7.6.7.6.7.7.

WHEN for me the silent oar
  Parts the silent river,
And I stand upon the shore
  Of the strange forever,
Shall I miss the loved and known,
Shall I vainly seek mine own ?

Can the bonds that make us here
 Know ourselves immortal,
Drop away like foliage sere
 At life's inner portal?
What is holiest below
Must for ever live and grow.

He who plants within our hearts
 All this deep affection,
Giving, when the form departs,
 Fadeless recollection,
Will but clasp the unbroken chain
Closer when we meet again.

Therefore dread I not to go
 O'er the silent river :
Death, thy hastening oar I know ;
 Bear me, thou life-giver,
Through the waters to the shore
Where mine own have gone before.

       Lucy Larcom.

387   *There is no death.*   8.8.8.6.

THERE is no death. The stars go down
To rise upon some fairer shore,
And bright in heaven's jewelled crown
 They shine for evermore.

There is no death. The dust we tread
Shall change beneath the summer showers
To golden grain, or mellow fruit,
 Or rainbow-tinted flowers.

There is no death. An angel form
Walks o'er the earth with silent tread ;
He bears our best loved things away,
 And then we call them " dead."

He leaves our hearts all desolate,
He plucks our fairest, sweetest flowers ;
Transplanted into bliss, they now
    Adorn immortal bowers.

Born into that undying life,
They leave us but to come again ;
With joy we welcome them—the same,
    Except in sin and pain.

And ever near us, though unseen,
The dear immortal spirits tread ;
For all the boundless universe
    Is life ; there are no dead.

                        E. Bulwer Lytton.

388   *The grave.*   8.8.8.4.

THERE is a calm for those who weep,
  A rest for weary pilgrims found :
They softly lie, and sweetly sleep,
    Low in the ground.

The storm that wrecks the winter sky
  No more disturbs their deep repose,
Than summer evening's latest sigh
    That shuts the rose.

Ah, mourner, long of storms the sport,
  Condemned in wretchedness to roam,
Hope ; thou shalt reach a sheltering port,
    A quiet home.

Seek the true treasure, seldom found,
  Of power the fiercest griefs to calm,
And soothe the bosom's deepest wound
    With heavenly balm.

A bruisèd reed God will not break ;
  Afflictions all his children feel ;
He wounds them for his mercy's sake,
      He wounds to heal.

O traveller in the vale of tears,
  To realms of everlasting light,
Through time's dark wilderness of years,
      Pursue thy flight.

J. Montgomery.

389   *For evermore.*   7.7.7.5.

WHEN the toil of day is done,
When the race of life is run,
Father, grant thy wearied one
      Rest for evermore.

When the strife of sin is stilled,
When the foe within is killed,
Be thy gracious word fulfilled—
      Peace for evermore.

When the darkness melts away
At the breaking of thy day,
Bid us hail the cheering ray,
      Light for evermore.

When the heart, by sorrow tried,
Feels at length its throbs subside,
Grant us, where all tears are dried,
      Joy for evermore.

When for vanished days we yearn,
Days that never can return,
Teach us in thy love to learn
      Love for evermore.

When the breath of life is flown,
When the grave must claim its own,
Lord of life, be ours thy crown—
    Life for evermore.

J. Ellerton.

390   *The whole family in heaven and earth.*   C.M.

LET saints on earth in concert sing,
  With those whose work is done;
For all the servants of our King,
  In heaven and earth are one.

One family, we dwell in Him,
  One Church, above, beneath;
Though now divided by the stream,
  The narrow stream of death.

One army of the living God,
  To his command we bow;
Part of the host have crossed the flood,
  And part are crossing now.

E'en now to their eternal home
  There pass some spirits blest;
While others to the margin come,
  Waiting their call to rest.

By faith we join our friendly hands
  With those that went before;
And greet the pure, triumphant bands
  On the eternal shore.

O that we now might grasp our Guide;
  O that the word were given;
Come, Lord of Hosts, the waves divide,
  And land us all in heaven.

C. Wesley.

391   *All live unto God.*   8s.

. GOD of the living, in whose eyes
Unveiled thy whole creation lies,
All souls are thine : we must not say
That those are dead who pass away ;
From this our world of sense set free,
Our dead are living unto Thee.

Released from earthly toil and strife,
With Thee is hidden still their life ;
Thine are their thoughts, their works, their
      powers,
All thine, and yet most truly ours ;
For well we know where'er they be,
Our dead are living unto Thee.

Not spilt like water on the ground,
Not wrapped in dreamless sleep profound,
Not wandering in unknown despair,
Beyond thy voice, thine arm, thy care ;
In life, in joy, in peace they be ;
Not dead, but living unto Thee.

Thy word is true, thy will is just ;
To Thee we leave them, Lord, in trust ;
And thank Thee for the love which gave
Thy Son to fill a human grave,
That none might fear the world to see
Where all are living unto Thee.

O Breather into man of breath,
O Holder of the keys of death,
O Giver of the life within,
Save us from death, the death of sin ;
That body, soul, and spirit be,
For ever living unto Thee.

                                    J. Ellerton.

392   *All live unto Him.*   8.8.8.4.

O LORD of Life, where'er they be,
Safe in thine own eternity,
Our dead are living unto Thee.
         Hallelujah!

All souls are thine, and, here or there,
They rest within thy sheltering care;
One providence alike they share.
         Hallelujah!

Thy word is true, thy ways are just;
Above the requiem, " dust to dust,"
Shall rise our psalm of grateful trust.
         Hallelujah!

O happy they in God who rest,
No more by fear and doubt oppressed;
Living or dying they are blest.
         Hallelujah!
            H.

393   *All souls are mine.*   C.M.

THEY passed away from sight and hand,
   A slow successive train;
To memory's heart—a gathered band—
   Our lost ones come again.

Their spirits up to God we gave,
   With eyes as wet as dim,
Confiding in his power to save,
   For all do live to Him.

Beyond all we can know or think,
   Beyond the earth and sky,
Beyond time's lone and dreaded brink
   Their deathless dwellings lie.

Dear thoughts that once our union made,
 Death does not disavow ;
We prayed for them while here they stayed,
 And what shall hinder now ?

Our Father, give them perfect rest
 And portions with the blest ;
O. pity if they went astray,
 And pardon for the best.

As they may need still deign to bring
 The helping of thy grace,
The shadow of thy guardian wing
 Or shinings of thy face.

For all their sorrows here below
 Be boundless joy and peace,
For all their love, a heavenly glow
 That nevermore shall cease.

      N. L. Frothingham.

394   *Beyond the veil.*   10.8.10.6.

THEY are all gone into the world of light,
 And I alone sit lingering here ;
Their very memory is fair and bright,
 And my sad thoughts doth clear.

It glows and glitters in my cloudy breast,
 Like stars upon some gloomy grove,
Or those faint beams in which this hill is drest,
 After the sun's remove.

I see them walking in an air of glory,
 Whose light doth trample on my days :
My days, which are at best but dull and hoary,
 Mere glimmering and decays.

O holy Hope, and high Humility,
   High as the heavens above,
These are your walks and you have showed them
      me,
   To kindle my cold love.

Dear, beauteous Death, the jewel of the just,
   Shining nowhere but in the dark,
What mysteries do lie beyond thy dust,
   Could man outlook that mark.

He that hath found some fledged bird's nest may
     know,
   At first sight, if the bird be flown ;
But what fair well or grove he sings in now,
   That is to him unknown.

And yet, as angels in some brighter dreams
   Call to the soul, when man doth sleep ;
So some strange thoughts transcend our wonted
     themes,
   And into glory peep.

If a star were confined into a tomb,
   Her captive flames must needs burn there ;
But when the hand that locked her up, gives
     room,
   She'll shine through all the sphere.

O Father of eternal life and all
   Created glories under Thee,
Resume thy spirit from this world of thrall
   Into true liberty.

H. Vaughan.

395   *The angels of grief.*   11.4.

WITH silence only as their benediction,
    God's angels come
Where, in the shadow of a great affliction,
    The soul sits dumb.

Yet would we say, what every heart approveth,—
    Our Father's will,
Calling to Him the dear ones whom He loveth,
    Is mercy still.

Not upon us or ours the solemn angel
    Hath evil wrought;
The funeral anthem is a glad evangel;
    The good die not.

God calls our loved ones, but we lose not wholly
    What He has given;
They live on earth in thought and deed, as truly
    As in his heaven.

                              J. G. Whittier.

396   *The parting here, the greeting there.*   L.M.

GOD giveth quietness at last;
The common way once more is passed
From pleading tears and lingerings fond
To fuller life and love beyond.

Fold the rapt soul in your embrace,
Dear ones familiar with the place;
While to the gentle greetings there
We answer here with murmured prayer.

What to shut eyes hath God revealed?
What hear the ears that death has sealed?
What undreamed beauty passing show
Requites the loss of all we know?

O Silent Land to which we move,
Enough, if there alone be love,
And mortal need can ne'er outgrow
What it is waiting to bestow.

O white soul from that far-off shore
Float some sweet song the waters o'er ;
Our faith confirm, our fears dispel,
With the dear voice we loved so well.

J. G. Whittier.

397   *Beside the grave.*   6.6.4.

Lowly and solemn be
Thy children's cry to Thee,
  Father divine,
A hymn of suppliant breath,
Owning that life and death
  Alike are thine.

O Father, in that hour
When earth all succouring power
  Shall disavow ;
When spear and shield and crown
In faintness are cast down ;
  Sustain us, Thou.

By Him who bowed to take
The death-cup for our sake,
  The thorn, the rod ;
From whom the last dismay
Was not to pass away ;
  Aid us, O God.

Tremblers beside the grave,
We call on Thee to save,
  Father divine ;
Hear, hear our suppliant breath,
Keep us in life and death,
  Thine, only thine.
Felicia D. Hemans.

398   *Farewell, Brother.*   8.7.

FAREWELL, brother ; deep and lowly
  Rest thee on thy bed of clay.
Kindred saints and angels holy
  Bore thy heavenward soul away.
Sad, we gave thee to that number
  Laid in yonder icy halls,
Where, above thy peaceful slumber,
  Many a shower of sorrow falls.

Hear our prayer, O God of glory,
  Lowly breathed in sorrow's song ;
Bleeding hearts lie bare before Thee,
  Come in holy trust made strong.
Hark, a voice moves nearer, stronger,
  From the shadowy land we dread :
' Mortals, upward, seek no longer
  Those that live among the dead.'

Farewell, brother ; soon we meet thee
  Where no cloud of sorrow rolls :
For glad tidings float, how sweetly,
  From the glorious land of souls.
Death's cold gloom—it parts asunder :
  Lo, the folding shades are gone.
Mourner, upward ; yonder, yonder,
  God's broad day comes pouring on.
E. H. Sears.

399   *Of such is the kingdom of God.*   7.7.4.

Let no hopeless tears be shed,
Holy is this narrow bed.
                    Hallelujah !

Death eternal life bestows,
Open heaven's portal throws.
                    Hallelujah !

And no peril waits at last
Him (*her*) who now away hath past.
                    Hallelujah !

Not salvation hardly won,
Not the meed of race well run ;
                    Hallelujah !

But the pity of the Lord
Gives his child a full reward ;
                    Hallelujah !

Grants the prize without the course ;
Crowns without the battle's force.
                    Hallelujah !

God, who loveth innocence,
Hastes to take his darling hence.
                    Hallelujah !

Lord, when this sad life is done,
Join us to thy little one ;
                    Hallelujah !

And in thine own tender love,
Bring us to the home above.
                    Hallelujah !

Paris Missal, tr. R. F. Littledale.

400 . *The children going.* 8.7.

THEY are going,—only going :
    Jesus called them long ago ;
All the wintry time they're passing
    Softly as the falling snow.
When the violets in the spring-time,
    Catch the azure of the sky,
They are carried out to slumber
    Sweetly where the violets lie.

They are going,—only going,—
    When with summer earth is drest,
In their cold hands holding roses
    Folded to each silent breast ;
When the autumn hangs red banners
    Out above the harvest sheaves,
They are going, ever going,
    Thick and fast, like falling leaves.

All along the mighty ages,
    All adown the solemn time,
They have taken up their homeward
    March to that serener clime,
Where the watching, waiting angels
    Lead them from the shadow dim,
To the brightness of his presence,
    Who has called them unto Him.

They are going—only going—
    Out of pain and into bliss ;
Out of sad and sinful weakness
    Into perfect holiness.
Snowy brows,—no care shall shade them ;
    Bright eyes,—tears shall never dim ;
Rosy lips,—no time shall fade them ;
    Jesus called them unto Him.

Little hearts for ever stainless ;
   Little hands as pure as they ;
Little feet, by angels guided,
   Never a forbidden way :
They are going,—ever going,—
   Leaving many a lonely spot ;
But 'tis Jesus who has called them,—
   Suffer, and forbid them not.

401   *The angels' welcome.*   C.M.

'THE children come,' the angels cry ;
   'They leave a world of sin ;
At heaven's gate our armies wait,
   To let the travellers in.
They dwelt in darkness, but there came
   A glorious, golden light ;
It shone on high, it filled the sky,
   It chased away their night.

They come, they come, redeemed and free,
   From every land they come ;
By night, by day, a bright array,
   They're welcomed one by one.
From sultry climes and frozen shores,
   Green fields or barren sands,
With eager feet we haste to greet
   Their souls from distant lands.'

And still they sing, those angels bright,
   While here we toil and pray :
But we ere long may join their song,
   When we have passed away.
Then children's hands will lead us home
   When work on earth is done,
And heaven will ring while angels sing—
   The new great life begun.

J. P. Hopps.

402 *Angels.* 6.5.

HAND in hand with angels .
   Through the world we go ;
Brighter eyes are on us
   Than we blind ones know.

Tenderer voices cheer us
   Than we deaf will own ;
Never, walking heavenward,
   Can we walk alone.

Hand in hand with angels ;
   Some are out of sight,
Leading us, unknowing,
   Into paths of light.

Some soft hands are carried
   From our mortal grasp,
Soul in soul to hold us
   With a firmer clasp.

Hand in hand with angels
   Walking every day ;
How the chain may brighten,
   None of us can say.

Yet it doubtless reaches
   From earth's lowest one
To the loftiest seraph,
   Standing near the throne.
                   Lucy Larcom.

403 *Ministering angels.* Irr.

BROTHER, the angels say,
   Peace to thy heart ;
We, too, O brother, have
   Been as thou art,

Hope-lifted, doubt-depressed,
  Seeing in part,
Tried, troubled, tempted,
  Sustained, as thou art.

Brother, they softly say,
  Be our thoughts one ;
Bend thou with us and pray,
  ' Thy will be done.'
Our God is thy God ;
  He wills the best ;
Trust as we trusted,
  Rest as we rest.

Ye, too, they gently say,
  Shall angels be ;
Ye, too, O brothers,
  From earth be free ;
Yet in earth's loved ones
  Ye shall have part,
Bearing God's strength and love
  To the torn heart.

Thus when the spirit, tried,
  Tempted and worn,
Finding no earthly aid,
  Heavenward doth turn,
Come these sweet angel-tones
  Falling like balm,
And on the troubled heart
  Steals a deep calm.

404   *Why seek ye the living among the dead ?*   L.M.

AH, why should bitter tears be shed
  In sorrow o'er the mounded sod,
When verily there are no dead
  Of all the children of our God ?

They who are lost to outward sense
   Have but flung off their robes of clay,
And, clothed in heavenly radiance,
   Attend us on our lowly way.

And oft their spirits breathe in ours
   The hope and strength and love of theirs,
Which bloom as bloom the early flowers
   In breath of summer's viewless airs.

And silent aspirations start,
   In promptings of their purer thought,
Which gently lead the troubled heart
   To joys not even hope had wrought.

Let living Faith serenely pour
   Her sunlight on our pathway dim,
And Death can have no terrors more ;
   But holy joy shall walk with him.
                        G. S. Burleigh.

405   *The call of the dead.*   C.M.

ANOTHER hand is beckoning us,
   Another call is given ;
And glows once more with angel-steps
   The path that reaches heaven.

Alone unto our Father's will
   One thought hath reconciled ;
That He whose love exceedeth ours
   Hath taken home his child.

Fold her, O Father, in thine arms,
   And let her henceforth be   ·
A messenger of love between
   Our human hearts and Thee.

Still let her mild rebuking stand
  Between us and the wrong,
And her dear memory serve to make
  Our faith in goodness strong.

J. G. Whittier.

406   *The memory of the dead.*   6.7.

O IT is sweet to think
  Of those that are departed,
While whispered yearnings sink
  To silence·tender-hearted,
While tears that hath no pain
  Are tranquilly distilling,
And the dead live again
  In hearts that love is filling.

Dear dead ! they have become
  Like guardian angels to us ;
And distant heaven, like home,
  Through them begins to woo us :
Love, that was earthly, wings
  Its flight to holier places :
The dead are sacred things
  That multiply our graces.

They whom we loved on earth
  Attract us now to heaven ;
Who shared our grief and mirth
  Back to us now are given.
They move with noiseless foot
  Gravely and sweetly round us,
And their soft touch hath cut
  Full many a chain that bound us.

O dearest dead, to heaven
  With grudging sighs we gave you,
To Him,—be doubts forgiven—
  Who took you there to save you :
O for his grace to love
  Your memories yet more kindly,
Pine for our homes above,
  And trust to God more blindly.

F. W. Faber.

407   *Venturi salutamus.*   8.8.7.

OUR beloved have departed,
While we tarry, heavy-hearted,
  In the dreary, empty house :
They have ended life's brief story,
They have reached the home of glory,
  Over death victorious.

Hush that sobbing, weep more lightly ;
On we travel, daily, nightly,
  To the rest that they have found.
Are we not upon the river,
Sailing fast, to meet for ever
  On more holy, happy ground ?

On in haste, to home invited,
There with friends to be united
  In a surer bond than here ;
Meeting soon, and met for ever !
Glorious Hope, forsake us never,
  For thy glimmering light is dear.

Ah, the way is shining clearer,
As we journey ever nearer
  To the everlasting home ;

Comrades, who await our landing,
Friends, who round the throne are standing,
We salute you, and we come.

German, tr. Anon.

408   *Auld Lang Syne.*   C.M.

IT singeth low in every heart,
  We hear it each and all,—
A song of those who answer not,·
  However we may call.
They throng the silence of the breast;
  We see them as of yore,—
The kind, the true, the brave, the sweet,
  Who walk with us no more.

'Tis hard to take the burden up,
  When these have laid it down:
They brightened all the joy of life,
  They softened every frown.
But O 'tis good to think of them
  When we are troubled sore;
Thanks be to God that such have been,
  Although they are no more.

More homelike seems the vast unknown,
  Since they have entered there;
To follow them were not so hard,
  Wherever they may fare.
They cannot be where God is not,
  On any sea or shore;
Whate'er betides, thy love abides,
  Our God for evermore.

J. W. Chadwick.

409   *Heavenward.*   6.4.6.4.6.6.6.4.

Lord, to live life again
  Is not our cry,
One tear to memory given,
  Onward we hie.
Life's dark flood forded o'er,
All but at rest on shore,
Say, should we plunge once more,
  With home so nigh?

Why should we, if we might,
  Retrace our way?
Wander through stormy wilds,
  Faint and astray?
Night's gloomy watch is fled,
Morning's all burning red,
Hope's smiles are round us shed;
  Heavenward, away!

Where then are those dear ones,
  Our joy and delight?
Dear and more dear, though now
  Hidden from sight;
Where they rejoice to be,
There is the land for me.
Fly, time, fly speedily;
  Come, life and light!

Lady Nairn.

410   *My Dead.*   C.M.

I cannot think of them as dead
  Who walk with me no more;
Along the path of Life I tread,
  They have but gone before.

The Father's house is mansioned fair
  Beyond my vision dim ;
All souls are his, and here or there,
  Are living unto Him.

And still their silent ministry
  Within my heart hath place,
As when on earth they walked with me
  And met me face to face.

Their lives are made forever mine ;
  What they to me have been
Hath left henceforth its seal and sign
  Engraven deep within.

Mine are they by an ownership
  Nor time nor death can free ;
For God hath given to Love to keep
  Its own eternally.

F. L. Hosmer.

411   *Green pastures and still waters.*   8.7.

CLEAR in memory's silent reaches
  Lie the pastures I have seen,
Greener than the sun-lit spaces
  Where the May has flung her green :
Needs no sun and needs no starlight
  To illume these fields of mine,
For the glory of dead faces
  Is the sun, the stars, that shine.

More than one I count my pastures
  As my life-path groweth long ;
By their quiet waters straying
  Oft I lay me, and am strong.

And I call each by its giver,
   And the dear names bring to them
Glory as from shining faces
   In some New Jerusalem.

Yet, O well I can remember,
   Once I called my pastures, Pain,
And their waters were a torrent
   Sweeping through my life amain :
Now I call them Peace and Stillness,
   Brightness of all Happy Thought,
Where I linger for a blessing
   From my faces that are nought.

Nought ?   I fear not.   If the Power
   Maketh thus his pastures green,
Maketh thus his quiet waters,
   Out of waste his heavens serene,
I can trust the mighty Shepherd
   Loseth none He ever led ;
Somewhere yet a greeting waits me
   On the faces of my dead.
                        W. C. Gannett.

412   *All Saints.*   8.7.8.7.7.7.

Who are these like stars appearing,
   These, before God's Throne who stand ?
Each a golden crown is wearing,
   Who are all this glorious band ?
     Alleluia, hark ! they sing,
     Praising loud their heavenly King.

Who are these in dazzling brightness,
   Clothed in God's own righteousness,
These, whose robes of purest whiteness
   Shall their lustre still possess,
     Still untouched by time's rude hand ?
     Whence came all this glorious band ?

These are they who have contended
  For the Saviour's honour long,
Wrestling on till life was ended,
  Following not the sinful throng ;
    These who well the fight sustained,
    Triumph with the Lamb have gained.

These are they whose hearts were riven,
  Sore with woe and anguish tried,
Who in prayer full oft have striven
  With the God they glorified ;
    Now, their painful conflict o'er,
    God has bid them weep no more.

These, the Almighty contemplating,
  Did as priests before Him stand,
Soul and body always waiting
  Day and night at his command :
    Now in God's most holy place
    Blest they stand before his Face
        H. T. Schenck, tr. Frances E. Cox.

413   *Our dead.*   C.M.

OUR dead are like the stars by day,
  Withdrawn from mortal eye,
Yet holding unperceived their way
  Through the unclouded sky.

By them, through holy hope and love,
  We feel in hours serene
Connected with a world above,
  Immortal and unseen.

Though death his sacred seal hath set
  On bright and bygone hours,
Still those we love are with us yet,
  Are more than ever ours ;—

Ours by the pledge of love and faith,
   By hopes of heaven on high,
By trust triumphant over death,
   In immortality.

                        B. Barton.

414   *Our dead.*   8.7.

FROM the eternal shadow rounding
   All our sun and starlight here,
Voices of our lost ones sounding
   Bid us be of heart and cheer,
Through the silence, down the spaces,
   Falling on the inward ear.

Let us draw their mantles o'er us
   Which have fallen in our way ;
Let us do the work before us,
   Cheerly, bravely, while we may,
Ere the long night-silence cometh,
   And with us it is not day.

                       J. G. Whittier.

415   *Earth's nameless martyrs.*   8s.

THE kings of old have shrine and tomb
In many a minster's haughty gloom ;
And green, along the ocean-side,
The mounds arise where heroes died ;
But show me on thy flowery breast,
Earth, where thy nameless martyrs rest :

The thousands that, uncheered by praise,
Have made one offering of their days ;
For truth, for heaven, for freedom's sake,
Resigned the bitter cup to take ;
And silently, in fearless faith,
Have bowed their noble souls to death.

Where sleep they, earth? by no proud stone
Their narrow cell of rest is known;
The still, sad glory of their name
Hallows no fountain unto fame;
No, not a tree the record bears
Of their deep thoughts and lowly prayers.

Yet what if no light footstep there,
In pilgrim-love and awe repair,
And the old woods and sounding waves
Are silent of those hidden graves?
They sleep in secret, but their sod,
Unknown to man, is marked of God.

Felicia D. Hemans.

416　　　　　　　*Our guides.*　　　　　　6.4.

ALL hail, God's angel, Truth,
In whose immortal youth
　　Fresh graces shine :
To her sweet majesty,
Lord, help us bend the knee,
And all her beauty see,
　　And wealth divine.

Thanks for the names that light
The path of Truth and Right
　　And Freedom's way :
For all whose life doth prove
The might of Faith, Hope, Love,
Thousands of hearts to move,
　　A power to-day.

Thanks for the heart of Love,
Kin to thine own above,
　　Tender and brave ;

Ready to bear the cross,
To suffer pain and loss,
And earthly good count dross,
   In toils to save.

May their dear memory be
True guide, O Lord, to Thee,
   With saints of yore;
And may the work they wrought,
The truth of God they taught,
The good for man they sought,
   Spread evermore.

W. Newell.

417   *Thanks for All Saints.*   S.M.

For all thy saints, O God,
Who strove in Thee to live,
Who followed Thee, obeyed, adored,
   Our grateful hymn receive.

For all thy saints, O God,
Accept our thankful cry,
Who counted Thee their great reward,
   And yearned for Thee to die.

They all, in life and death,
With Thee, Lord, in their view,
Learned from thy Holy Spirit's breath
   To suffer and to do.

For this thy name we bless,
And humbly pray that we
May follow them in holiness,
   And live and die in Thee.

Bishop Mant.

418   *The stream of faith.*   C.M.

FROM heart to heart, from creed to creed,
    The hidden river runs ;
It quickens all the ages down,
    It binds the sires to sons,—
The stream of Faith, whose source is God,
    Whose sound, the sound of prayer,
Whose meadows are the holy lives
    Upspringing everywhere.

How deep it flowed in olden time,
    When men by it were strong
To dare the untrod wilderness,
    Charmed on by river-song ;
Where'er they passed by hill or shore,
    They gave the song a voice,
Till all the craggy land had heard
    The Father's Faith rejoice.

And still it moves, a broadening flood :
    And fresher, fuller grows
A sense as if the sea were near,
    Towards which the river flows :
O Thou, who art the secret Source
    That rises in each soul,
Thou art the Ocean too,—thy charm,
    That ever deepening roll.

                    W. C. Gannett.

419   *All Saints.*   11.11.10.10.

SING with our might and uplift our glad voices ;
Sing while the heart with thanksgiving rejoices ;
Sing of all saints spreading goodness abroad,
Prophets and holy ones, sons of the Lord.

Thanks to the Lord for his prophets and sages,
Thanks for the saints He hath raised in all ages,
Hark to their voices ;—they utter One Name ;
One Lord, one Brotherhood, one Hope proclaim.

Often forsaken and outcast and friendless,
Wounded and dying in sufferings endless,
Bear they their witness or raise their high song,
Fervent in faithfulness, patient and strong.

From age to age the glad tidings are spoken,
Shore calls to shore that the line is unbroken ;
One holy army, one glorious cry,—
On earth be peacefulness, praises on high.
J. V. Blake.

420   *All Saints.*   8.6.8.6.8.8.

O SING with loud and joyful song,
   The seers of every name ;
O sing the prophets high and true,
   And saints of sacred fame.
From age to age their voice is heard,
One solemn cry, one living word.

They come, the Lord's anointed ones,
   In every age and shore,
And ever-blessèd tidings brought,
   And holy witness bore,
Witness of Love's celestial light,
Of duty and eternal right.

O thanks that all the ages down
   The same love is outpoured ;
O thanks that every prophet-voice
. Proclaims one truth, one Lord ;
O holy throng, ye show the store
Of endless life from more to more.
J. V. Blake.

421 *All Saints.* 8s.

ONE feast, of holy days the crest,
　Unbound by creeds, we love to keep;
All Saints,—the unknown good that rest
　In God's still memory folded deep;
The bravely dumb that did their deed,
　And scorned to blot it with a name,
Men of the plain, heroic breed,
　That loved heaven's silence more than fame.

Such lived not in the past alone,
　But thread to-day the unheeding street,
And stairs to sin and famine known,
　Sing with the welcome of their feet;
The den they enter grows a shrine,
　The grimy sash an oriel burns,
Their cup of water warms like wine,
　Their speech is filled from heavenly urns.

About their lowly brow appears
　An aureole traced in tenderest light,
The rainbow-gleam of smiles through tears
　In dying eyes by them made bright,
Of souls that shivered on the edge
　Of that chill ford repassed no more,
And in their mercy felt the pledge
　And sweetness of a further shore.

J. R. Lowell.

422 *Fellowship.* L.M.

WHEREVER through the ages rise　•
The altars of self-sacrifice,
Where love its arms hath opened wide,
Or man for man has calmly died,

We see the same white wings outspread
That hovered o'er the Master's head ;
And in all lands beneath the sun
The heart affirmeth, ' Love is one.'

Up from undated time they come,
The martyr-souls of heathendom,
And to his cross and passion bring
Their fellowship of suffering.

And the great marvel of their death
To the one order witnesseth,—
Each, in his measure, but a part
Of thy unmeasured Over-Heart.

J. G. Whittier.

423 *Martyrs.* 7.6.

LET our choir new anthems raise,
    Wake the song of gladness ;
God Himself to joy and praise
    Turns the Martyrs' sadness :
Bright the day that won their crown,
    Opened heaven's bright portal,
As they laid the mortal down
    To put on the immortal.

Never flinched they from the flame,
    From the torture never ;
Vain the foeman's sharpest aim,
    Evil's best endeavour :
For by faith they saw the land
    Decked in all its glory,
Where triumphant now they stand
    With the victor's story.

Up and follow, Christian men ;
  Press through toil and sorrow ;
Spurn the night of fear, and then,
  O the glorious morrow.
Who will venture on the strife?
  Blest who first begin it ;
Who will grasp the land of life ?
  Warriors, up and win it.

J. M. Neale.

424   *Martyrs.*   6.4.

THEIR names are names of kings
  Of heavenly line ;
The pride of earthly things
  They dared resign.

They bore the Spirit's sword
  And faith's strong shield ;
They fought for God the Lord
  On many a field.

Though hard their earthly lot,
  'Mid hate and scorn,
In life regarded not,
  In death forlorn ;

Yet blest that end of woe,
  And those sad days ;
Only man's blame below ;
  Above, God's praise.

So did the life of pain
  In glory cease ;
Lord God, may we attain
  Their home of peace.

S. J. Stone.

425   *Close of the year.*   8.7.

ACROSS the sky the shades of night
　　This winter's eve are fleeting:
We deck thine house, O Lord, with light,
　　In solemn worship meeting:
And as the year's last hours go by,
We lift to Thee our earnest cry,
　　Once more thy love entreating.

Before thy mercy, Lord, we bow,
　　To Thee our prayers addressing;
Recounting all thy mercies now,
　　And all our sins confessing;
Beseeching Thee, this coming year,
To hold us in thy faith and fear,
　　And crown us with thy blessing.

And, while we kneel, we lift our eyes
　　To dear ones gone before us;
Safe housed with Thee in Paradise,
　　Their spirits hovering o'er us:
And beg of Thee, when life is past,
To re-unite us all, at last,
　　And to our lost restore us.

We gather up, in this brief hour,
　　The memory of thy mercies;
Thy wondrous goodness, love and power,
　　Our grateful song rehearses:
For Thou hast been our Strength and Stay,
In many a dark and dreary day
　　Of sorrow and reverses.

In many an hour, when fear and dread,
　　Like evil spells have bound us,
And clouds were gathering overhead,
　　Thy Providence hath found us:

In many a night when waves ran high,
Thy gracious Presence drawing nigh
　　Hath made all calm around us.

Then, O great God, in years to come,
　　Whatever fate betide us,
Right onward through our journey home
　　Be Thou at hand to guide us:
Nor leave us till, at close of life,
Safe from all perils, toil, and strife,
　　Heaven shall unfold and hide us.

J. Hamilton.

426　　　　　*Close of the year.*　　　　10.4.10.6.

ANOTHER year is swallowed by the sea
　　Of sunless waves ;
Another year, thou past eternity,
　　Hath rolled o'er new-made graves.

They open yet, to bid the living weep
　　Where tears are vain :
While they, unswept into the ruthless deep
　　Storm-tried and sad, remain.

And we are spared in love to wear away
　　By noble deeds
Vile traces, left beneath the upbraiding spray
　　Of empty shells and weeds.

But there are things which time devoureth not—
　　Thoughts whose green youth
Flowers o'er the ashes of the unforgot,
　　And words whose fruit is truth.

Are ye not imaged in the eternal sea,
  Things of to-day?
Deeds, which are harvest for eternity,
  Ye cannot pass away.

E. Elliott.

427   *The New Year.*   7s.

FOR thy mercy and thy grace,
  Constant through another year,
Hear our song of thankfulness,
  Father and Redeemer, hear.

In our weakness and distress,
  Rock of strength, be Thou our stay;
In the pathless wilderness
  Be our true and living way.

Who of us death's awful road
  In the coming year shall tread?
With thy rod and staff, O God,
  Comfort Thou his dying head.

Keep us faithful, keep us pure,
  Keep us evermore thine own;
Help, O help us to endure;
  Fit us for the promised crown.

So within thy palace gate
  We shall praise, on golden strings,
Thee, the only Potentate,
  Lord of lords, and King of kings.

H. Downton.

428   *The New Year.*   7.5.

FATHER, here we dedicate
  All this year to Thee,
In whatever worldly state
  Thou wilt have us be:

Not from sorrow, pain, or care,
　　Freedom dare we claim ;
This alone shall be our prayer,
　　' Glorify thy Name.'

Can a child presume to choose
　　Where or how to live ?
Can a Father's love refuse
　　All the best to give ?
More Thou givest every day
　　Than the best can claim,
Nor withholdest aught that may
　　Glorify thy Name.

If in mercy Thou wilt spare
　　Joys we yet partake ;
If on life, serene and fair,
　　Brighter rays may break ;
Thee our hearts, while glad they sing,
　　Shall in all proclaim,
And whate'er the future brings,
　　Glorify thy Name.

If Thou callest to the cross,
　　And its shadows come,
Turning all our gain to loss,
　　Shrouding heart and home ;
Let me think how thy dear Son
　　To his glory came,
And in deepest woe pray on,
　　' Glorify thy Name.'

　　　　　　　　　　L. Tuttiett.

429　　　　*The New Year.*　　　　7s.

BACKWARD looking o'er the past,
　　Forward, too, with eager gaze,
Stand we here to-day, O God,
　　At the parting of the ways.

Tenderest thoughts our bosoms fill ;
  Memories all bright and fair
Seem to float on spirit wings,
  Downward through the silent air.

Hark, through all their music sweet,
  Hear you not a voice of cheer?
'Tis the voice of Hope which sings,
  ' Happy be the coming year.'

Father, comes that voice from Thee,
  Swells it with thy meaning vast,
Good in all thy Future stored,
  Fairer than in all the Past.
                              J. W. Chadwick.

430   *Another year.*   C.M.

ANOTHER year of setting suns,
  Of stars by night revealed,
Of springing grass, of tender buds
  By Winter's snow concealed.

Another year of Summer's glow,
  Of Autumn's gold and brown,
Of waving fields, and ruddy fruit
  The branches weighing down.

Another year of happy work,
  That better is than play,
Of simple cares, and love that grows
  More sweet from day to day.

Another year of baby mirth,
  And childhood's blessèd ways,
Of thinker's thought, and prophet's dream,
  And poet's tender lays.

Another year at Beauty's feast,
　At every moment spread,
Of silent hours when grow distinct
　The voices of the dead.

Another year to follow hard
　Where better souls have trod,
Another year of life's delight,
　Another year of God.
J. W. Chadwick.

431　　*New Year (or Anniversary) Hymn.*　　C.M.

THE old year's long campaign is o'er,
　Behold a new begun;
Not yet is closed the holy war,
　Not yet the triumph won.
Not yet the end, not yet repose!
　We hear our Captain say,
'Go forth again to meet your foes,
　Ye children of the day.'

'Go forth, firm faith on every heart,
　Bright hope on every helm;
Through that shall pierce no fiery dart,
　And this no fear o'erwhelm.
Go in the Spirit and the might
　Of Him who led the way;
Close with the legions of the night,
　Ye children of the day.'

So forth we go to meet the strife
　We will not fear nor fly;
We love the holy warrior's life,
　His death we hope to die.
We slumber not, that charge in view,
　'Toil on while toil ye may,
Then night shall be no night to you,
　Ye children of the day.'

LORD GOD, the High and Holy One,
    Thine own sustain, defend;
And give, though dim this earthly sun,
    Thy true light to the end;
Till morning tread the darkness down,
    And night be swept away,
And infinite, sweet triumph crown
    The children of the day.

S. J. Stone.

432   *The children.*   7.6.8.6

GOD bless the little children,
    The faces sweet and fair,
The bright young eyes, so strangely wise,
    The bonny silken hair.

God love the little children,—
    The angels at the door,
The music sweet of little feet
    That patter on the floor.

God help the little children,
    Who cheer our saddest hours,
And shame our fears for future years,
    And give us winter flowers.

God keep the little children
    Whom we no more can see;
Fled from their nest and gone to rest,
    Where we desire to be.

J. P. Hopps.

433   *The little ones.*   C.M.

ALL hidden lie the future ways
    Their little feet shall fare;
But holy thoughts within us stir
    And rise on lips of prayer.

To us beneath the noonday heat,
  Dust-stained and travel-worn,
How beautiful their robes of white,
  The freshness of their morn.

Within us wakes the childlike heart,
  Back rolls the tide of years;
The silent wells of memory start
  And flow in happy tears.

O little ones, ye cannot know
  The power with which ye plead,
Nor why, as on through life we go,
  The little child doth lead.
F. L. Hosmer.

434   *Baptism.*   C.M.

In token that thou shalt not fear
  Christ crucified to own,
We print the cross upon thy brow,
  And stamp thee his alone.

In token that thou shalt not blush
  To glory in his name,
We blazon here upon thy front
  His glory and his shame.

In token that thou shalt not flinch
  Christ's quarrel to maintain,
But 'neath his banner manfully,
  Firm at thy post remain;

In token that thou, too, shalt tread
  The path He travelled by;
Endure the cross, despise the shame,
  And sit thee down on high;

Thus outwardly and visibly
We seal thee for his own ;
And may the brow that wears his cross,
Hereafter share his crown.

Dean Alford.

435   *The Good Shepherd.*   8.7.

FATHER, who thy flock art feeding,
With the shepherd's kindest care,
All the feeble gently leading,
While the lambs thy bosom share,—

Thou, our little ones receiving,
Fold them in thy gracious arm ;
There, we know,—thy word believing,—
Only there, secure from harm.

Never, from thy pasture roving,
Let them be to sin a prey ;
Let thy tenderness, so loving,
Keep them in life's doubtful way :

Then, within thy fold eternal,
Let them find a resting-place,
Feed in pastures ever vernal,
Drink the rivers of thy grace.

W. A. Muhlenberg.

436   *Baptism.*   S.M.

To Thee, O God in heaven,
This little one we bring ;
Giving to Thee what Thou hast given,
Our dearest offering.

Into a world of toil
These little feet will roam,
Where sin its purity may soil,
Where care and grief may come,

O then, let thy pure love,
With influence serene,
Come down, like water, from above,
To comfort and make clean.

J. F. Clarke.

437   *Baptism.*   S.M.

To Him who children blessed,
And suffered them to come,—
To Him who took them to his breast
We bring these children home.

To Thee, O God, whose face
Their spirits still behold,
We bring them, praying that thy grace
May keep, thine arms enfold.

And as this water falls
On each unconscious brow,
Thy Holy Spirit grant, O Lord,
To keep them pure as now.

J. F. Clarke.

438   *Baptism.*   L.M.

THE very blossoms of our life,
The treasures that no wealth could buy,
We freely bring them here to-day
And give them up to Thee, Most High.

Not, as in olden times, to death,
To hermit life, or darksome days ;
But unto beauty, goodness, truth,
To all high thoughts and noble ways.

To find and serve Thee in the world,
By seeking truth and helping men,—
To this we consecrate them now,
And day by day will o'er again.

Thus do we keep them while we give,
  And make them still of nobler worth.
When all the world is given thus,
  Heaven will indeed have come on earth.

M. J. Savage.

439   *Baptism.*   7.4.

STANDING forth on life's rough way,
  Father, guide them ;
O we know not what of harm
  May betide them ;
'Neath the shadow of thy wing,
  Father, hide them ;
Waking, sleeping, Lord, we pray,
  Go beside them.

When in prayer they cry to Thee,
  Thou wilt hear them :
From the stains of sin and shame
  Thou wilt clear them ;
'Mid the quicksands and the rocks,
  Thou wilt steer them ;
In temptation, trial, grief,
  Be Thou near them.

Unto Thee we give them up,
  Lord, receive them ;
In the world we know must be
  Much to grieve them,
Many striving oft and strong
  To deceive them :
Trustful, in thy hands of love
  We must leave them.

W. C. Bryant.

440   *Confirmation.*   8.7.

FATHER, look upon thy children,
   Who before thy footstool bow,
Coming as thy sons and daughters
   To renew their solemn vow.

Thou who knowest all our weakness,
   Strengthen us with heavenly might,
Temples of thy Holy Spirit,
   Fill us with its life and light.

Fill us with all understanding,
   Give us wisdom from above,
All the powers of ill to vanquish,
   Strong in faith, and hope, and love.

Give to us all heavenly knowledge,
   Fill us with thy holy fear;
With hushed spirits, yet as children,
   For thy blessing we draw near.

Set thy holy seal upon us,
   Write upon us thy new name;
Guide us wheresoe'er Christ leadeth,
   Undefiled and free from blame.

Steadfast to the end enduring,
   May we win the blest reward,
Even an abundant entrance
   To the kingdom of our Lord.
                      Esther A. Wiglesworth.

441   *Confirmation.*   8.7.

HOLY Father, Thou hast taught me
   I should live to Thee alone;
Year by year thy hand hath brought me
   On through dangers oft unknown;

When I wandered Thou hast found me ;
　When I doubted, sent me light ;
Still thine arm has been around me,
　All my paths were in thy sight.

In the world will foes assail me,
　Craftier, stronger far than I ;
But thine aid will never fail me,
　While on Thee I shall rely :
Therefore, Lord, I come, believing
　Thou canst give the power I need,
Through the prayer of faith receiving
　Strength,—the Spirit's strength indeed.

I would trust in thy protecting,
　Wholly rest upon thine arm,
Follow wholly thy directing,
　Thou mine only guard from harm.
Keep me from my own undoing,
　Help me turn to Thee when tried ;
Still my footsteps, Father, viewing,
　Keep me ever at thy side.

Anon.

442 *Confirmation.* 7s.

HAPPY who in early youth,
　While yet pure and innocent,
Stores his mind with heavenly truth,
　Life's unfading ornament.

Happy who in tender years
　Leans on God for his support ;
Who life's bark in virtue steers,
　That it reach salvation's port.

Guide, O guide this hopeful band,
 Father, in thy truth and light ;
May these children ever stand
 Firm in goodness and in right.

Thine, O God, these souls are thine,
 Undefiled they came from Thee ;
Guide them in thy love divine,
 Heirs of immortality.

J. K. Gutheim.

443   *Confirmation.*   L.M.

Go forth to life, O child of earth,
Still mindful of thy heavenly birth ;
Thou art not here for ease, or sin,
But manhood's noble crown to win.

Though passion's fires are in thy soul,
Thy spirit can their flames control ;
Though tempters strong beset thy way,
Thy spirit is more strong than they.

Go on from innocence of youth
To manly pureness, manly truth ;
God's angels still are near to save,
And God Himself doth help the brave.

Then forth to life, O child of earth,
Be worthy of thy heavenly birth ;
For noble service thou art here ;
Thy brothers help, thy God revere.

S. Longfellow.

444   *Holy Communion.*   7s

WHEN the paschal evening fell
Deep on Kedron's hallowed dell,
When around the festal board
Sate the apostles with their Lord,

Then his parting word He said,
Blessed the cup and broke the bread—
'This whene'er ye do or see,
Evermore remember Me.'

Years have passed : in every clime,
Changing with the changing time,
Varying through a thousand forms,
Torn by factions, rocked by storms,
Still the sacred table spread,
Flowing cup and broken bread,
With that parting word agree,
'Drink and eat ; remember Me.'

When by treason, doubt, unrest,
Sinks the soul, dismayed, oppressed ;
When the shadows of the tomb
Close us round with deepening gloom ;
Then bethink us at that board
Of the sorrowing, suffering Lord,
Who, when tried and grieved as we,
Dying, said, ' Remember Me.'

When in this thanksgiving feast
We would give to God our best,
From the treasures of his might
Seeking life and love and light ;
Then, O Friend of human-kind,
Make us true and firm of mind,
Pure of heart, in spirit free ;
Then may we remember Thee.

Dean Stanley.

445   *Holy Communion.*   C.M.

O HERE, if ever, God of love,
  Let strife and hatred cease ;
And every heart harmonious move,
  And every thought be peace.

Not here, where met to think of Him
  Whose latest thoughts were ours,
Shall mortal passions come to dim
  The prayer devotion pours.

No, gracious Master, not in vain
  Thy life of love hath been ;
The peace Thou gav'st may yet remain,·
  Though Thou no more art seen.

' Thy kingdom come : ' we watch, we wait,
  To hear thy cheering call,
When heaven shall ope its glorious gate,
  And God be all in all.

Emily Taylor.

446   -   *One in Christ.*   C.M.

A HOLY air is breathing round,
  A fragrance from above ;
Be every soul from sense unbound,
  Be every spirit love.

O God, unite us heart to heart,
  In sympathy divine ;
That we be never drawn apart,
  And love not Thee or thine ;

But, by the cross of Jesus taught,
  And all thy gracious word,
Be nearer to each other brought,
  And nearer to the Lord.

So may thy kingdom come, with grace
  In every heart of man ;
Thy peace and joy and righteousness
  In all our bosoms reign :

The kingdom of established peace,
  Which can no more remove ;
The perfect power of holiness,
  The omnipotence of Love.

A. A. Livermore.

447   *The bond of love.*   C.M.

BENEATH the shadow of the cross,
  As earthly hopes remove,
His new commandment Jesus gives,—
  His blessèd word of love.

O bond of union, strong and deep,
  O bond of perfect peace !
Not e'en the lifted cross can harm,
  If we but hold to this.

Then, Jesus, be thy Spirit ours,
  And swift our feet shall move
To deeds of pure self-sacrifice,
  And the sweet tasks of love.

S. Longfellow.

448   *God a Refuge.*   8s.

FORTH from the dark and stormy sky,
Lord, to thine altar's shade we fly :
Forth from the world, its hope and fear,
Father, we seek thy shelter here :
Weary and weak, thy grace we pray,
Turn not, O Lord, thy guests away.

Long have we roamed in want and pain ;
Long have we sought thy rest in vain ;

'Wildered in doubt, in darkness lost,
Long have our souls been tempest-tossed;
Low at thy feet our sins we lay;
Turn not, O Lord, thy guests away.

Bishop Heber.

449　　　*One Fold and One Shepherd.*　　　7.6.

Now is the time approaching,
　By prophets long foretold,
When all shall dwell together,
　One Shepherd and one fold.
Now, Jew and Gentile, meeting
　From many a distant shore,
Around one altar kneeling,
　One common Lord adore.

Let all that now divides us
　Remove and pass away,
Like shadows of the morning
　Before the blaze of day.
Let all that now unites us
　More sweet and lasting prove,
A closer bond of union
　In a blest land of love.

O long-expected dawning,
　Come with thy cheering ray:
Then shall the morning brighten,
　The shadows flee away.
O sweet anticipation,
　It cheers the watchers on
To pray and hope and labour
　Till the dark night be gone.

Jane Borthwick.

450   *Holy Communion.*   C.M.

' No, not for these alone I pray,'
   The dying Master said ;
Though on his breast that moment lay
   The loved disciple's head ;

Though to his eye that moment sprung
   The kind, the pitying tear
For those that eager round Him hung,
   His words of love to hear.

No, not for these alone, He prayed ;
   For all of mortal race,
Whene'er their fervent prayer is made,
   Where'er their dwelling-place.

Sweet is the thought, when thus we meet
   His feast of love to share ;
And 'mid the toils of life, how sweet
   The memory of his prayer.
                       Emily Taylor.

451   *Holy Communion.*   C.M.

WE gather to the sacred board,
   Perchance a scanty band ;
But with us in sublime accord
   What mighty armies stand.

In creed and rite howe'er apart,
   One Master still we own,
And pour the worship of the heart
   Before our Father's throne.

A thousand spires o'er hill and vale
   Point to the same blue heaven ;
A thousand voices tell the tale
   Of grace through Jesus given.

High choirs, in Europe's ancient fanes,
   Praise Him for man who died ;
And o'er the boundless Western plains
   His name is glorified.

Around his tomb, on Salem's height,
   Greek and Armenian bend ;
And through all Lapland's months of night
   The peasants' hymns ascend.

Are we not brethren, Master dear ?
   Then may we walk in love,
Joint subjects of thy kingdom here,
   Joint heirs of bliss above.
                      S. G. Bulfinch.

452   *Communion Hymn.*   C.M.

'REMEMBER Me,' the Master said,
   On that forsaken night,
When from his side the nearest fled,
   And death was close in sight.

Through all the following ages' track,
   The world remembers yet ;
With love and worship gazes back,
   And never can forget.

But none of us has seen his face,
   Or heard the words He said ;
And none can now his looks retrace
   In breaking of the bread.

O blest are they who have not seen,
   And yet believe Him still ;
They know Him, when his praise they mean,
   And when they do his will.

We hear his word along our way;
  We see his light above;
Remember when we strive and pray,
  Remember when we love.

N. L. Frothingham.

53   *Marriage.*   7.6.

O Love divine and golden,
  Mysterious depth and height,
To Thee the world beholden,
  Looks up for life and light;
O Love divine and gentle,
  The blesser and the blest,
Beneath whose care parental
  The world lies down in rest.

The fields of earth adore Thee,
  The forests sing thy praise,
All living things before Thee
  Their holiest anthems raise:
Thou art the joy of gladness;
  The Life of life Thou art;
The dew of gentle sadness,
  That droppeth on the heart.

O Love divine and tender,
  That through our homes doth move,
Veiled in the softened splendour
  Of holy household love,
A throne without thy blessing,
  Were labour without rest,
And cottages possessing
  Thy blessedness, are blest.

God bless these hands united,
　　God bless these hearts made one;
Unsevered and unblighted
　　May they, through life, go on:
Here, in earth's home, preparing
　　For the bright Home above;
And there, for ever sharing
　　Its joy, where 'God is love.'

J. S. B. Monsell.

454　　　*Marriage Hymn.*　　　7s.

FATHER, in thy presence now
Has been pledged the nuptial vow;
Heart to heart, as hand in hand,
Linked in one thy children stand.

God of love, this union bless,
With earth's purest happiness;
With those joys whose heavenly spring
Shall diviner raptures bring.

May these blended souls be found
Firm in duty's active round;
Daily every burden share,
Nightly seek thy shadowing care.

When against their trembling forms
Shoot the arrows of life's storms;
Or when age or sickness waits
Herald at life's parting gates;

In the fulness of belief,
May they look beyond the grief;
And together fearless tread
In the path where Thou shalt lead.

455 *Golden Wedding.* 7.6.8.6.

Two summer streams were flowing
    Bright in the morning sun,
And in their course, with gentle force,
    They mingled into one.

Now flows the blended river
    Beneath the western sky,
And manifold the hues of gold
    Calm on its bosom lie.

So, friends beloved and honoured,
    Your stream of life has flowed,
And now may rest upon its breast
    The golden peace of God.

Warm hearts are beating round you ;
    And in our fervent song,
Here do we pray, your closing day
    May linger late and long ;

That warmest benedictions
    May soothe its latest stage,
And wreathe with flowers of summer hours
    The snowy crown of age ;

Till, clothed in wedding garments,
    You stand before the throne,
Whence cometh down the bridal crown,
    And the sweet voice, 'Well done.'
                                        E. H. Sears.

456 *Ordination Hymn.* C.M.

O GOD, thy children, gathered here,
    Thy blessing now we wait ;
·Thy servants, girded for their work,
    Stand at the temple's gate.

A holy purpose in their hearts
  Has deepened calm and still;
Now from their childhood's Nazareth
  They come to do thy will.

O Father, keep their souls alive
  To every hope of good;
And may their lives of love proclaim
  Man's truest brotherhood.

O Father, keep their spirits quick
  To every form of wrong;
And in the ear of sin and self
  May their rebukes be strong.

O give them, in thy holy work,
  Patience to wait thy time,
And, toiling still with man, to breathe
  The soul's serener clime.

And grant them many hearts to lead
  Into thy perfect rest;
Bless Thou them, Father, and their work;
  Bless and they shall be blest.

S. Longfellow.

457   *The fathers' House of God.*   C.M.

WE love the venerable house
  Our fathers built to God:
In heaven are kept their grateful vows;
  Their dust endears the sod.

Here holy thoughts a light have shed
  From many a radiant face,
And prayers of humble virtue made
  The perfume of the place.

And anxious hearts have pondered here
  The mystery of life,
And prayed the eternal Light to clear
  Their doubts, and aid their strife.

From humble tenements around
  Came up the pensive train,
And in the church a blessing found,
  That filled their homes again.

For faith, and peace, and mighty love,
  That from the Godhead flow,
Showed them the life of heaven above
  Springs from the life below.

They live with God, their homes are dust;
  Yet here their children pray,
And in this fleeting life-time trust
  To find the narrow way.

On him who by the altar stands,
  On him thy blessing fall;
Speak through his lips thy pure commands,
  Thou Heart, that lovest all.
                   R. W. Emerson.

458   *Dedication Hymn.*   L.M.

O GOD, accept the gift we bring,
  This house of prayer at last complete;
Now as a grateful offering
  We gladly lay it at thy feet.

All was thine own ere it was ours,
  And since 'tis ours, 'tis thine the more,
For we are thine, and all our powers,
  O Thou, our Life, whom we adore.

Long be these walls a loving home,
　Where rich and poor shall brothers be ;
Where strife and envy may not come ;
　Where all may dwell in charity.

Long be this spot a sacred place,
　Where burdened hearts shall meet to pray,
Look upward to a Father's face,
　And find their burdens melt away.

This church we dedicate to Light,
　To Light of Truth and Light of Love,
To Hope, to Faith, to Prayer, to Right,
　To man on earth, to God above.

As shines the lighthouse by the sea
　To guide the sailor on his way,
So may this church a beacon be
　To light man onward toward the day.

J. T. Sunderland.

459　　　*Dedication Hymn.*　　　8s.

To Light, that shines in stars and souls,
To Law, that rounds the world with calm,
To Love, whose equal triumph rolls
Through martyr's prayer and angel's psalm,—
We wed these walls with unseen bands,
In holier shrines not made with hands.

May purer sacrament be here
Than ever dwelt in rite or creed ;
Hallowed the hour with vow sincere
To serve the time's all-pressing need,
And rear, its heaving seas above,
Strongholds of freedom, folds of love.

Here be the wanderer homeward led,
Here living streams in fulness flow,
And every hungering soul be fed,
That yearns the Eternal Will to know,
Here conscience hurl her stern reply
To mammon's lust and slavery's lie.

Speak, Living God, thy full command
Through prayer of faith and word of power,
That we with girded loins may stand
To do thy work and wait thine hour,
And sow, 'mid patient toils and tears
For harvests in serener years.

S. Johnson.

460　　　　*All things are thine.*　　　　L.M.

ALL things are thine : no gift have we,
Lord of all gifts, to offer Thee ;
And hence with grateful hearts to-day,
Thy own before thy feet we lay.

Thy will was in the builders' thought ;
Thy hand unseen amidst us wrought ;
Through mortal motive, scheme and plan,
Thy wise eternal purpose ran.

No lack thy perfect fulness knew ;
From human needs and longings grew
This house of prayer, this home of rest
In the fair garden of the West.

In weakness and in want we call
On Thee for whom the heavens are small ;
Thy glory is thy children's good,
Thy joy thy tender Fatherhood.

O Father, deign these walls to bless;
Fill with thy love their emptiness:
And let their door a gateway be
To lead us from ourselves to Thee.

J. G. Whittier.

461 *Dedication Festival.* L.M.

O THOU, whose liberal sun and rain
Come not upon the earth in vain,
Now let thy quickening word come down
The worship of this hour to crown.

O hear this church renew its vow,
Its solemn consecration now,
To work, with heart and soul and might,
For truth and freedom, love and right;

To listen with a willing faith
To whatsoe'er the Spirit saith,
And year by year to be more true
To Him who maketh all things new.

S. Longfellow.

462 *Harvest Thanksgiving.* 8s.

LORD of the harvest, Thee we hail;
Thine ancient promise doth not fail;
The varying seasons haste their round;
With goodness all our years are crowned;
  Our thanks we pay
  This holy day;
O let our hearts in tune be found.

If Spring doth wake the song of mirth;
If Summer warm the fruitful earth;

When Winter sweeps the naked plain,
Or Autumn yields its ripened grain ;
 Still do we sing
 To Thee, our King ;
Through all their changes Thou dost reign.

But chiefly when thy liberal hand
Scatters new plenty o'er the land,
When sounds of music fill the air,
As homeward all their treasures bear ;
 We too will raise
 Our hymn of praise,
For we thy common bounties share.

Lord of the harvest, all is thine,—
The rains that fall, the suns that shine,
The seed once hidden in the ground,
The skill that makes our fruits abound.
 New, every year,
 Thy gifts appear ;
New praises from our lips shall sound.
J. H. Gurney.

463   *Harvest Festival.*   7.6.

 Lord of the silent winter,
  Beneath whose skies of gray
 The frost-bound fields lie cheerless,
  But wait a brighter day :
 If human hearts are dreary,
  By mists of sorrow chilled,
 Give patience to the weary,
  Till they with peace be filled.

 Lord of the joyous spring-time,
  When leaves and buds appear,
 And lengthening days of beauty
  Renew the softened year.

Breathe on our hearts in blessing ;
  Away our sadness roll ;
And send, all pain redressing,
  A spring-time to the soul.

Lord of the glowing summer,
  When waves the corn on high,
And fruits in valleys ripen
  Beneath a cloudless sky ;
Shine on our hearts' endeavour
  To give our strength to Thee,
That in our spirits ever
  A richer life may be.

Lord of the bounteous autumn,
  When vineyards yield their store,
And golden sheaves, new-gathered,
  Pass to the garner door :
Grant now a full fruition
  To every seed of truth,
Which fell, with blessed mission,
  Upon our souls in youth.

Lord of the changing seasons,
  Lord of our passing days,
Wake Thou in us abundance
  Of duty, love, and praise :
That hearts of wintry sadness
  May feel the breath of spring,
And summer's time of gladness
  The autumn glories bring.

D. Agate.

464   *The year of the Lord.*   7s.

PRAISE to God and thanksgiving !
Hearts, bow down, and voices, sing !
Praises to the Glorious One,
All his year of wonder done !

Praise Him for his budding green,
April's resurrection-scene :
Praise Him for his shining hours,
Starring all the land with flowers :

Praise Him for his summer rain,
Feeding, day and night, the grain :
Praise Him for his tiny seed,
Holding all his world shall need :

Praise Him for his garden root,
Meadow grass and orchard fruit :
Praise for hills and valleys broad,
Each the Table of the Lord :

Praise Him now for snowy rest,
Falling soft on Nature's breast :
Praise for happy dreams of birth
Brooding in the quiet earth :

For his year of wonder done,
Praise to the All-Glorious One :
Hearts, bow down, and voices, sing
Praise and love and thanksgiving.

W. C. Gannett.

465   *Thanksgiving in harvest.*   7.6.

WE plough the fields, and scatter
    The good seed on the land,
But it is fed and watered
    By God's Almighty hand ;
He sends the snow in winter,
    The warmth to swell the grain,
The breezes and the sunshine,
    And soft refreshing rain,

All good gifts around us
  Are sent from heaven above,
Then thank the Lord, O thank the Lord,
  For all his love.

He only is the Maker
  Of all things near and far;
He paints the wayside flower,
  He lights the evening star;
The winds and waves obey Him,
  By Him the birds are fed;
Much more to us, his children,
  He gives our daily bread.
    All good gifts around us
      Are sent from heaven above,
    Then thank the Lord, O thank the Lord,
      For all his love.

We thank Thee then, O Father,
  For all things bright and good,
The seed-time and the harvest,
  Our life, our health, our food;
Accept the gifts we offer
  For all thy love imparts,
And, what Thou most desirest,
  Our humble, thankful hearts.
    All good gifts around us
      Are sent from heaven above,
    Then thank the Lord, O thank the Lord,
      For all his love.
          M. Claudius, tr. Jane M. Campbell.

466   *Harvest.*   C.M.

WE own thy hand, O God, in all
  The wide-spread harvest-yield,
The loving-kindness that has crowned
  Our garden and our field.

We bless Thee for our sheltered homes,
  With their affections true,
With all their wealth of social joy,
  And scope thy work to do;

For all that tends to spirit-growth
  And larger liberty,
Anoints our eyes to clearer sight,
  And holds us nearer Thee;
For all that makes thy comfort dear,
  That brings us strength and grace,
And aids us, e'en through clouds, to see
  The shining of thy face.

We bless Thee for the tiny feet
  That walk beside us here;
For childhood's merry music sweet
  Its trust that knows no fear;
And for the little ones who stayed
  Within our homes awhile,
And left with us the angel-grace
  Of parting word and smile.

Not for our pain, our breaking hearts,
  O God, we cannot bring
Our thanks for these, but, over all,
  The shadow of thy wing.
Thou hast not left our souls alone;
  In ways unknown, unsought,
Thy love sustaining power hath shown,
  Its nameless comfort brought.

That they have lived, we thank Thee, Lord,
  That they are still our own;
And thin the veil that hides from us
  The glory round them thrown,

The glory of thy gift and grace,
  That now, with clasping hand,
We walk within, and see thy face
  And need not understand;

That not afar doth lie their home,
  Nor ever change their love;
Our Father's mansions hold us all,
  Though seeming to remove.
Thanks for our sweet home-gatherings, Lord,
  Our cup that runneth o'er;
For the communion of thy saints
  We bless Thee even more.

We bless Thee for our faith and hope,
  The promise Thou hast given,
And for the glorious Harvest Home
  That waits for us in heaven.
For Him who came that home to point,
  To lead the living way,
The child in Bethlehem's manger born,
  We thank Thee most to-day.
                              Mary Johnson.

467   *In time of dearth.*   7s.

Thou that sendest sun and rain,
  Ruling over land and sea,
May we ne'er of Thee complain,
  Whatsoe'er our lot may be.

Whether sun or rain in turn
  Ripen or destroy the grain,
May we still this lesson learn,
  Ne'er to murmur or complain.

Fewer flocks or fewer herds,
  Scanty though our store may be,
Still we seem to hear thy words,
  'Trust, ye faithful, trust in Me.'

All we have we know is thine,
  Thine to give and take away;
Feed us then with food divine,
  Feed us this and every day.

Thus, as changeful seasons bring
  Wealth or want, whiche'er it be,
Uncomplaining still we'll sing,
  Simply trusting all to Thee.

G. Thring.

468   *Flower Service.*   11.10.

HERE, Lord, we offer Thee all that is fairest,
  Bloom from the garden and flowers from the
    field,
Gifts for the stricken ones, knowing Thou carest
  More for the love than the wealth that we yield.

Send, Lord, by these to the sick and the dying,
  Speak to their hearts with a message of peace,
Comfort the sad who in weakness are lying,
  Grant the departing a gentle release.

Raise, Lord, to health again those who have
    sickened,
  Fair be their lives as the roses in bloom :
Give of thy grace to the souls Thou hast quickened
  Gladness for sorrow and brightness for gloom.

We, Lord, like flowers, must bloom and must
    wither ;
We, like these blossoms, must fade and must die ;
Gather us, Lord, to thy bosom for ever,
    Grant us a place in thy house in the sky.

A. G. W. Blunt.

469   *For those at sea.*   8.7.8.4.

STAR of peace to wanderers weary,
    Bright the beams that smile on me :
Cheer the pilot's vision dreary,
    Far, far at sea.

Star of hope, gleam on the billow ;
    Bless the soul that sighs for thee :
Bless the sailor's lonely pillow,
    Far, far at sea.

Star of faith, when winds are mocking
    All his toil, he flies to thee ;
Save him on the billows rocking,
    Far, far at sea.

Star divine, O safely guide him ;
    Bring the wanderer home to thee ;
Sore temptations long have tried him,
    Far, far at sea.

Jane Cross Simpson.

470   *His wonders in the deep.*   6.6.8.4.

O THOU who didst prepare
    The ocean's caverned cell,
And teach the gathering waters there
    To meet and dwell :

Tossed in our reeling bark
Upon the treacherous sea,
Thy wondrous ways, O Lord, we mark,
And sing to Thee.

How terrible art Thou,
In all thy wonders shown ;
Though veiled is thine eternal brow,
Thy steps unknown :
Invisible to sight—
But O to faith how near—
Beneath the gloomiest cloud of night
Thou shinest here.

To peaceful rest we go,
And close our tranquil eyes,
Though deep beneath the waters flow,
And circling rise.
Though swells the flowing tide,
And threatens far above,
We know in whom our souls confide
With fearless love.

Snatched from a darker deep
And waves of wilder foam,
Thou, Lord, our trusting souls wilt keep,
And waft them home :
Home where no storm can sound,
Nor angry waters roar,
Nor troublous billows heave around
That peaceful shore.

Charlotte E. Tonna.

471   *Ibi festivitas sine fine.*   **L.M.**

'Tis thus we press the hand and part,
Thus have we bid farewell again ;
Yet still we commune, heart with heart,
Linked by a never-broken chain.

Still one in life and one in death,
　One in our hope of rest above;
One in our joy, our trust, our faith,
　One in each other's faithful love.

Yet must we part, and parting, weep;
　What else has earth for us in store?
These farewell pangs, how sharp and deep;
　These farewell words, how sad and sore.

Yet shall we meet again in peace,
　To sing the song of festal joy,
Where none shall bid our gladness cease,
　And none our fellowship destroy;

Where none shall beckon us away,
　Nor bid our festival be done;
Our meeting-time the eternal day,
　Our meeting-place the eternal throne.

Then, hand in hand, firm linked at last,
　And, heart to heart, enfolded all,
We'll smile upon the troubled past,
　And wonder why we wept at all.

Then let us press the hand and part,
　The dearly loved, the fondly loving,
Still, still in spirit and in heart,
　The undivided, unremoving.

H. Bonar.

472　　　*Farewell service.*　　　6.6.8.4.

　With the sweet word of peace
　　We bid our brethren go;
　Peace, as a river to increase,
　　And ceaseless flow.

With the calm word of prayer
We earnestly commend
Our brethren to thy watchful care,
　　Eternal Friend.

With the dear word of love
We give our brief farewell :
Our love below, and thine above,
　　With them shall dwell.

With the strong word of faith
We stay ourselves on Thee :
That Thou, O Lord, in life and death
　　Their help shalt be.

Then the bright word of hope
Shall on our parting gleam,　.
And tell of joys beyond the scope
　　Of earth-born dream.

Farewell, in hope, and love,
In faith, and peace, and prayer,
Till He whose home is ours above
　　Unite us there.
　　　　　　　　　　G. Watson.

473　　　　　　*Our country.*　　　　6.4.

GOD bless our native land ;
Firm may she ever stand
　　Through storm and night :
When the wild tempests rave,
Ruler of wind and wave,
Do Thou our country save,
　　By thy great might.

For her our prayers shall be,
Our fathers' God, to Thee ;
　　On Thee we wait :

Be her walls Holiness;
Her rulers, Righteousness;
Her officers be Peace;
God save the State.

Lord of all truth and right,
In whom alone is might,
On Thee we call :
Give us prosperity;
Give us true liberty;
May all the oppressed go free;
God save us all.

C. T. Brooks and J. S. Dwight.

474   *National Hymn.*   L.M.

PRAISE to our God, whose bounteous hand
Prepared of old our glorious land;
A garden fenced with silver sea;
A people prosperous, bold, and free.

Praise to our God; through all our past
His mighty arm hath held us fast;
Till wars and perils, toils and tears,
Have brought the rich and peaceful years.

Praise to our God; the vine He set
Within our coasts is fruitful yet;
On many a shore her seedlings grow;
'Neath many a sun her clusters glow.

Praise to our God; his power alone
Can keep unmoved our ancient throne,
Sustained by counsels wise and just,
And guarded by a people's trust.

Praise to our God; though chastenings stern
Our evil dross should throughly burn;
His rod and staff, from age to age,
Shall rule and guide his heritage.

J. Ellerton.

INDEX OF FIRST LINES.

	HYMN
A fitly spoken word	323
A holy air is breathing round	446
A thousand years have come and gone	47
A voice by Jordan's shore	35
A voice upon the midnight air	68
Abide with me; fast falls the eventide	22
Across the sky the shades of night	425
Again, as evening's shadow falls	21
Ah, why should bitter tears be shed	404
All are architects of fate	345
All around us, fair with flowers	346
All as God wills, who wisely heeds	296
All before us lies the way	221
All hail, God's angel, Truth	416
All hidden lie the future ways	433
All that's good, and great, and true	116
All things are thine; no gift have we	460
Alone, to land alone upon that shore	384
Angels holy, high and lowly	119
Another hand is beckoning us	405
Another year is swallowed by the sea	426
Another year of setting suns	430
Art thou weary, art thou languid	55
As darker, darker, fall around	20
As shadows, cast by cloud and sun	46
Ask and receive,—'tis sweetly said	148
At first I prayed for Light	233
Awake our souls, away our fears	356
Backward looking o'er the past	429
Beneath the shadow of the cross	447
Beside the shore of Galilee	52
Blessed be thy name for ever	117
Breathe on me, Breath of God	87
Brief life is here our portion	374
Brother, hast thou wandered far	217
Brother, the angels say	403
Call the Lord thy sure salvation	208
Calm me, my God, and keep me calm	252
Calm, on the listening ears of night	41

	HYMN
Christian, seek not yet repose	344
City of God, how broad and far	361
Clear in memory's silent reaches	411
Come, labour on	329
Come, O Thou Traveller unknown	247
Come, Thou Holy Spirit, come	84
Come unto Me, ye weary	53
Commit thou all thy griefs	294
Courage, brother; do not stumble	343
Dark is the sky that overhangs my soul	295
Dear Lord and Father of mankind	253
Descend to thy Jerusalem, O Lord	63
Easter flowers, Easter carols	81
Eternal Life, whose love divine	353
Eternal Ruler of the ceaseless round	246
Evensong is hushed in silence	19
Every day hath toil and trouble	342
Fairer grows the earth each morning	130
Farewell, brother; deep and lowly	398
Father Almighty, bless us with thy blessing	93
Father and Friend, thy light, thy love	113
Father, give thy benediction	32
Father, hear the prayer we offer	244
Father, here we dedicate	428
Father, I am so weak	293
Father, I know that all my life	292
Father in heaven, thy dwelling-place	147
Father, in thy mysterious presence kneeling	243
Father, in thy presence now	454
Father, let thy kingdom come	273
Father, look upon thy children	440
Father, now the day is over	11
Father, O hear us, seeking now to praise Thee	120
Father Omnipotent, joyful and thankful	82
Father Supreme, Thou high and holy one	18
Father, the sweetest, dearest name	102
Father, Thou art calling, calling to us plainly	172
Father, thy wonders do not singly stand	184
Father, to Thee we look in all our sorrow	291
Father, who thy flock art feeding	435
Firm, in the maddening maze of things	289
For all thy saints, O God	417
For ever with the Lord	369
For the beauty of the earth	124
For the dear love that kept us through the night	5
For thy mercy and thy grace	427
Forth from the dark and stormy sky	448
From heart to heart, from creed to creed	418
From the eternal shadow rounding	414
From the recesses of a lowly spirit	241
Go down, great sun, into thy golden west	17
Go forth to life, O child of earth	443
Go not far from me, O my God	287
Go not, my soul, in search of Him	98
God bless our native land	473

	HYMN
God bless the little children	432
God draws a cloud over each gleaming morn	74
God Eternal, changing never	240
God giveth quietness at last	396
God is love; his mercy brightens	228
God is near thee, therefore cheer thee	216
God moves in a mysterious way	215
God of ages and of nations	183
God of the earnest heart	214
God of the earth, the sky, the sea	121
God of the living, in whose eyes	391
God of Truth, thy sons should be	326
God's trumpet wakes the slumbering world	340
Gracious Father, hear our prayer	239
Gracious Power, the world pervading	128
Gracious Spirit, dwell with me	86
Hail, sacred day of earthly rest	1
Hand in hand with angels	402
Happy soul, that free from harms	255
Happy who in early youth	442
Hark, hark, my soul; angelic songs are swelling	382
Hark the glad sound! the Saviour comes	33
Hast thou, 'midst life's empty noises	339
Have you heard the golden city	362
He cometh not a king to reign	178
He hides within the lily	181
He is gone—beyond the skies	83
He knows the bitter, weary way	276
He leads us on	213
He liveth long who liveth well	338
He prayeth well who loveth well	337
He whom the Master loved has truly spoken	302
Heir of all the ages, I	182
Help me, my God, to speak	150
Here is the sorrow, the sighing	375
Here, Lord, we offer Thee all that is fairest	468
Holy Father, Thou hast taught me	441
Holy Father, who this day	16
Holy Spirit, Truth divine	89
Hope on, hope on, the golden days	320
How happy is he born or taught	322
How pleasant are thy paths, O Death	385
How shall come thy kingdom holy	272
How shalt thou bear the cross that now	167
I bless Thee, Lord, for sorrows sent	280
I cannot find Thee. Still on restless pinion	105
I cannot think of them as dead	410
I do not ask, O Lord, that life may be	285
I have no comfort but thy love	223
I hear it often in the dark	191
I heard the voice of Jesus say	54
I know not if the dark or bright	309
I little see, I little know	308
I live for those who love me	336
I long for household voices gone	288
I look to Thee in every need	304
I pray to know thy peace	144

HYMN

I read of many mansions 199
I saw the beauty of the world 107
I wake this morn, and all my life 8
I was wandering and weary 58
I worship Thee, sweet will of God 145
If only God I have 146
Immortal by their deed and word 48
Immortal, invisible, God only wise 109
Immortal Love, for ever full 177
Immortal Love, within whose righteous will 254
In quiet hours the tranquil soul 256
In the bitter waves of woe 162
In the cross of Christ I glory 65
In the hour of my distress 85
In the old time, runs the story 40
In Thee my powers, my treasures live 360
In this world, the Isle of dreams 380
In token that thou shalt not fear 434
In trouble and in grief, O God 307
Infinite Spirit, who art round us ever 200
It came upon the midnight clear 39
It fell upon a summer day 51
It is finished—all the pain 71
It is finished! Man of sorrows 72
It singeth low in every heart 408

Jerusalem, my happy home 376
Jerusalem, the golden 379
Jesu, Lover of my soul 310
Jesus, by thy simple beauty 49
Jews were wrought to cruel madness 70

Knocking, knocking! who is there 59

Lead, kindly Light, amid the encircling gloom . . . 264
Let all men know, that all men move 226
Let me count my treasures 242
Let my life be hid in Thee 198
Let no hopeless tears be shed 399
Let our choir new anthems raise 423
Let saints on earth in concert sing 390
Let the merry church-bells ring 80
Let the whole creation cry 110
Let us with a gladsome mind 111
Life of Ages, richly poured 192
Life of our life, and Light of all our seeing . . . 157
Live for something; be not idle 351
Lo, we stand before Thee now 126
Long did I toil, and knew no earthly rest 225
Long, long ago, in manger low 38
Look from thy sphere of endless day 274
Lord God Almighty 108
Lord God, by whom all change is wrought 348
Lord God of morning and of night 6
Lord, I hear of showers of blessing 270
Lord, in this sacred hour 4
Lord of all being, throned afar 112
Lord of might and Lord of glory 154
Lord of power, Lord of might 10

	HYMN
Lord of the harvest, Thee we hail	462
Lord of the silent winter	463
Lord, to live life again	409
Lord, when through sin I wander	149
Love for all; and can it be	218
Lowly and solemn be	397
Many things in life there are	306
Men whose boast it is, that ye	170
My God, how wonderful Thou art	96
My God, I rather look to Thee	250
My God, my Father, while I stray	305
My God, why dost Thou longer stay	222
My song and city is	381
Mysterious Presence, Source of all	193
Mysterious Spirit, unto whom	196
Nearer, my God, to Thee	197
No human eyes thy face may see	248
No longer forward or behind	297
No, not for these alone I pray	450
Not always on the mount may we	60
Not so fearful, doubting pilgrim	249
Not so in haste, my heart	160
Now is the time approaching	449
Now on land and sea descending	13
Now slowly, slowly darkening	370
Now that day its wings has furled	14
Now the joyful Christmas morning	37
O blessed life! the heart at rest	195
O deem not they are blest alone	301
O Eternal Life, whose power	194
O everlasting Light	266
O fairest-born of Love and Light	311
O Father of our spirits	138
O Freedom, on the bitter blast	169
O God, accept the gift we bring	458
O God, in whom we live and move	138
O God of Truth, whose living Word	325
O God, the Rock of Ages	368
O God, Thou art my fortress high	219
O God, Thou art my God alone	139
O God, thy children, gathered here	456
O God, thy power is wonderful	103
O God, unseen, but ever near	220
O God, whose love is near	224
O God, whose presence glows in all	127
O God, whose thoughts are brightest light	318
O grant us light, that we may know	263
O happy band of pilgrims	303
O here, if ever, God of love	445
O it is hard to work for God	268
O it is sweet to think	406
O Life that maketh all things new	188
O Light of life, O Saviour dear	28
O little town of Bethlehem	36
O Lord of life, where'er they be	392
O Lord, Thou art not fickle	334

	HYMN
O Love divine and golden	453
O Love divine, how sweet Thou art	227
O Love divine, of all that is	13
O Love divine, that stoop'st to share	300
O Love divine, whose constant beam	91
O Love, O Life, our faith and sight	179
O Name, all other names above	97
O pure Reformers, not in vain	267
O send me not away ; for I would drink	260
O Shadow in a sultry land	12
O sing with loud and joyful song	420
O sometimes comes to soul and sense	186
O sometimes gleams upon our sight	187
O Source divine, and Life of all	185
O Star of Truth, down shining	324
O still, in accents sweet and strong	333
O strong upwelling prayers of faith	164
O that Thou would'st the heavens rend	259
O the clanging bells of time	367
O Thou from whom all goodness flows	251
O Thou great Friend to all the sons of men	57
O Thou in all thy might so far	95
O Thou not made with hands	359
O Thou to whom our voices rise	132
O Thou who art of all that is	299
O Thou who didst prepare	470
O Thou whose liberal sun and rain	461
O timely happy, timely wise	7
O who is this that on a tree	73
O worship the King, all glorious above	114
Oft, as we run the weary way	349
On our way rejoicing	363
Once to every man and nation	328
One by one the sands are flowing	347
One feast, of holy days the crest	421
One gift, my God, I seek	153
One holy Church of God appears	358
One Lord there is, all lords above	100
One sweetly solemn thought	372
One thought I have, my ample creed	92
Only waiting till the shadows	371
Onward, Christians, onward go	352
Onward, onward, though the region	354
Onward ! upward ! Christian soldier	355
Our beloved have departed	407
Our day of praise is done	9
Our dead are like the stars by day	413
Our Friend, our Brother, and our Lord	180
Our God, our help in ages past	94
Out from the heart of nature rolled	90
Out of the dark the circling sphere	269
Part in peace ! is day before us	31
Past are the cross, the scourge, the thorn	76
Pleasant are thy courts above	131
Praise, my soul, the King of heaven	115
Praise to God and thanksgiving	464
Praise to our God, whose bounteous hand	474
Press on, press on, ye sons of light	357

HYMN

Pure in heart and free of sin 321
Purer yet, and purer 298

Rejoice, the Lord is King 122
Rejoice, ye pure in heart 364
Remember Me, the Master said 452
Routine of duties 341

Saviour, again to thy dear name we raise 29
Saviour, blessed Saviour 365
Shall we grow weary in our watch 314
Sign of a glorious life afar 64
Silent, like men in solemn haste 353
Sing forth his high eternal name 104
Sing with our might and uplift our glad voices 419
Slowly by thy hand unfurled 27
Souls of men, why will ye scatter 229
Spirit divine, attend our prayer 88
Spirit of Grace, Thou Light of Life 212
Sport of the changeful multitude 168
Standing forth on life's rough way 439
Standing on the shore at morning 77
Star of peace to wanderers weary 469
Stay, Master, stay upon this heavenly hill 61
Still, still with Thee, when purple morning breaketh . . . 176
Still the night, holy the night 45
Still will we trust, though earth seem dark and dreary . . 284
Still with Thee, O my God 158
Strive ; yet I do not promise 245
Sweet is the solace of thy love 283

Take my life, and let it be 265
Teach me, my God and King 262
Tell me not in mournful numbers 350
Tell me the old, old story 56
That mystic word of thine, O sovereign Lord 189
The buds are bursting on the trees 79
The child leans on its parent's breast 163
The children come, the angels cry 401
The flowing soul, nor low nor high 99
The God of love my Shepherd is 203
The hills and vales grow dark 23
The kings of old have shrine and tomb 415
The land beyond the sea 383
The Lord be with us as we bend 30
The Lord is in his Holy Place 175
The ocean looketh up to heaven 133
The old year's long campaign is o'er 431
The past is dark with sin and shame 161
The radiant morn hath passed away 26
The roseate hues of early dawn 312
The Shadow of the Rock 206
The shadows of the evening hours 25
The thought of God, the thought of Thee 106
The toil of brain, or heart, or hand 330
The twilight falls, the night is near 24
The very blossoms of our life 438
The winds that o'er my ocean run 209
The world may change from old to new 319

Their names are names of kings . . . .
There is a book, who runs may read . . . . . .
There is a calm for those who weep . . . .
There is gladness in the air . . . .
There is no death. The stars go down . . . . .
There is no night in heaven . . . .
There were ninety and nine that safely lay . . . .
They are all gone into the world of light . . . . .
They are going,—only going . . . .
They passed away from sight and hand . . . . . .
Thirsting for a living spring . . . .
This is the day of light . . . .
Thou art, O God, the light and life . . . . . .
Thou givest thy rest, O Lord; the din is stilled . .
Thou grace divine, encircling all . . . . . .
Thou hidden love of God, whose height . . . . .
Thou knowest, Lord, the weariness and sorrow . . .
Thou Life within my life, than self more dear . . . .
Thou long disowned, reviled, oppressed . . . . . .
Thou Lord of Hosts, whose guiding hand . . . . .
Thou One in all, Thou All in one . . . . . .
Thou say'st, Take up thy cross . . . .
Thou that sendest sun and rain . . . .
Thou who in life below . . . .
Thou who on that wondrous journey . . . . .
Thou, whose glad summer yields . . . . . .
Thou, whose name is blazoned forth . . . . . .
Thou workest on, Eternal God . . . .
Though we long in sin-wrought blindness . . . .
Through the night of doubt and sorrow . . . . .
Through the starry midnight dim . . . .
Thy seamless robe conceals Thee not . . . . . .
Thy task may well seem over hard . . . .
Thy way, not mine, O Lord . . . .
'Tis a beautiful world which God has made . . . .
'Tis thus we press the hand and part . . . . . .
To do thy holy will . . . .
To Him who children blessed . . . .
To Light, that shines in stars and souls . . . . .
To thine eternal arms, O God . . . .
To Thee, O God in heaven . . . .
To weary hearts, to mourning homes . . . . . .
To-day be joy in every heart . . . .
To-day beneath thy chastening eye . . . . . .
Two summer streams were flowing . . . .

Unheard the dews around me fall . . . . . .
Unto Thee abiding ever . . . .
Unto thy temple, Lord, we come. . . . . . .

Walk in the light ! so shalt thou know . . . . . .
Watchman, tell us of the night . . . .
We are but pilgrims here . . . .
We ask not that our path be always bright . . . .
We believe in Human Kindness . . . .
We bless Thee for thy peace, O God . . . . . .
We cannot always trace the way . . . .
We come unto our fathers' God . . . .
We gather to the sacred board . . . .

	HYMN
We love the venerable house	457
We name thy name, O God	173
We own thy hand, O God, in all	466
We plough the fields, and scatter	465
We pray for truth and peace	165
We pray no more, made lowly wise	174
We read upon the lettered page	282
We wait in faith, in prayer we wait	281
We wake each morn as if the Maker's grace	233
We will not weep; for God is standing by us	280
What is that goal of human hope	377
What is this that stirs within	313
What means this glory round our feet	44
What Thou wilt, O Father, give	238
When courage fails, and faith burns low	327
When for me the silent oar	386
When hope grows dim and shadows fall	155
When my love to God grows weak	69
When on my day of life the night is falling	207
When the Lord of love was here	50
When the night is still and far	101
When the paschal evening fell	444
When the toil of day is done	389
When the weary, seeking rest	237
When up to nightly skies we gaze	210
When winds are raging o'er the upper ocean	257
Where dost Thou feed thy favoured sheep	205
Where is thy God, my soul	171
Wherever through the ages rise	422
Who are these like stars appearing	412
Wilt Thou not visit me	152
With silence only as their benediction	395
With the sweet word of peace	472
Without haste and without rest	331
Work, it is thy highest mission	332
Ye happy bells of Easter day	75
Yes, for me, for me He careth	231
Yes, God is good; in earth and sky	232
Yes, Thou art with me, and with Thee	151
Young souls, so strong the race to run	159

UNWIN BROTHERS, PRINTERS, CHILWORTH AND LONDON.

27

CHILDREN'S SERVICES,

WITH

HYMNS AND SONGS.

EDITED BY THE

REV. A. W. OXFORD, M.A.

Second Edition.

A

SHORT INTRODUCTION

TO THE

History of Ancient Israel.

BY THE

REV. A. W. OXFORD, M.A.

9 780265 741414